Queering Theology Series

Editors
Marcella Althaus-Reid
Lisa Isherwood

Associate Editors
Robert Goss
Carter Heyward
Beverley Harrison
Ken Stone
Mary Hunt
Tom Hanks
Gerard Loughlin
Graham Ward
Elizabeth Stuart

The Sexual Theologian

Essays on Sex, God and Politics

Edited by
Marcella Althaus-Reid
Lisa Isherwood

T & T CLARK INTERNATIONAL
A Continuum imprint
LONDON • NEW YORK

Published by T&T Clark International
A Continuum imprint
The Tower Building, 11 York Road, London SE1 7NX
15 East 26th Street, Suite 1703, New York, NY 10010

www.tandtclark.com

British Library Cataloguing-in-Publication Data
A catalogue record for this book is available from the British Library

Typeset by Fakenham Photosetting Ltd, Fakenham, Norfolk
Printed on acid-free paper in Great Britain by CPI Bath

ISBN 0567082229 (hardback)
     0567082121 (paperback)

Contents

Introduction: Queering Theology
Thinking Theology and Queer Theory

Lisa Isherwood and Marcella Althaus-Reid

Queer theology and love-talk

It was a conference organized on themes of sexuality and theology. A group of theologians had gathered to discuss in a semi-informal way questions related to sexual ethics, politics and theology. Experiences and reflections were shared from the different perspectives of the participants and as the day advanced, many stereotypes were unveiled. For instance, that Third World theologians care about sexual ethics only in the context of heterosexuailty. Or that European theologians work only in bourgeois contexts. At one point, knowing that a couple of political theologians currently engaged with queer theory were sitting together at the same table, someone approached them to reproach them for – apparently – having departed from a radical but 'common-sense' theology. They were asked provocative questions: 'What has sexuality to do with the current economic crisis of your countries? How can you talk about sexuality when the global expansion of capitalism is destroying so many lives?' Suddenly remembering Tina Turner, the Latin American theologian ironically replied: 'You are asking me what love has to do with this?'

It was a time when the theological praxis was understood as fragmented and made by struggles which excluded each other. Therefore, to be a liberationist and engage in a praxis of political and economic transformation couldn't coexist with a feminist pursuit of gender equality. In similar fashion, to be committed to an environmental theology was seen as separate from the struggle of, for instance, Hispanic women in the USA, or from Black theology. However, we have come to the point of understanding better the complexity of any theological reflection committed to a serious dialogue with critical reality. Especially, because the theological praxis of liberation to which many of us have been committed for many years helped us to understand how different struggles have more in common than previously assumed. For instance, the fact that women's discrimination is related to the environmental crisis, or that classist structures in society are reflected in the hierarchical organization of the Church. Using a perspective from queer theology, we may say that to reflect theologically is always an activity done with a presupposition of love. To talk theology is to talk about a loving style of relationship. Theological themes are themes of love, even if perhaps this has been obscured by centuries of using a terminology which may have lost its original transparency. Redemption, for instance, is the work of giving freedom; salvation, of deliverance from suffering and danger. Grace is the work of freeing and delivering people and nature for free; conversion, the transformation of a person into a great lover of justice, equality and peace. It is in this frame that we would like to present queer theology as a radical form of the 'love-talk of theology', that is, a theology which introduces a profound questioning into the ways of love in our lives as individuals and as society, and the things love can do in our world.

Queering theology provides us with more than a reflection: it is a Christian praxis which aims to rethink alternative and radical ways of transformation in our present world so shaken by the contradictions of globalization. Following that question of 'What has love to do with this?' it can simply say: 'Love has everything to do with everything theology does.' Questioning the love-talk of theology means here to go deeper into the structures of the Church, and the way that theology helps to present, support and understand the meaning of love in practice, that is, friendship, solidarity and the political strategies and organization of the social structures necessary to foster a theological praxis of love in action. Some years ago, the late Latin American theologian Guillermo Cook commented that the main criticism of the Church by Maya indigenous people from Central America was concerned, basically, with the organizational arrogance of the Western Church. According to Cook, the Christian Mayas criticized the fact that in more than five centuries of Christianity in Latin America, the Church has taken no account of the traditional structure of Mayan society into its organization. The Western Church did not even consider incorporating into its theology the Mayan ways to love: that is, their traditions of solidarity, their identity-building process depending on communal frames. Nor was it prepared to learn from Mayan perspectives on sexuality, marriage and the family. In short, the Christian Church pervaded the Maya society with an epistemology or love/knowledge assuming certain universality, and translated theologically as divinely normative. However, the normative love/knowledge of the Church does necessarily need to come from straight heavens. Not only has Christian theology been informed by an ideologically constructed love-knowing and a particular sexual understanding of human and divine truth, but this knowledge is also constitutive of a way of thinking/acting theology. That is, it assumes as normal or natural what is temporary and culturally organized in an ideological frame. Feminist, Black, Aboriginal, Disabled and other political theologies have denounced that theology as an idolatry. A gender thinking, a white-race colouring of reflection and a class bias have lain behind the making of many reflections in the Church, without having been explicitly acknowledged.

However, what the Church has been lacking is the querying of what Rosemary Hennessy calls the politics of profit and pleasure in its history.[1] What a theology of radical sexuality, such as queer theology, has to do with the present capitalist expansion, the destruction of the environment and the politics of exclusion lies in the relationship between capitalism and sexuality, economic and heterosexual

---

1. Rosemary Hennessy, *Profit and Pleasure: Sexual Identities in Late Capitalism* (London: Routledge, 2000).

thinking and the traditional theological ethics which sustain many of the exclusive Christian praxis. However, queer theology takes its place not at the centre of the theological discourses conversing with power but at the margins. It is a theology from the margins which wants to remain at the margins. To recognize sexual discrimination in the Church and in theological thinking (by selective thematic of reflection or by de-authorization of other discourses) does not mean that a theology from the margins should strive for equality. Terrible is the fate of theologies from the margin when they want to be accepted by the centre! Queer theology strives instead for differentiation and plurality. Queer theology is in this sense equivalent to a call for biodiversity in theology, that is, life and love in all its diversity, which at the end transforms and renews all its praxis. From that perspective, queer theology is a political and sexual queering of theology which goes beyond the gender paradigm of thinking of the early years of feminist theology but also transcends the fixed assumptions of lesbian and gay theology. To regulate sexuality in the name of divinities means to regulate the order of affectionate exchanges but also other human exchanges such as the political and economic systems. Queering theology, that is, questioning the (hetero)sexual underlying of theological reflections exceeds the sphere of the private and also goes into the heart of the understanding of the exchange vision of the IMF and the understanding of what does it mean to be human in the globalization philosophy. Queering theology is not a rhetorical pastime but a political duty.

Queering theology is therefore a deep questioning or an exercise of multiple and diverse hermeneutical suspicions. Queer theory has been described as an umbrella term gathering together diverse issues within a common struggle: a resistance against heterosexual knowing. Theology has been adding issues of reflection under a common concern for justice, for instance, but while class, race and issues of gender have become part of the exercise of reflecting critically on issues of God and human history, sexuality remains one of the most difficult and pervasive ideological areas of assumed understandings. Somehow, queering theology requires us to challenge the existent link between theology and sexual domestication. Queering theology requires courage. In the same way that people sometimes need to renounce a beloved who has ill treated them, we face here the challenge of renouncing beloved sexual ideologies, systems of belief that even if built upon injustice have become dear to us, especially if associated with the will of God. Theology itself has a long history of struggling from the liberation of former ideological abusive loves, such as racism, sexism, indifference towards the poor (if not active collusion in their oppression) and colonialism.

While liberation theologies have been traditionally gender- and sex-blinded, the problem has been more than the fact that millions of women in poor countries have continued suffering abuse and exclusion under the indifference of a praxis which used the concept of the 'poor' as a blanket statement. The problem has been that the many creative forms of women's organization, successful in practice, are consistently excluded from the main stream of the top-level organization of society. Recently, Hebe Bonafini (a founder of the Movimiento de Madres de Plaza de Mayo in Buenos Aires) made a similar point while speaking in relation to the total breakdown of Argentina, as a nation under the control of the IMF and the economic experiments of neoliberalism. As Argentina faces an unprecedented chaotic situation, where social exclusion has reached limits only seen before in science-fiction movies, Mrs Bonafini shared the way that the excluded are organizing themselves by *asambleas populares* (neighbourhood gatherings, without political representatives or hierarchies) and cooperative work. The important point that she made was, however, to highlight how a different way of thinking is now needed: the alternative, radical thinking that tells us that the excluded know that at the root of the crisis is a way of relating to each other, of networking and dismantling hierarchical thought. This is something that liberation theologies still find hard to accept. Feminist theologies proposed a relational paradigm too, based on gender. However, the gender paradigm, even if in dialogue with a liberationist one, has never been enough to produce radical transformations. The problem is that gender paradigms tend to normalize theologies in the long term by subsuming differences into equalities. There is a revolutionary challenge, however, when we confront the sexual ideological normativity of theology. At this point, queer theory has produced what might be considered a qualitative change in theological thinking by unveiling the extension of the influence not just of heterosexuality but of heteronormativity in radical theology and specifically feminist theology.

Queer theory and theology

> Queer is a continuing moment, movement, motive – recurrent, eddying, *trou-blant*. The word 'queer' itself means *across* – it comes from the Indo-European root *twerkw*, which also yields the German *quer* (transverse) ... The immemorial current that *queer* represents is antiseparatist as it is antiassimilationist. Keenly, it is relational, and strange.[2]

Theology has always been contextual, and it has always depended on a theoretical framework of interpretation of the world. The fact is that theology is not enough and in itself is insufficient as a discipline to provide us with a basis for explaining critically the reality in which we live. Traditionally in the West, philosophy has provided theology not only with a theoretical framework of interpretation but also with a particular kind of questioning. Had that been a Maya philosophy or an African wisdom corpus in dialogue with theology we would have a different style of doing theology and also a distinctive set of questions and problematic to discuss than the one we inherited. The theoretical framework of interpretation which theology uses varies in time, or at least it should do. New awakenings of consciousness challenge previous ones. They become subversive, and in that sense can be considered problem-posing or *troublant*. Such is the case with queer theory as a radical theoretical field which has provided a style and a questioning that crucially destabilizes theological praxis. From the urban protests of the carnival against capitalism to the reflections on sexuality at the margins, queer theory has deregulated the binary myths of the subjects of theology, and in doing that it has deregulated our representations of God. The point is that theories of sexuality function as myths which organize a representation of history.[3]

---

2. Eve Kosofsky Sedgwick, *Epistemology of the Closet* (London: Penguin, 1993), p. xii.
3. Hennessy, *Profit and Pleasure*, p. 166.

Against that, other sexual thinking is rendered as deviant. However, the given coherence of certain social order and institutional life as the Church also depends on the mythical heteronormal matrix[4] which constitutes private and corporative identities. In theology, the question is, how do the politics of heteronormal identities (political and divine) pre-empt our representation of God and the reflection into the key themes of Christianity?

By queer studies we mean an alliance of diverse interests and studies with one common struggle: the struggle to liberate the dualistic patterns of sexual identity (present even in gay and lesbian discourses). Judith Butler, in her influential book *Gender Trouble*, presented a powerful argument for queer theory. Butler considers that it has been accepted that gender is learned in society, and that sexuality is something with which we are born. Gender, as behavioural patterns established in different societies, is transmitted from generation to generation. Different times and cultures produce different gender stereotypes, which, in encountering Christianity, became entangled with the old gender structures of identity and behaviour accumulated in the Bible, sometimes even in contradiction of each other. Feminist theology has made a point of denouncing the sacralization of oppressive gender patterns, but it didn't understand that it is a 'heterosexual matrix' which gives coherence and stability to the myth of heterosexuality as a natural or a given, while genders are useful in so far as they 'play' masculine and feminine oppositions. What happened here is that queer theory has introduced the concept of sexuality as learned and as more unstable than previously assumed. The question for us is, how do we learn theology and sexuality? (And how can we unlearn it?)

Queer theory has three characteristics: the emphasis on the construction of sexuality; the element of plurality, which needs to be present in any reflection; and the idea of ambivalence or the fluidity of sexual identities.[5] But theology has been organized around a givenness, a monotheism and an exercise of the authority of the metanarratives of heteronormativity. Therefore, queer theory works as a new 'mediator science' in radical theologies. As Gustavo Gutierrez spoke of liberation theology as the irruption of the poor in theology, queer theory has facilitated the irruption of the ultimate marginalized in Christianity: people and institutional forms of organization at the margins of heteronormativity (gay, lesbians, transgenders), but also knowledge at the margin of heterosexuality too. Different ways of amatory knowing express themselves in different ways of befriending, imagining God and compassion and creating different structures of relationships.

By queer theology, then, we mean a movement and an alliance of people who question the sexual construction of theology. Queer theology takes seriously the queer project of deconstructing heterosexual epistemology and presuppositions in theology, but also unveiling the different, the suppressed face of God amidst it. It is not only that theology has been traditionally obsessed with ordering sexuality but

---

4. Judith Butler, *Gender Trouble: Renaissance and the Subversion of Identity* (London: Routledge, 1990).

5. Fabio Cleto, *Camp. Queer Aesthetics and the Performing Subject: A Reader* (Edinburgh: Edinburgh University Press, 1999), p. 9.

much of theology has developed forms of sexual orderings into doctrinal reflections or the reading of the Scriptures.

If we were to mention some common characteristics in the process of doing
queer theology, we will need to consider issues concerning theology as a genre,
that is, how people write theology, and the focus of reflection of this theology. As
a genre, queer theology partakes of the irony, humour and self-disclosure type of
discourse of the camp genre and queer literature. The self-disclosure style means
also that queer theology is an '*I*' theology. The theologian doesn't hide in a gram-
matical essentialism, for instance, to use a 'we' which presumes the authority of
an academic body. In this way, queer theology is a form of autobiography because
it implies an engagement and a disclosure of experiences which traditionally have
been silenced in theology. For instance, issues of SM (sadomasochism), trans-
vestism, or the denunciation of heterosexuality as a construction which does not
even properly apply to the real experiences of heterosexual people. It uses ways
of expression which are the camp, ironic genres of the sexual dissidents. Camp
is a discourse of excess, an exaggerated style which puts together eroticism and
humour. Camp is 'A queer, twisted discursive building' which does not want firm
foundations. A camp theology is an unsettled one.

Queer theology is, then, a sexual theology with a difference: a passion for the
marginalized. That passion is compassion but also a commitment to social justice,
because there is a wider understanding of human relationships involved. The way
that mechanisms of production and consumption have been analysed, for instance
in Latin American liberation theology, now incorporates a different perspective
which has been excluded and pertains to the exploitation, but also to the solidarity
and cooperation, of people at the margins of society and theology. Therefore, it
is not correct to say that queer theology lacks agency. Queer theology is an agent
for transformation. As Hennessy has pointed out, heteronormativity has a labour-
division policy presupposed in gender hierarchies and the reification of sexual
identities in our societies are linked to capitalism.[6] Queer theology is a political
theology.

As a subversive force, queer theology focuses on theological closets, in what has
not been said or has been hidden. It is a theology which denounces the domestic
sexual violence of theology on its dissidents. Its strategy is to read theology, dismantling dualist readings and plays of oppositions. It may read the Scriptures in a
specific sexual way which departs from heteronormativity; it identifies moments
of sexual resistance in church traditions, or even alternative church traditions; it
exposes the profound homophobia of theology and the sexual assumptions in doctrines; and finds neglected areas of attention in theological discussions. More than
anything else, queer theology is an incarnated, body theology which deals with
desire, but also pleasure. And pleasure is after all, the incarnation of desires.

6.   Hennessy, *Profit and Pleasure*, p. 105.

Queer theology and incarnation

Queer theology is an emerging discipline which takes as its starting-point the radical, and as yet unexplored, nature of incarnation. That the divine left the heavens and entered flesh once and for all is the queer ground that we inhabit – what other god does such a thing? (There is always the safety of a heavenly home!) That God is in flesh changes everything, yet it has been a message of salvation in the hands of the Church which by its very nature does not like change – it is too destabilizing for its power base. The church hierarchy clings to power and makes impotent the revolutionary potential of the human/divine nature. Christian theology and tradition hold fast to very rigid ideas about the nature of the world, sexuality, sin and human nature, and fail to see the radical implications that they declare. God dwells in flesh and when this happens all our myopic earth-bound ideas are subject to change; the dynamic life-force which is the divine erupts in diversity and the energy of it will not be inhibited by laws and statutes. Far from creating the same yesterday, today and tomorrow, this dynamism is always propelling us forward into new curiosities and challenges. It does not shut us off from the world; it is the world drawing us into more of ourselves as we spiral in the human/divine dance.

This world is queer indeed, and those who wish to play it straight are failing to see that new horizons are declared holy and we are propelled on in courage not certainty. Where are those who will sit with the fear and uncertainty and not flee in the face of a queer god – the early followers fled in the face of a crucified god, very queer in the Jewish world! They fled to 'life as normal' but it didn't work – it can never work because life if fully engaged with is far from normal. Norms are easy conveniences for those who like surveys and statistics, they are not for those who live. Life can never be normal for those who embrace the flesh as divine, those who are lovers of god through that flesh in all its diverse glory.

Theology that has incarnation at its heart is queer indeed. What else so fundamentally challenges the nature of human and divine identity? That the divine immersed itself in flesh, and that flesh is now divine, is queer theology at its peak. There can be no sanitization here, or something of the divine essence will be lost – it is not the genetically modified, metaphysical Son of God that declares the divine-human conjunction, but the screaming baby born amidst the cow shit and fleas, covered in his birthing blood and received into the uncertain arms of his child/mother, who declares salvation for all. Male theologians have preferred to distance themselves from these all too earthy moments and in so doing have missed the point – the divine is earthy, messy and partial and is to be found there in all its glory, not in splendid doctrine stripped of all humanness.

Queer theologians are perhaps afraid but nevertheless courageous enough to plunge into flesh in its unrefined fullness in order to embrace and be embraced by the divine. Bodies tell very complex and challenging stories, and these now become the stuff of the salvific tale. We are all too well aware of how we have constructed bodies within boundaries that could never contain them but have at times distorted and mutilated them. Queer theology challenges the boundaries and wishes to propel us into a much wider paradise, one no longer walled and narrow like that in Genesis. Incarnation will not be thus confined. It throws down a challenge to imprisoned and imprisoning theology. We too are challenged to let go of the doctrines and dogmas we have constructed on our fear of the divine that pulsates within and between us. We don't have to embody Greek virtues any longer, and so are free of the fear instilled by metaphysical perfection and ultimate ends. 'I came that you may have life in abundance' is a profoundly fleshly statement, and one that releases us into the passionate embrace of our own incarnation.

We are challenged to move beyond metaphysics and the comfortable world that it creates. Queer theory with its postmodern roots asks us to distrust any master-narrative, and there is no bigger one than metaphysics – it fixes everything in its place and gives a place to everything. When we move beyond it we shake the foundations of the theological world. But are we doing something profoundly anti-Christian? Graham Ward provides a suggestion which allows us to argue that we are not. The Christian god/man does not have a fixed nature, even though subsequent theology has argued that he does, but a permeable and unstable nature. Ward alerts us to the many changes that took place, the queer transformations that showed the unstable categories involved in God incarnate. It is through changes from divine to flesh, flesh and blood to bread and wine, and from human to cosmic spirit, that the full incarnation of redemptive praxis takes place. What is fixed and stable and overarchingly metaphysical about this? By guarding these stories with a protective shield of Greek metaphysics and exclusivity we have made them stable and clear categories, thus negating them. Queer theology would like to take them in the raw and examine how we between us embody these and other forms of incarnation. Queer theologians wish to take seriously the stories we tell ourselves and each other; these include the collective narrative we have shared over two millennia as well as the stories of our lives and our communities. There are no boundaries: all stories tell us of the incarnation we share and the redemptive space we strive for.

Our narrative heritage is rich and full of cautionary tales for the tentative queer theologian!!! The temptation stories are particularly interesting and inspirational as here we see stated plainly the rejection of incarnation with the help of metaphysics! Turning stones into bread, flying without wings, giving over one's own power to another in order to have earthly power is all very easy and perhaps even expected if we continue to operate within a metaphysical framework: after all isn't this what many a fundamentalist tale is made of? How many conversion stories have we heard that contain elements of the truly fantastic? (And what of the aggressively grasping capitalism of many of those who espouse a fundamentalist faith?) But we find that all these extrovert trappings, so completely unremarkable for an almighty god, are rejected by the one who is declared the divine incarnate. Instead, there is a life committed to the struggle for justice and liberation in the real lives of real people. People in time and place struggling with their own incarnate demons of prejudice, poverty, colonialization, terror, fear and the desire to be themselves in situations that won't always allow this. If we engage with this story from our heritage do we conclude that those who work in the field of metaphysics have sold out to the devil? Queer theology does not operate in easy answers and tidy doctrine: truly honouring our incarnation does not allow for such neat packaging and comfort. Incarnation and queer theory are splendid, passionate and risk-compelling companions – they promise nothing and they offer everything.

Queer theory/theology and its critics

So why is there so much concern about the coupling of queer theory and theology? Surely there is only room for celebration, space for the dance of liberation to continue. Naturally there will be criticism from traditionalists who are happier with tight boundaries and neat edges around their theology, but it is surprising to note that there is concern about the queer rhetoric from a number of areas. We both have our roots in feminist liberation theology and so find it interesting that there is some concern emanating from both these camps. These concerns are perhaps, at this stage, no more than theoretical warning noises, since the true praxis of queer theology needs some time before it can be assessed.

Like postmodernism, queer theology asks that we demystify, undo and subvert. Far from being seen as unhelpful this approach is viewed as crucial to our well-being, and we are encouraged to embrace it as a very healthy path by those who work within liberation and feminist theology. However, there is a line drawn in the sand by both sets of theologians when it comes to postmodernism and its apparent lack of moral judgement. Beverley Harrison highlights this by contrasting a feminist liberation theologian's response to the story of a torture victim: she says it would be an outrage and a determination to act to alter the situation. The postmodernist, she claims, when told the story would simply reply, 'How interesting.' Can queer theory/theology as a child of this movement avoid the same pitfalls? In finding everything interesting and expanding of the human story, can queer theology be expected to draw a line and still be true to its queer agenda? This can be highlighted, I suspect, with the example of paedophilia: people do it and no doubt many declare it to be a spiritual path, certainly historically it has had great cultural significance (a significance that usually underpinned the continuation of patriarchal society, although this was not always the case). Are feminists and other liberation theologians right to be concerned that this particular incarnational tale may be opening the way for abuse?

There are of course other concerns, Sheila Jeffreys is in the forefront of those who ask, where do women go if we transform the discourse from feminism to queer? If gender is nothing more than a performance that can be adopted at will then, she argues, the edge is taken off feminist politics.[7] Indeed, she suggests that the queer agenda has arisen from a gay lifestyle where women are not only absent but also at best disliked and at worst parodied and despised, and so women are not central to any queer theory. She warns that history shows us that women do not survive well in male-dominated politics, be they queer or any other type.

We may accept that her suggested genesis for queer theory is correct, but we do not necessarily agree that this means all is lost. Coming at this issue from theology as we do means that we have different categories in which to take refuge, such as the very queer notion that the divine and human flesh are interchangeable and that

7.   See Sheila Jeffreys, *Unpacking Queer Politics* (Cambridge, Polity Press, 2003), p. 33.

in Christ there is neither male nor female. As feminist theologians, we are only too well aware that this has been abused and used in favour of one gender and not the other, but it also provides an opportunity for us to think beyond gender in a whole and empowering way.

Another of Jeffreys' concerns is that in considering gender as a performance we are still stuck within binary opposites when looking for ways to perform. She is therefore not at all convinced that anything is challenged, but rather that the categories male and female are reinforced. She highlights her point by examining butch-femme relationships and transsexual surgery – she does not in the ordinary way connect both issues, but is concerned that a number of older butches are opting for surgery as their bodies soften and they look more female: in order to overcome this they go under the knife. Jeffreys is understandably concerned that both womanhood and lesbianism are being undermined here in an attempt to opt into male power and privilege.[8] She is also aware than when academic language is used and sexuality is spoken of in academic language it becomes difficult to criticize without being labelled as out of touch. Her concern arises from the feminist understanding that gender as we know it is based on power relations and she questions how this is to be overcome if basic gender construction is simply performed and not challenged. Far from quoting Joan Nestle as the one who may explain how gender is subverted through butch-femme role-playing she cites her as one who popularizes role-playing as a watered-down form of SM in which dominance and submission are embraced as delights and not political problems.[9] Jeffreys is distressed that many SM dykes take their ideas from gay male culture where they are formed in a world of hypermasculinity. This is a culture that often assesses real masculinity in terms of the amount of pain that can be borne and is often acted out with fascist insignia as sexual props. Jeffreys is unconvinced that this is a healthy culture and she warns women against it.

Using the testimony of an ex-femme, Jeffreys is able to demonstrate that there is a creation of 'otherness' in role-playing that feminists have always striven against: one that can easily result in violence, be it sex-play or domestic abuse. Indeed, she goes further and asks if role-playing allows women to fit into recognized sexual scenarios, and as a consequence if it hinders the liberation that feminists pursue.[10] Masculinity and femininity have no meaning on their own: they need each other for difference, and it is precisely this perceived difference that has not served women well over the centuries. Jeffreys is concerned that butch-femme and even transsexual surgery appropriates heterosexual binarism in order to assume sexual realism – to look to the historical oppressor for legitimacy.

We do not wish to dismiss Jeffreys' concerns or to assume that there is a simple solution when theologians are dealing with these issues; after all it has been pointed out that theology itself is heterosexual.[11] We will do well to heed her concerns and to bring into play the less stable categories that at its inception

---

8.   Ibid., p. 130.
9.   Ibid., p. 127.
10. Ibid., p. 129.
11. See Marcella Althaus-Reid, *Indecent Theology* (London: Routledge, 2001).

underpinned Christianity – those already mentioned: incarnation, transfiguration, transubstantiation, and so on. Will we be successful? Who knows? Queer theology is, like all theology, an act of faith and reason with no guarantee of success for either.

Feminists are not the only ones to highlight concerns in relation to queer theory. Liberation theologians are worried that queer politics has no interest in analysing capitalism, viewing the main issue as one of access and not the system itself. As we both come from a liberation background we would be more than reluctant to engage with any theory that overlooked the genocidal realities of advanced capitalism. However, as feminist liberation theologians we make the connections between sex, gender and capitalism, and so in incorporating queer theory into our theology we hope to expand the area of issues that come under scrutiny and not actually reduce them. We are no longer naïve enough to think that Foucault's claim that pleasure resists power is unproblematic: after all pleasure costs and we are not left unaided in our choice of pleasures. Pleasure is profit! We hope that queer theology develops true democracy, that is a system that has connection and mutuality at its heart, and that it does not simply become yet another form of liberal or neoliberal theology that puts consumerism in the place of real people touching and being touched.

Of course, fundamentalist Christians do a good line in holiness and the rewards of capitalism, and this too needs to be combated. It is no accident, we think, that a form of Christianity so based in family values is also wedded to consumption and financial reward for holy lives. If queer theology does no more than destabilize the assumed 'rightness' of family values it will have struck a solid blow against advanced capitalism. It will of course do much more than that!

Those who are involved in justice-seeking theologies are anxious that queer theory and therefore queer theology will contribute to liberation theologies losing their political and justice-seeking edge. Two examples of how this may happen can be highlighted by Jeffreys, although her concern is not theological. She examines the issues of public sex and bare-backing (having anal sex without a condom). Both issues are very much in the queer arena for discussion. Her stance on both issues has drawn accusations of conservatism from those who view themselves as part of the radical sex movement. Jeffreys claims that public sex is more than simply sex outdoors: it is also commercialized through taking place in back-rooms, and so on. Much of it takes place with prostitutes and this once more is a commercialization of pleasure. Jeffreys also has a fundamental feminist concern which is that public sex makes the public space less safe for women. She sees the zeal for public sex as a move from community to a masculine cult of the individual and a replacement of community with the market sector.[12]

Bare-backing with HIV partners is advertised on the web in sites such as 'Pozcum' and 'The Fuck of Death', where seeking it is eroticized and seen as hypermasculine. Martin Levine has attempted to explain this behaviour by suggesting that a great deal of gay male sexuality is an unreconstructed version of adolescent male sexuality, which in turn is about

12. Jeffreys, *Unpacking Queer Politics*, p. 57.

risk-taking.[13] He sees this as a form of aggressive masculinity which is enacted vigorously to prove one's maleness. It is therefore detached, phallocentric, privatized and objectifying which means that sexuality is relatively unintegrated. Jeffreys is horrified to think that such a model could be put forward as queer and therefore with liberating potential for women. What she thinks about a woman bare-backing an HIV man with the aid of a dildo she does not say.

As liberation theologians it is natural that an initial reaction to men seeking death and others willing to oblige has to be sadness and even horror. However, the picture is rarely straightforward, and Bob Goss has some interesting insights from personal experience which make us think again. His partner Frank became HIV-positive and was reluctant to bare-back in order to preserve Bob's health, feeling that to infect him would be immoral and irresponsible.[14] Bob had no such reservations, indeed he records that there was a deep spiritual longing left unfulfilled by his partner's reluctance. Goss cites other gay men who speak about bare-backing in spiritual as well as physical ways, and he reflects again on what at first seems a straightforward question of justice.

For Goss, an ethic of what he terms 'communal survivability' is not necessarily good enough, and may not even be Christian. He points out that it was not an ethic that Jesus held dear when he went up to Jerusalem and disrupted the temple. There were more compelling reasons than survival that brought Jesus to that place and those actions.[15] Goss suggests that these were love and solidarity, and he claims that just such reasons can be in play when considering bare-backing. This goes beyond the love and solidarity that one feels for an infected partner and extends to love and solidarity with one's community so grievously affected by HIV/AIDS. What is called for is not a knee-jerk reaction but rational, conscious and committed reflection and action which, even in times of great risk, propel sex beyond the bounds of mere reductionism and into a space that sees and weighs up the complex motivations that make sex a human act of intimacy. Safety then may pale into insignificance next to sexual union that affirms the uniqueness of the individuals, the realness of God and the deep spiritual love, trust, giving and vulnerability of the couple wrapped in the presence of their God. While Goss is offering this challenge from within a long-term relationship he is by no means suggesting that it can only be understood within such a context.

We are not claiming that all Jeffreys' concerns can be laid to one side by adopting the approach that Goss suggests, but we are highlighting the fact that some issues are not as easily dealt with as may at first appear to be the case.

We are mindful of the critics of queer theology/theory, and their concerns fuel our own investigations. We hope that one anxiety can be laid to rest by this book alone. Many critics suggest that queer theory is obscure and does not serve activist theology. We hope that the articles gathered here demonstrate that there is a critical-activist edge to queer theology, and that it is accessible and flexible enough truly

13. Quoted ibid., p. 72.

14. Robert Goss, *Queering Christ. Beyond Jesus Acted Up* (Cleveland, OH: Pilgrim Press, 2002).

15. Ibid., p. 85.

to transform. It is our hope that queer theory aids theology in the task of moving from metaphysics to metamorphing, not just for the sake of it but in order that more space may be made for the glorious and diverse creation of the divine to dance and be celebrated.

The essays collected here demonstrate the way in which queer theory impacts on theology and opens its horizons. They show that all areas of theology can be touched by a queer approach: from death to Mary, from embodiment to biblical study. The aim is not to shock but to honestly engage with one of the most challenging theoretical approaches in the contemporary world. After all, theology is contextual and that context includes the intellectual climate of the secular world, not just its own small and cloistered domain. The time of only asking the right and safe questions in order to generate the right and safe answers is over. Theology has, over the years, forgotten that it is a brave subject and one that should lead the way as 'queen of the sciences'. It has become self-referential and therefore cut off, afraid to look outside itself in case its own irrelevance becomes abundantly clear. Sadly this becomes a self-fulfilling prophecy: the less it looks and ventures out, the more irrelevant it becomes. This can never be acceptable, particularly for a theology that declares incarnation to be at the heart of its reflections. Those engaged in queer theology are stating publicly their faith in the relevance of theology in all areas of life; they are not afraid of the disintegration of the discipline through engagement with what is real in the lives of people – this after all is how the whole thing started, people's ponderings were based on the stuff of their lives and their place in the greater whole. And so the authors in this book take a hard look at real lives and dare to theologize.

Marie Cartier demonstrates that by looking with queer eyes, the life, poetry and theology of Sor Juana take on a set of different dimensions. Cartier is bold in her assertion that if scholars are not engaging with queer theory they are in fact presenting historically inaccurate research. They miss the clues, and so the theology that they present to us becomes disembodied, less rooted in reality and less effective as a resource for generations of Christians. Cartier shows how scholars engaged with the work of Sor Juana have at times been reluctant to take her at her word because they do not have a mindset that allows them to do so.

Martín Hugo Córdova Quero attempts a queer reading of the life and theology of Aelred of Rievaulx. He shows how brotherly love is spoken of in the language of the Song of Songs, and far from being spiritualized this should be taken as what it is – love between men. What we see with a queer reading is that friendship is a combination of affection and reason but comes from an existing love of God that both parties experience before their own friendship. Far from shunning love between men, Aelred, Quero argues, makes a virtue out of it and certainly understands it as a holy path. Quero argues that queer readings allow us to ask different questions of the past and therefore to plot different courses for the future.

Lisa Isherwood uses the story of Margery Kempe to examine the pervasive and oppressive nature of heteropatriarchy and to ask whether we can keep the rules and be people dedicated to liberation and life in abundance. She demonstrates how very private acts underpin very public actions and social assumptions. Margery queered the pitch through her intimate relationship with the divine in all its aspects. She moved from being the traditional wife and mother to a wild and challenging free woman, creating a space for herself that was almost unimaginable. In so doing she raises exciting questions for theologians who dare to take her story and the story of incarnation seriously – she queers the divine.

Elizabeth Stuart engages with death and takes the reader camping around the crem. Stuart argues that the Church has lost its wider vision through an overengagement with Enlightenment thought; it is only through reinstating much that was lost that it will once again offer hope by challenging many of the constructions, including gender, that hold us captive. Death is essential to the queer project as it allows for a life beyond, where gender itself is overcome. The perspective of death frees Christians from the endless repetitions of unfulfilled desires and opens a new and real future, a future that is in the now, for, as Stuart claims, Christians have already entered death and resurrection through their baptism.

Graham Ward reminds us that sexual language is used when referring to the body of Christ, and he asserts that this is because of a fundamental erotics driving the enquiry into that body by Christian scholars. As scholars we are all drawn by a longing, a desire for knowledge of that into which we enquire. Lest we get carried away with our ability to merge with the knowledge that we seek, Ward reminds us that knowledge is not stable – it is different according to time, place and culture. Ward engages with the stories of Jesus's circumcision and contemporary theorists in order to demonstrate that the composition of an argument is never innocent and that there is indeed a politics of faith.

Gerard Loughlin challenges the criticism that the Church is obsessed with sex by suggesting that it is good that the Church has sex. The Church has not merely fallen prey to a modern secular obsession: it has always been a fully embodied community, a eucharistic community that is most itself when eating together the body of God. In addition, the Church is the Bride of Christ: a relationship that calls for physical union, which is queer indeed when one considers the multigendered nature of the Church as community – the bride is made up of many bodies all called to this union. Loughlin sees the union not as theoretical but as placental, one in which we are in the body of God. He argues that the view of sex fostered by evolutionary biology will not do theologically, since asexual reproduction is the most effective, because there is more to it than babies. Sex after nature, he claims, calls us to the infinite joy of our consummation with and in God.

Marcella Althaus-Reid wishes to lift the skirts of God, and does so. She asks if this is indeed the vocation of the theologian: to lovingly go beneath the skirts of the Beloved in forging the intimacy that transforms. Intimate connection with the divine is not a new concept and is the foundation of both biblical and Patristic understandings. What is new is that Althaus-Reid destabilizes the assumed heterosexual underpinnings of these longings and connections with the divine. She demonstrates the necessity for queering the heterosexual ideology that operates in theology in order to welcome the strangers, embrace the queer God and disrupt unjust power systems.

Ken Stone applies queer theory to biblical texts and concludes that it encourages us to question religious identities, not just sexual and gender identities. He encourages queer readers of the Bible to concentrate on stories that reveal the ambiguity of religious and ethnic identity rather than those which see religious identity in polarized terms. The queer reader has an opportunity to interrupt the demonization of others that goes on when those who are dominant in culture or religion are faced with the presence of those unlike themselves. Stone argues that demands for inclusion are all very well in the short term, but all this does is to reinforce the boundaries between inside and outside. The best long-term strategy is to turn boundaries inside out through presence on the margins.

All these articles offer another way of looking and therefore another way of being in the world. None claims to be *the answer* and the authors themselves continue their journeys, queering the pitch as they go.

　　　THE NECESSITY FOR FICTION IN RESURRECTING QUEER
LINEAGE: *SOR JUANA'S SECOND DREAM*

Marie Cartier

Was Sor Juana de la Cruz, a cultural symbol second only in popularity to the
Virgin of Guadalupe in Mexico, a *lesbian*?[1] How can we know – *for sure*? Does
it matter and, if so, to whom? How does queer theory add to the discussion of
how historians have interpreted the romantic poetry of Sor Juana, the love poetry
admittedly and unabashedly addressed to women?[2] How do we interpret those
endearments today?

Did monastic culture offer a situation that queer theory cannot interpret outside
the culture itself? In attributing 'queerness' to Sor Juana's writings, are we then
taking her out of her time? For all time? Can queer theory add to the interpretation
of such a contested figure? These are the questions that began to intrigue me as I
undertook the task of completing a review of the literature available in English of
Sor Juana de la Cruz. Apart from my surprise at the mammoth nature of the task
– she is second only in popularity to the Virgin of Guadalupe, Mexico's patron
saint – I was intrigued by how all of the major scholars interpreted her work.

I have two distinct agendas in this study. The first is a defence of fiction as a
legitimate methodological approach for unravelling the complexities in the life of
a historical figure. The second involves using queer theory to explicate Sor Juana's
sexuality. My argument is that while there are methodological problems with
fiction and queer theory, their usefulness is more than compelling.

In examining the secondary sources on Sor Juana I found that there was an
almost universal inability to engage the possibility of Sor Juana's queerness *as
queer*. The majority of scholars executed what in any other context would be
deemed decidedly poor scholarship in their opening chapters by declaring that Sor
Juana, while having written romantically to women and having been linked with
lesbian tendencies, was too important a figure to allow a discussion of her sexuality
to occur in their studies. For example, in the Introduction to her book, *Sor Juana
Ines de la Cruz: Religion, Art and Feminism*, Pamela Kirk writes that she

---

1.　Alicia Gaspar de Alba, 'Author's Postscript', *Sor Juana's Second Dream* (Albuquerque,
NM: University of New Mexico Press, 1999), p. 460.

2.　Sor Juana, *Love Poems/Poemas de Amor*, trans. Joan Larkin and Jaime Manrique (New
York: Painted Leaf Press, 1997). The poems in this selection have been culled from Sor Juana's
extensive body of poetry on the many kinds of love, 'some of them clearly addressed to women'.

... will not be examining in any detail Sor Juana's relationships with the women she knew. This includes the Countess of Paredes, whom I will consider only as Sor Juana's patroness without exploring the dimensions of the friendship of the two women which has led to considerable (and inconclusive) speculation based on some of Sor Juana's poems addressed to the Countess. These poems are not part of Sor Juana's religious work, and therefore are not under consideration here. I will, however, be taking care to *consider the writings of the men* with whom Sor Juana interacted in order to give the reader a sense of the degree to which Sor Juana was their equal, or even their superior in logical argumentation, breadth of culture, and brilliance of language.[3]

A discussion of Sor Juana's sexuality seems somehow *beneath* this scholar, and other scholars[4] and beneath the dignity of the source herself, Sor Juana. As is seen in the above quotation, her relationship and writings with the Countess are relegated to that of patroness and so seen as unworthy of consideration in a book about 'religion and art'. However, in Kirk's own words, Sor Juana's relationships and writings with men – although many also cannot be included under Kirk's general umbrella of 'religion and art' – are considered worthy because they demonstrate Sor Juana's 'equality' with men.

Two things are important to consider here with regard to this line of argument. First, in terms of relationships of *power*, the Countess had much more power, even as a woman, than many of the men of the Church who associated with Sor Juana. Specifically because of her relationship with the Countess, Sor Juana had the protection that *allowed* her male visitors, and because of her relationship with the vicereine *she was published*. To deny the importance of that relationship seems to be decidedly ahistorical, and denies the Countess the power of the office that she chose to wield in a very *feminist* fashion – she supported Sor Juana's right to write and speak. I would argue that were it not for the Countess, we would have no *historical author* Sor Juana, because it is doubtful that she would have been published any other way. That alone seems to suggest that her relationship with the Countess de Paredes is historically *the most important relationship* Sor Juana had.

Perhaps because Kirk is a theologian (and states this several times in her Introduction) she cannot engage Sor Juana's sexuality and power *with women*. Electa Arenal and Amanda Powell, in their Introduction to their translation of *The Answer/La Respuesta*, Sor Juana's most clearly feminist document, have no such qualms about attributing at least the power that these two vicereines were able to wield in Sor Juana's *favour*, even while they do not critically engage with *why* these courtly women would choose to wield this type of power – *for a cloistered nun*.

> Her most ardent love poems were dedicated to the two vicereines. Well-educated and sophisticated readers, it was they who most energetically encouraged her scholarly and literary pursuits. [The Countess de Paredes] ... was an avid

3.   Pamela Kirk, *Sor Juana Ines de la Cruz: Religion, Art and Feminism* (New York: Continuum, 1998), p. 11. (Emphasis added.)
4.   I am quoting the Kirk example here because of its obvious exclusion of discussion of Sor Juana's sexuality, and its blatant 'reasons' for this. However, Kirk is not the only scholar to posit this type of reasoning as justification for refusing to consider seriously Sor Juana's *own words* in the context that she might have meant exactly what she wrote.

supporter of Sor Juana. It was she who took Sor Juana's poems to Spain and
arranged for her first book to be published.[5]

I would suggest that it is unusual and uncomfortable for many authors, even
avowedly feminist authors such as Kirk, to attribute power to women in relationships and particularly difficult to unpack the *manipulated* power in relationships
such as those that the vicereines had to engage with in order to be able to support
Sor Juana. After all, the first vicereine with whom Sor Juana had a relationship was
the Marquise de Mancera, who reportedly said[6] that she was not able to 'live an
instant without her Juana Ines'.[7] How did she *manage* this, not being able to 'live
an instant' without a cloistered nun? Most biographers seem to find it uncomfortable to consider the answer.

I believe that part of the reason for this discomfort is because of Sor Juana's
masculinity. I believe that at the time of her relations with the vicereines she was
engaged in what today we would consider a relationship structure known in the
lesbian community as butch-femme, in which one partner creates (not imitates)
a new form of masculinity, and one partner creates (not imitates) a new form of
femininity. This structure is uncomfortable not only for the general populace but
also for most feminists. Since the 1970s feminists have wanted everyone to be
female in a *feminine*, not *masculine,* fashion.

Historian Lillian Faderman brings to light the American history of disdain for
the butch woman by unpacking its 1950s into its 1970s lineage in the following
excerpt from her book, *Odd Girls and Twilight Lovers, A History of Lesbian Life
in Twentieth-Century America.*

> Middle-class lesbians ... seem to have avoided butch/femme relationships
> and styles because they did violence to their often unarticulated but neverthe-
> less deeply felt feminism. As a Los Angeles lesbian woman, who is now a
> psychologist, remembers of her response to butch/femme in the '50s, 'I didn't
> think anything could be that simple with the polarities of sheer masculine and
> sheer feminine between two women. I didn't like it between men and woman
> but between two lesbians it really seemed strange to me.' The disdain was
> mutual. Butches and femmes thought these 'kiki' women were the ones who
> were buckling under by dressing like conventional women. *It was something of
> a class war ...* [8]

I would suggest that Sor Juana's attitude, dress and relationships with women were
not feminine in a feminine fashion but masculine in the *only* masculinity she could
create at the time – that of a cross-dressing nun. It is also interesting to note that
class distinctions between Sor Juana and the vicereines 'mimic' or mirror class
distinctions between traditional 1950s butch and femme couples – with the femme

    5.   Electa Arenal and Amanda Powell, *The Answer/La Respuesta: Including a Selection of
Poems: Sor Juana Ines de la Cruz*, critical edn and trans. (New York: The Feminist Press, 1994),
pp. 9–11.
    6.   According to her biographer, Calleja.
    7.   Ibid.
    8.   Lillian Faderman, *Odd Girls and Twilight Lovers* (New York: Penguin, 1991), pp. 181,
186. (Emphasis added.)

often needing to provide protection and money for the butch who often could not find or hold down a job in the homophobic 1950s.

Unpacking the relationships Sor Juana had with the vicereines, I believe, leads feminist scholars like Kirk to begin to expose what they see as the underbelly of Sor Juana's sexual preference: not only did she have Sapphic tendencies, she was *butch,* i.e., she was masculine and she was proud of that – proud enough to write poetry about it. For example on the death of the vicereine she wrote:

> Laura, desire dies with you
> Never to be slacked. My eyes die
> Stripped of the sight of you
> And the light you lent them.[9]

And, at another time, she wrote:

> My breasts answer yours
> Magnet to magnet
> Why make love to me, then leave?
> Why mock me?[10]

Did Sor Juana identify as a *butch* woman? Was she courting a *femme*?

> Self-identified butches and femmes have always been sexual outlaws. Straight society simply could not tolerate the idea of a feminine, 'normal'-looking woman who got her needs for sex and masculine companionship and protection met by a strong and erotically skilled woman. Shrinks, cops and fundamentalists have always hated butch women, who threatened male privilege by successfully competing with men for pussy and domestic care-taking.[11]

Were the vicereines providing Sor Juana with the domestic care-taking and 'pussy' (i.e., sexual satisfaction and/or world *of desire*) that was therefore threatening to the power structure in Sor Juana's world?

Is identifying that *possibility* so damning to her status as a cultural icon that any sexuality in her poetry is simply not to be looked at in case it might reveal *this* lineage? I do not want to essentialize butch-femme. It is a construction of public same-sex relations that begins primarily in America in the 1950s. I am using it here as a heuristic model to understand the complexities of Sor Juana's sexuality. I also argue, however, that this is perhaps a type of relationship that transcends history and culture – particularly strict patriarchal history and culture.

As I have stated, although the majority of her work, especially poetry, addresses issues of corporeality, specifically the significance of desire and her love for women, the nature of that work is raised and then regularly dismissed without explanation. One exception perhaps is her major biographer, Octavio Paz, who in his *Sor Juana or the Traps of Faith* takes a psychological stance and declares

9. Joan Larkin and Jaime Manrique, *Sor Juana's Love Poems*, p. 75.
10. Ibid., p. 35.
11. Pat Califia, 'Butch Desire', *Dagger: On Butch Women*, ed. Lily Burana and Roxxie Linnea Due (San Francisco, CA: Cleis Press, 1994), p. 220.

that Sor Juana could not have made the decision to be lesbian – it was much too complicated a choice for a woman of her age.

> To think that she felt a clear aversion to men and an equally clear attraction to women *is absurd*. In the first place, because even if that supposition were true, *it is not likely that while she was still so young she knew* her true inclinations; in the second, because only by attributing to her an intellectual and sexual license more appropriate to a Diderot heroine than to a girl of Juan Ines' age and social class in New Spain could she *cold-bloodedly* have chosen as refuge an institution inhabited exclusively by persons of the sex that supposedly attracted her … it is futile to try to learn what her true sexual feelings were. *She herself did not know.*[12]

Alicia Gaspar de Alba quotes this same passage in her article 'The Politics of Location of the Tenth Muse of the America: An Interview with Sor Juana Ines de La Cruz', in the volume *Living Chicana Theory*. Following this quotation by Paz, Gaspar de Alba writes, 'I am convinced however, that Sor Juana *did* know the contours of her own desire, and I identify her as a lesbian separatist feminist who cross-dressed as a nun to hide, even from herself, what in seventeenth-century Spanish America would have been interpreted as heresy.'

In other words, *Sor Juana meant what she wrote.* I am also suggesting here that perhaps as we unpack the lineage of Sor Juana, we see not only a cross-dressing woman but also a butch woman. I don't believe she cross-dressed merely to gain entrance to the convent and to educate herself. Of course, this is important, perhaps primary. But Sor Juana *herself* declared again and again the primacy of love, of physical love and of desire in her life. I believe we must ask, if we are to do worthy scholarship on this particular subject, what purpose did the nun's habit hold for her in allowing that choice to be at least partially fulfilled, if only in its ability *to be declared*?

The censure and *erasure of a sexualized* female masculinity, not just a created masculinity that allows access to power structures such as education, is still very difficult for people – even feminists – to acknowledge. I believe this may account for the reluctance of even feminist scholars to deconstruct Sor Juana's masculinity. If we do deconstruct her creation of masculinity, we also unpack her relationships. For a butch is a butch most *next to a femme*, and I would suggest Sor Juana was at her *most* masculine self not in her education but in her love for the vicereines.

Who engages this and why?

The only Sor Juana scholars I could find who engage her lesbianism in a truly academic fashion, and for me that means they do not write it off but choose to explore the words she wrote as if she meant them,[13] are the lesbian scholar Joan Larkin and the gay male scholar Jaime Manrique and the lesbian scholar Alicia

---

12. Octavio Paz, *Sor Juana or the Traps of Faith*, trans. Margaret Sayers Peden (Cambridge, MA: Harvard University Press, 1988), p. 111. (Emphasis added.)

13. These are the only scholars that I was able to find in my extensive review of the literature available on Sor Juana to the *non-Spanish-speaking reader*. There may be more work available in English that I did not find, and especially in Spanish, particularly in the growing Chicana lesbian community – but I did not have access to it.

Gaspar de Alba, who engage Sor Juana from the perspective of their *dual careers* as academics and artists. This intrigued me.

Manrique and Larkin collected Sor Juana's work in a volume clearly called 'love poems', which announces throughout that these poems were written for women. By pulling the poetry out and announcing it this way Larkin and Manrique stand *by the work*, saying yes *she means what she says* – these poems were addressed to women, for they *were* addressed to women. While this seems elementary, it is not. It is actually a brave and innovative step that Larkin and Manrique took by declaring that this woman, Sor Juana, while a cultural icon and national symbol, did in fact *mean what she said* when she spoke of loving women.

From their Introduction, written by editor Jaime Manrique:

> As a poet, she is, I think one of the most carnal bards of all time: bawdy, tactile, fiery, elegiac, she hits multiple notes, *always insisting on the importance of desire* ... Sor Juana's first volume of poetry, *Inundacion castalida*, was published in Spain by the Vicereine Maria Luisa Manrique de Lara y Gonzaga, Countess of Paredes, Marquise de la Laguna. Maria Luisa was also the source of inspiration for the Mexican poet, the 'Lysi' of the love poems. It gives me enormous pleasure to link once more the Manrique name to Sor Juana's trajectory ... [14]

Does Sor Juana's desire for women need to be rescued *by a queer relation*, as above, in order to be seen? Or by a member of her avowed, at least in her own writing, queer tribe, as with the work of Gaspar de Alba? *It appears so.* An examination of the secondary sources reveals her queer history is banished as at worst *unspeakable*, or at best, as with Paz's work, *impossible*.

It is the intention of this chapter to look at the source which I believe takes the reader the furthest out on a limb in this regard, and that is Gaspar de Alba's novel, *Sor Juana's Second Dream*. The title refers back to Sor Juana's seminal work, *The Dream*, which is perhaps one of the first philosophical treatises on life and our place in the cosmos. This work has been successfully translated and commented on, most notably by Luis Harss.[15] Sor Juana has been quoted as writing that it is the only poem she had ever written for her own pleasure. 'I dreamed that I wanted to understand at once all things that make up the universe.' Harss is not sure this quote can be attributed to Sor Juana herself; perhaps, he suggests, *The Dream* is not a record of an ordinary dream, unless by 'dream' we mean a lifetime's unfulfilled desire.[16]

If this is her first dream, an exploration into a 'lifetime's unfulfilled desire', then Gaspar de Alba explores the *fulfilment* of at least one of Sor Juana's articulated desires. Perhaps it is the unfulfilled desire of the first *Dream* that is fulfilled in *Sor Juana's Second Dream*. What is *Sor Juana's Second Dream* after all? Gaspar de Alba suggests it is the dream of her love for women, and not just that but a dream

14. Jaime Manrique, 'Forward: Sor Juana and Love', in Larkin and Manrique, *Sor Juana's Love Poems*, p. 11. (Emphasis added.)

15. Luis Harss, *Sor Juana's Dream: Translation, Introduction and Commentary* (New York: Lumen Books, 1986).

16. Ibid., p. 2.

of a life where this love for women could be *actualized*. The author goes inside the head and heart of Sor Juana and lives the life we imagine is behind the love poems translated by Manrique and Larkin, the life that some critics are afraid to imagine, and some are titillated to imagine, but none have actually unpacked and *imagined* – i.e., *imaged* to life.

I want to explore the *necessity* for using the academic language of *fiction* as a valid device for uncovering queer lineage. Why is it, or is it not, necessary to fictionalize the contested subject in order to explore her contested *sexuality*? Is fiction a legitimate discourse and exploratory tool for this examination? What does this tool bring to light in the writings of, for example, a figure as hotly contested as Sor Juana? How does the fiction writer employ the known academic sources and when must she invent? When she does this, how, and indeed does she remain true to the known historical sources?

And, finally, how do the secondary sources impact on the lineage of a figure such as Sor Juana? I was particularly interested in looking at the intersection of primary and secondary sources in a figure like Sor Juana. For at what point does the lineage *become* the secondary sources and what the woman originally *said* become not *what she meant*?

In the example of Sor Juana it appeared that what she meant in her poetry had been *decided* not by the poetry itself but by the secondary sources' *interpretations* of what she meant. The secondary sources' impact upon the original primary sources remained fixed until scholars skilled in both academia and art employed *art* to impact upon not necessarily the primary work, *but also on the secondary sources' interpretations of the primary sources* – as is the case with *Sor Juana's Second Dream*. Gaspar de Alba uses art to *deconstruct* the secondary sources' *impact* on the primary sources and she therefore *returns the primary* sources to being primary. In other words, *Sor Juana's Second Dream* posits the radical notion that what Sor Juana wrote is what Sor Juana meant.

What Gaspar de Alba does is posit herself between and beyond the secondary interpretations. Certainly Sor Juana *is* intellectual, and yes she was a nun, and no she was not the saint that the early interpretations painted. However, Gaspar de Alba clearly sees that one of her personal contributions is giving Sor Juana *a body*. And she sees fiction as the tool that allows her 'access' to the reality of Sor Juana as first and foremost corporeal, *as inhabiting a body*.

> I've been a writer longer than an academic. I was already established in the field before I became an academic. Using fiction allowed me the kind of freedom that I would not have been allowed in an academic study. I wouldn't have been able to probe her heart and head in academic language as I was able to do in fiction. *I wanted to dis-clothes her. To look under her skirt. To see the woman.*[17]

As an example of *discarding* the body, consider *Juana Ines de la Cruz and the Theology of Beauty: The First Mexican Theology* by George Tavard (1997), which lifts up an interesting 'historical point' regarding her much contested 'conversion'.

---

17. Gaspar de Alba, interview, 14 July 2000.

In her deeds during the last years of her life, Sor Juan Ines de la Cruz was, no less than in her literary career, a child of the baroque age and imagination. The vow that she signed with her blood was taken, precisely in the seventeenth century, by innumerable confraternities of the immaculate conception that flourished in the cities of Spain. It was taken in 1617 by the universities of Granada, Alcala, Baeza, Santiago, Toledo and Saragossa, in 1618 by the university of Salmanca, in 1619 by the university of Huesca, in 1646 by King John IV of Portugal. The form of Sor Juan's self-renunciation and of consecration to the mother of God was borrowed from the accepted piety of her times. What she abandoned was unique to herself.[18]

While this viewpoint, that what was happening in Spanish universities can be easily translated into a motive for Sor Juana's actions, is not explored further, this explanation for her conversion does try to suggest links between her actions as a religious and some sense of 'normal' historical trajectory, rather than the hierarchal plot suggested by Paz and others. It does not account for the distance between Spain and Mexico in terms of influence, nor the fact that Paz is *crediting men at the universities for informing a nun in the convent.*

This negation of any 'heroics' on her part is explicated further in Tavard:

> one can learn a good deal from the theology of Sor Juan Ines de la Cruz in a number of areas … she affirms the rights of women to study, and to study theology; but she does not demand the right to teach. If she anticipates some aspects of women's emancipation, the question of the ordination of women does not come up. And *she seems to have no basic problem about the subordinate place of religious women in the Church's structure.* A number of conventions that would be questioned today she takes for granted … Juana is by no means a revolutionary.[19]

Again, he seems to not be reading the primary source, for if Sor Juana says anything in *La Respuesta*, she says she has many disagreements with the Church hierarchy, particularly with its insistence on women being silent in the Church. She handles a brilliant defence of women's right to learn throughout history and in Scripture, including among others Deborah and Ruth, in order for her to make the assertion that women's place is *not* to remain silent as Paul suggests, but *to learn.* If not, she asks, how does one explain Deborah?

One of Sor Juana's main lines of defence throughout *La Respuesta* was that she was not *alone*, she counts scriptural and Catholic female figures as prefiguring her and giving her a history for female authority and the authority to write – among them Deborah, but also Esther, Guadalupe, the Virgin and St Catherine. She did not have an investment in being *the* revolutionary but rather in preserving and continuing a lineage of radical women.

Tavard of course does not explain the *existence* of Sor Juana's erotica in his assertion that she is not a 'revolutionary'. While he contends that Juana's theology is the first to have chosen 'beauty – the fourth transcendental, as the chief attribute

---

18.   George H. Tavard, *Juana Ines de la Cruz and the Theology of Beauty: The First Mexican Theology* (Notre Dame, IN: University of Notre Dame Press, 1991), p. 183.

19.   Ibid., p. 184. (Emphasis added.)

of God',[20] he also suggests[21] that while her explication may be sufficient for the artist 'latent in all men and women' the theologian may wish for some clarification regarding 'her point where the physical and spiritual beauty of creatures that is a gift of God's love triggers a theophany through which the divine glory is perceived'.[22]

Perhaps if he had placed her work *in the context of her body of work*, as Gaspar de Alba and other queer scholars have done, he would have found the clarification he asks for: she clearly *continually* creates a space for her theology in her glorification of the body and of desire – the physical and spiritual. Through his own dismissal of a majority of her work he misses the very information he says she does not provide. What seems apparent here is that since Juana does not provide the information that Tavard *wants to find*, he feels he has the right to assert that she *did not provide* that information.

The actual debates about Sor Juana centre around three main themes:

1. Was Sor Juana's conversion forced from the outside, due to political intrigue beyond her control, or was it a religious statement she made towards strengthening a weakened faith due to excessive involvement in the profane? Did the pressure for her to 'convert' begin at the time of her confession, or much earlier, at the time she dismisses her confessor?
2. Was she primarily an intellectual? A nun on a religious path? An artist? How should she be classified and what is her most important body of work – the plays? The feminism? The poetry? The love poetry? The correspondence? What constitutes legitimate work worthy of theological consideration? Of queer studies contemplation? Of unique and not mediocre artistry? Of feminism?
3. Was Sor Juana a physically active lesbian, a lesbian *à la* 'Boston marriage', where the most intense emotional bond is with another woman but it is not a sexual bond, or should her 'love poetry' be reclassified as statements towards God, or simply removed from her canon for serious consideration?

I believe, as stated in the earlier sections, that Gaspar de Alba is most successful in unpacking several of these controversies, most notably Sor Juana's queer lineage, because she allows the primary sources to mean what they say. She does not interpret *over* the sources as much as the traditional secondary sources have done. And she is free from having to address the secondary sources because she is an artist and can go directly to the primary sources. This may be an important lesson for queer scholarship. Perhaps one of the ways to address contested lines of enquiry is through art.

While many of the 'serious' studies ask questions about 'the nature of the erotic friendship' in their preface, hinting that these questions will be addressed within the volume, none of them gives serious consideration to the topic and none of them

20. Ibid., p. 196.
21. Ibid., p. 215.
22. Ibid., p. 215.

mentions *previous work* on the topic – except for mentioning the film, *I, the Worst of All.* However, they do not address it as 'serious' scholarship, because it is 'art' and therefore can not be considered 'theory'.

They also do not take into account small-press scholarship, which is where most queer scholarship has been traditionally based, such as the anthology *Lesbian Nuns*, which in its Introduction places Sor Juana in the context of a lesbian lineage.

Gaspar de Alba's work, and recent work on the existence of lesbian nuns, such as Judith Brown's *Immodest Acts: The Life of a Lesbian Nun in Renaissance Italy*,[23] about a lesbian abbess in fifteenth-century Italy, give credence to a different 'interpretation'. This seminal work by Brown is quoted primarily only by Gaspar de Alba, even though the study does give credence to at least the possibility of a 'lesbian nun' in the medieval world.

As noted throughout, apparently only the queer studies scholars quote the 'queer studies' research. I would suggest that this position means that scholars who are not looking at queer studies research when researching a contested figure are usually not *historically accurate*, and do little to place a person authentically within his or her actual environment.

It is more than time for general scholarship in any field to consider seriously areas of queer scholarship. This is particularly important in an academic space as loaded with speculation as the field of Sor Juana. It should no longer be considered legitimate or worthy scholarship to lop off areas of enquiry that might make the scholar him or herself uncomfortable, or which do not fit his or her 'theory'.

For instance, it is not worthy scholarship to neglect Juana's correspondence with women when discussing 'religion, art and feminism' in favour of her correspondence with men, and not provide examples of each, in favour of merely stating that the correspondence with men is more important in its 'brilliance'.

As noted, if it weren't for Sor Juana's relationship with the vicereine, the majority of her work would never have been published – including *La Respuesta*, the most contested piece of her work. This relationship is not minor, but rather is *the central relationship* that scholars must study, and the relationship that scholarship *owes* the most to – for without the vicereine's patronage we have little Sor Juana to study.

The field of queer scholarship is young, and it needs a fresh look at the primary work. Right now, what is obvious is that the majority of the secondary work in this particular field, *outside of artistic endeavour*, as witnessed in this unpacking of Gaspar de Alba's *Sor Juana's Second Dream,* cannot provide answers – especially as it has refused serious entertainment of the questions.

23. Judith Brown, *Immodest Acts: The Life of a Lesbian Nun in Renaissance Italy* (Oxford: Oxford University Press, 1986).

2

FRIENDSHIP WITH BENEFITS: A QUEER READING OF AELRED OF
RIEVAULX AND HIS THEOLOGY OF FRIENDSHIP

Martín Hugo Córdova Quero

> It is no mean consolation in this life to have someone with whom you can be
> united by an intimate attachment and the embrace of very holy love ... You may
> be so united to him and approach him so closely and so mingle your spirit with
> his, that the two become one.
>
> (Aelred of Rievaulx)

To queer the past implies to ask different questions of it. It implies to que(e)r(y)
the past, attempting to find answers that go beyond what has traditionally been
accepted. This entitles a *risk of anachronism* when looking at *texts* that come
to us from the past: writings, stories, legends, episodes ... different *texts* in
different *devices* with which we attempt to (re)construct that past. In using the
term *(re)construct* for medieval sexuality, Mark Jordan states that it means:
'at least, that a sexuality is the kind of thing that must be constructed; that
the medievals, if they had such a thing, had to construct it for themselves;
that we have to (re)construct their constructions; that we (re)construct what
they constructed as a "sexuality"'[1] This *(re)construction* also implies a
(de)construction of the ways we traditionally have *(re)constructed* the past.
Heteronormativity is not absent from the base of the latter process.[2] It is present
in the tools and the lenses through which past events are analysed and brought
to our present times. The presence of heteronormativity in all activities of
human beings represents a conditioning especially for the academic work. To
queer, then, is to *disrupt* the presence of heteronormativity in academic work,
positing a different approach, attempting to discover the conflicts that are not

---

1.   Mark D. Jordan, 'Homosexuality, *Luxuria*, and Textual Abuse' in Karma Lochrie *et
al.*, *Constructing Medieval Sexuality*, Medieval Cultures Series No. 11 (Minneapolis, MN:
University of Minnesota Press, 1997), p. 24.

2.   We need to consider throughout this chapter that in exploring the past we face language as
a conditioning. Words that explain concepts to us in the present time did not exist in past times.
Concepts from the past are understood differently in present times. To speak in the same way that
past societies did is practically impossible. In this chapter, I will try to pay particular attention to
this fact of language. However, in the case of *heteropatriarchalism* and *heteronormativity* I will
use those terms as heuristic elements from present times to understand the matrix of social and
sexual order in the past, whilst being aware that, as categories, such concepts were nonexistent
in Aelred's life and work as well as in his society and monastery.

being articulated by the sanctioned discourse of academia in relation to the case studied.[3]

In this sense, Judith Butler, in her book *Bodies that Matter*,[4] talks about the term *queer*, understanding it as a process of (re)appropriation and reversal/contestation. She starts with a series of questions about the term *queer* that really posit a deep reflection on how the queering is related to that *matrix* – the heteronormativity – which the term attempts to *disrupt*. Butler wonders not only about how this process of reversal arose and functioned but also about the implications related to that process. In agreeing with Eve Kosofsky Sedgwick, Butler states an affirmation related to the central question for the process of queering: 'Eve Sedgwick's recent reflections on queer performativity ask us not only to consider how a certain theory of speech acts applies to queer practices, but how it is that "queering" persists as a defining moment of performativity.'[5] This is related to the implications of the queering, basically as regards the limits of queering in order not to reiterate the performances of the *matrix* that it is trying to *disrupt*/queer. Butler states further in defining the process of queering:

> Within queer politics, indeed, within the very signification that is 'queer', we read a resignifying practice in which the desanctioning power of the name 'queer' is reversed to sanction a contestation of the terms of sexual legitimacy. Paradoxically, but also with great promise, the subject who is 'queered' into public discourse through homophobic interpellations of various kinds *takes up* or *cites* that very term as the discursive basis for an opposition. This kind of citation will emerge as theatrical to the extent that it mines and renders hyperbolic the discursive convention that it also reverses. The hyperbolic gesture is crucial to the exposure of the homophobic 'law' that can no longer control the terms of its own abjecting strategies.[6]

My point here is that in the process of queering the past, we need to deal not only with the historical event we attempt to analyse – which is reiterated inside the heteronormativity of its own time – but also with the sciences related to the analysis and (re)construction of that event – whether history, theology, anthropology, etc., in relation to their own heteropatriarchal lenses. It is a double process that implies the opening up of the space of the historical event to new discourses as well as the opening up of the methods and procedures of the sciences attempting to analyse that case. Here the work of Sedgwick helps us. In her book *Tendencies* she states that 'queering is a performance that exploits and exposes "the open mesh of

---

3. I think that we need to begin by losing our way in order to discover the conflicts of motives and the surplus of stories that beset us whenever we approach these topics. Conflicting motives of historical accuracy, political advocacy, personal enunciation. Surplus stories of misreadings corrected, repressions overcome, sufferings redeemed. The motives and stories cannot be reconciled or reduced in advance. We can begin only by displaying the conflicts and enacting the stories. (Jordan, 'Homosexuality', p. 24.)

4. Judith Butler, *Bodies that Matter: On the Discursive Limits of 'Sex'* (New York: Routledge, 1993), p. 223.

5. Ibid., p. 224. In this sentence, Butler is referring to Sedgwick's article 'Queer Performativity' in *GLQ*, 1.1 (spring 1993).

6. Ibid., p. 232. (Emphasis in original.)

possibilities, gaps, overlaps, dissonances and resonances, lapses and excesses of meaning when the constituent elements of anyone's gender, or anyone's sexuality aren't made (or *can't be* made) to signify monolithically"'.[7]

Therefore, to queer the past is a *performative disruption* in order to open up spaces for other discourses from the past to arise and be heard in the conversation nowadays, as well as dealing with the performances of different discourses in the academy. To queer the past is not to transplant *gays, lesbians, bisexuals* or *trans-sexuals* into the past, but to *disrupt* monolithic discourses that oppress historical periods. It also refers to the fact that we need to be conscious that our own lenses should be *disrupted* and that the result of that process of *disruption* is not to re-iterate hegemonic heteropatriarchal discourses. As Lochrie affirms:

> Queering does not seek to discover or install lesbian and gay identities in pre-modern subjects of histories; rather, it *risks the anachronism* of speaking of sexuality in the first place to unsettle the heterosexual paradigms of scholarship; to contest medieval representational practices across sexual, gender, and class lines; and to produce readings of medieval texts that trouble our assumptions about medieval culture and textual practices.[8]

In the present writing I attempt to turn to one specific case and speak of 'sexuality, gender and class lines' in order to *disrupt* the heteronormative protocols of repre-sentation and to question historicist and literary assumptions, especially in relation to a religion such as Christianity, by assuming that *risk of anachronism*.

Queer theory helps us to realize that bodies, sexualities, sexual orientations and the performances of gender have all been colonized by heterosexism, which pervades all dimensions of life in a way that oppresses all human beings. Bodies have been the *geography* of this occupation, the place where colonialism has kept sexuality captive. When we talk about colonization of sexuality and bodies, we are talking primarily about the colonization of identities and performances. The violence of this process is revealed in the process of *normalization* which, in this case, can also be called *heterosexualization*. Whatever does not fit into the binary produced by heterosexism must be mistreated.

Butler makes queer theory by using *gender performance* based on the repetition of practices. 'The rules that govern intelligible identity, i.e. that enable and restrict the intelligible assertion of an "I", rules that are partially structured along matrices of gender hierarchy and compulsory heterosexuality, operate through repetition.'[9] Her *performing* resistance to *compulsory heterosexuality* points to the opening up of spaces of *disruption* in the midst of a situation that will continue being ruled by heterosexism: 'If the rules governing signification not only restrict, but enable the assertion of alternative domains of cultural intelligibility, i.e., new possibilities for gender that contest the rigid codes of hierarchical binarisms, then it is only within the practices of repetitive signifying that a subversion of identity becomes

7.   Eve Kosofsky Sedgwick, *Tendencies* (Durham, NC: Duke University Press, 1993), p. 8.

8.   Karma Lochrie, 'Mystical Acts, Queer Tendencies', in Lochrie *et al., Medieval Sexuality*, p. 180. (Emphasis added.)

9.   Judith Butler, *Gender Trouble: Feminism and the Subversion of Identity* (New York: Routledge, 1999), p. 185.

possible.'[10] Therefore, '[t]he critical task is, rather, to locate strategies of subversive repetition enabled by those constructions, to affirm the local possibilities of intervention through participating in precisely those practices of repetition that constitute identity and, therefore, present the immanent possibility of contesting them.'[11] We are inside the matrix, which implies participating actively in the repetition of practices, but, '[t]he task is not whether to repeat, but how to repeat or, indeed, to repeat and, through a radical proliferation of gender, *to displace* the very gender norms that enable the repetition itself'.[12] It is in the direction of this *disruption* that I turn to the case of Aelred in order to observe how he managed to *disrupt* the order of the norms of his time and to posit a different understanding of community at Rievaulx.

Aelred's *theology of friendship* cannot be fully understood when separated from his life. The experiences and feelings he shared in his works give meaning and substance to his theology. The fascinating integration of personal experiences in Aelred's life is an excellent case for unpacking the way past generations dealt with issues of gender, sexuality and religion. According to Walter Daniel, Aelred wrote 'twenty *opuscula*, two hundred sermons, thirty-three homilies on the burdens of Isaiah, as well as three hundred letters'.[13] None is an autobiography in the strict sense. When we want to know what Aelred says about his own life, we need to turn to those works of his that do contain certain autobiographical elements. These elements are so strong in *Speculum Caritatis* that Squire compares its first chapters with Augustine's *Confessions.*[14] Aelred's deepest confessions are also found in *De Spirituali Amicitia.* Many have written about the life of Aelred in relation to his spirituality and relationality[15] as well as his theology,[16] and monastic rule.[17] Rather than repeat what others have already done, in this chapter I will explore Aelred's life and theology by using queer theory.

In exploring Aelred's life and theology by using queer theory, we attempt to see how sexuality and gender performances are constructed in that specific case. That construction has connection to the way in which society is organized and its

---

10.   Ibid.

11.   Ibid., p. 188.

12.   Ibid., p. 189. (Emphasis in the original.)

13.   Peter Fergusson and Stuart Harrison. *Rievaulx Abbey: Community, Architecture, Memory* (New Haven, CT: Yale University Press, 1999), p. 65.

14.   Aelred Squire compares the first chapters of *Speculum Caritatis* with Chapters 9 and 10 of Augustine's *Confessions.* (Aelred Squire, *Aelred of Rievaulx: A Study* [London: SPCK, 1987], p. 43.)

15.   This is one of the most developed issues of Aelred's work. We can mention: Brian Bethume, 'Personality and Spirituality: Aelred of Rievaulx and Human Relations', *Cistercian Studies* 20 (1985): 98–112; Charles Dumont, 'St Aelred: The Balanced Life of the Monk', *Monastic Studies* 1 (1963): 25–38; and Amedee Hallier, 'God is Friendship: The Key to Aelred of Rievaulx's Christian Humanism', *American Benedictine Review* 18 (1967): 393–420.

16.   See, for example, Amedee Hallier, *The Monastic Theology of Aelred of Rievaulx: An Experiential Theology,* trans. C. Heaney (Kalamazoo, MI: Cistercian Publications, 1969); and O. Brooke. 'Towards a Theology of Connatural Knowledge', *Citeaux* 18 (1967): 275–90.

17.   Lawrence C. Braceland, 'Bernard and Aelred on Humility and Obedience', in *Erudition at God's Service,* ed. J.R. Sommerfeldt (Kalamazoo, MI: Cistercian Publications, 1987), pp. 149–60.

relationship to those constructions, attempting to understand and discover how the multiple possibilities and cultural interpretations of gender and sexuality are embodied and performed in a historical moment that differs from our own. Butler, in her book *Gender Trouble*, helps us to realize how queer theory deconstructs given categories and reconstructs a new meaning in order to allow for the multiple gender and sexual experiences of human beings, and open up identity to *fluidity* more near to *constructionism*[18] than to *essentialism.*[19]

Speculum Caritatis

Speculum Caritatis (*Mirror of Charity*) is one of the most important of Aelred's works, and perhaps the starting point of his *theology of friendship.*[20] The main purpose of this treatise is to help the novice mould himself for monastic life.[21] In addition to the clear, solidly based analysis that Aelred makes of charity and the beauty of the language he uses for contemplation,[22] this treatise is one of the first places where he starts to tell us about his intimate life.

In *Speculum Caritatis* Aelred tells us about his first close friend, Simon, a fellow monk. They developed a close and deep friendship, but it did not last long because Simon died very young. In his grief Aelred, at the loss of his most beloved one, wrote a lament for Simon that was included in the conclusion of the first book of *Speculum Caritatis*:

18.   Annamarie Jagose points out: 'Constructionists assume identity is fluid, the effect of social conditioning and available cultural models for understanding oneself … [They] assume that because same-sex sex acts have different cultural meaning in different historical contexts, they are not identical across time and space' (Annamarie Jagose, *Queer Theory: An Introduction* [New York: New York University Press, 1996], pp. 8–9).

19.   '[E]ssentialists regard identity as natural, fixed and innate … Essentialists assume that homosexuality exists across time as a universal phenomenon which has a marginalized but continuous and coherent history of its own' (Jagose, *Queer Theory*, pp. 8–9).

20.   Here, Aelred shows solid formation in Trinitarian and anthropological theology as well as the Scriptures and Patristic writings, especially of those Fathers who wrote in Latin. See M. Basil Pennington, *The Last of the Fathers: The Cistercian Fathers of the Twelfth Century. A Collection of Essays* (Still River, MI: St Bede's Publications, 1993), pp. 223–33. See also from the same author: 'A Primer on the School of Love', in *Citeaux* 31 (1980): 93–104.

21.   The treatise has 100 chapters divided into three books of different lengths. The first book addresses the nature of charity. The second treats the opposite of charity, that is, cupidity. Book III describes the various ways in which charity and cupidity are manifested, and compares them with each other. See William Michael Ducey, 'St Ailred of Rievaulx and the *Speculum Caritatis*', in *Catholic Historical Review* 17 (1931): 312–14.

22.   See the trilogy of John R. Sommerfeldt: 'The Vocabulary of Contemplation in Aelred of Rievaulx's *Mirror of Love*, Book I', in *Goad and Nail*, ed. E.R. Elder (Kalamazoo, MI: Cistercian Publications, 1987), pp. 241–50; 'Images of Visitation: The Vocabulary of Contemplation in Aelred of Rievaulx's *Mirror of Love*, Book II' and 'The Rape of the Soul: The Vocabulary of Contemplation in Aelred of Rievaulx's *Mirror of Love*, Book III', in *Erudition at God's Service*, ed. J.R. Sommerfeldt (Kalamazoo, MI: Cistercian Publications, 1987), pp. 161–8, 169–74.) See also Aelred Squire, 'Aelred of Rievaulx and the Monastic Tradition Concerning Action and Contemplation', *Downside Review* 72 (1954): 289–303; and M.L. Dutton, 'Christ Our Mother: Aelred's Iconography for Contemplative Union', in Elder, *Goad and Nail*, pp. 21–45.

My case is the same. I grieve for my most beloved, for the one-in-heart with me who has been snatched from me, and I rejoice that he is taken up to [the] eternal tabernacle. My attachment seeks his sweet presence which nourished it delightfully, but my reason does not agree that this soul, beloved by me, once free from the flesh should again be subject to the miseries of the flesh ... Here now, O Lord, I shall follow his ways, that in you I may enjoy his company. I was able to do so, Lord, though at a slow pace, when my eyes observed his devout way of life, when the sight of his humility blunted my pride, when the thought of his tranquility calmed my restlessness and when the bridle of his admirable seriousness checked my levity. I remember that often when my eyes were darting here and there, at one glimpse of him I was filled with such shame that, suddenly recovering my self, I checked all that levity by the strength of his seriousness and, pulling myself together, I began to employ myself in something useful. The authority of our Order forbade conversation; his appearance spoke to me, his walk spoke to me, his very silence spoke to me. His appearance was modest, his walk mature, his speaking serious and his silence without bitterness.[23]

The tone with which Aelred describes his feelings for Simon appears to be based on the *Song of Songs*. As is to be expected, Aelred expresses his feelings in words fitting for a medieval monastery. It could not be expected that he should use words directly from the *Song of Songs* in the way we might nowadays, especially through our lenses highly influenced by Victorian conceptions and (post)modernism. That would be simply anachronistic and pointless in the understanding of Aelred's case. Nonetheless, there is a homoerotic component that can be traced in the way that Aelred constructs his argument, which is surprisingly similar to the way that the argument is built on the *Songs of Songs*. For example, it is noteworthy that the mere *sight* of his friend instantly causes changes of great magnitude: a fact that could be also interpreted as the geography for homoerotic[24] feelings – something

23. *Speculum Caritatis* I.34: 106–7. (hereafter *Spec. Car.*), in Aelred of Rievaulx, *The Mirror of Charity*, trans. Elizabeth Connor (Kalamazoo, MI: Cistercian Publications, 1990), pp. 152–3.

24. The word *gay* applied to persons of same-sex eroticism is something that happens later in human history (nineteenth and twentieth-century). But, beyond the correct terminology, *homoeroticism* is something that could be found practically in all moments of human history. I do not use the term *gay* in this chapter, instead I choose to use the term *homoeroticism*. Certainly, the term *sodomite* could be used to describe homoerotically oriented persons, as it was used in some cases in medieval times, but it was not clear enough (i.e., it could be used also for bisexual persons or, even, for heterosexual persons) and was marked negatively by the censorship of Christian ideology, from Augustine and Thomas Aquinas to Peter Damian and the Fourth Lateran Council (1215) and beyond. (See later on in this chapter.) By any point of view the binary *straight/inverted* is acceptable, which ideologically marks the *rightness* of heteroerotic-oriented people (straights) and the *wrongness* of homoerotic-oriented people (inverted). While John Boswell (*Homosexuality, Sexual Tolerance and Christianity* [Chicago, IL: University of Chicago Press, 1980], pp. 41–5, 222) and Kenneth Russell ('Aelred, the Gay Abbot of Rievaulx', *Studia Mystica* 5 [1982]: 51) openly affirm that Aelred was gay; other scholars like E. Christiansen (*English Historical Review* 96 (1981): 852–4) deny this affirmation. I follow the definition of Nissinen: 'I use the term *homoeroticism*. By this term I mean all erotic–sexual encounters and experiences of people with persons of the same sex, whether the person is regarded as homosexual or not. This concept encompasses also bisexual behavior as long as it occurs in an erotic contact with a person of the same sex.' (Martti Nissinen, *Homoeroticism in the Biblical World: A Historical Perspective* [Minneapolis, MN: Fortress, 1998], p. 17. Emphasis in the original.)

that is already present in the description of the feelings and bodies of the two lovers in *Song of Songs*.

Comparison of Aelred's feelings of separation and bereavement with these same feelings as expressed in the *Song of Songs* adds evidence that the love Aelred felt towards Simon is an expression of brotherly as well as erotic love. In a strict sense, Aelred is trying to express his feelings for Simon in the context of his *brotherly love*, but because his vocabulary is so related to the *Song of Songs*, eroticism comes into scene through his writing. We need to remember that Aelred is attempting to manage life in the absence of the beloved, a fact deeply connected to his theology. How is it possible to live after the one you love has died? It is in this context that we come to understand Aelred's words: *'labor, gemitus, dolor, et afflictio spiritus'*.[25] All those words describe him at this moment of his life. Especially when they have their greatest meaning in relation to the loss of this person who meant so much to him.

This is where we begin to see the connections between Aelred's life and theology. As this chapter demonstrates later, for Aelred these two were not and should not be separated. As with the *Song of Songs* there is a tendency to spiritualize this passage, to make it noncorporeal and disconnected from the rest of life.[26] It is now commonly accepted that the primary meaning of love in the *Song of Songs* is erotic, but it is an eroticism that is not divorced from spirituality.[27] In other words,

---

25. *Spec. Car.* I.28: 79. Literally means 'work, mourning, pain and spiritual affliction'. An important description of Aelred's feelings, especially when he related them to his conversion.

26. In order to avoid the topic of erotic love in Holy Scriptures, the *Song of Songs* was read in only a spiritual sense, divorced from material existence and daily life. From Patristic times onwards, this highly erotic text was said to refer only to Christ and his Church, especially in the allegoric reading of the *hortus conclusus* (the enclosed garden) in relation to virginity. The writings of Origen and St Jerome are particular important. Origen understands the characters of *Song of Songs* as follows: 'By the Bridegroom understand Christ, and by the Bride the Church *without spot or wrinkle*, of whom it is written: *that he might present her to Himself a glorious Church, not having spot or wrinkle or any such a thing, but that she might be holy and without blemish*' (Origen, *The Song of Songs Commentary and Homilies*, trans. R.P. Lawson [London: Longman, 1957], pp. 267–8). St Jerome, on his side, also refers to this allegoric reading, especially in his letter to Eustachium on *The Virgin's Profession*, where he affirms:

> Let the seclusion of your own chamber ever guard you; ever let the Bridegroom sport with you within. If you pray, you are speaking to your Spouse: if you read, He is speaking to you. When sleep falls on you, He will come behind the wall and will put His hand through the hole in the door and will touch your flesh. And you will awake and rise up and cry: 'I am sick with love.' And you will hear Him answer: 'A garden enclosed [*hortus conclusus*] is my sister, my spouse, a spring shut up a fountain sealed' (*Ad Eustochium* 22: 25. In *Select Letters of St Jerome*, ed. T.E. Page *et al.* [London: William Heinemann, 1933], p. 109).

27. Elsa Tamez and Pablo Andiñach – among other scholars – point out that the first meaning of the *Song of Songs* is the erotic love between two persons. Both scholars have published commentaries on the *Song of Songs* taking into account the erotic aspect of the text. See Elsa Tamez, *Los Juegos del Erotismo del Texto* (unpublished dissertation, Universidad Biblica Latinoamericana, San José, Costa Rica); and Pablo Andiñach, *Cantar de los Cantares: El Fuego y la Ternura* (Buenos Aires: Lumen, 1997).

the eroticism of the text is embodied taking into account an incarnated anthropology.

Given the clarity and directness of the rest of his text, it is unlikely that Aelred meant to write about a disembodied, ethereal love in his words about Simon. The intensity of Aelred's love for Simon could be read as the same kind of intensity that is described in the *Song of Songs*; thus to 'spiritualize' Aelred's words and make them noncorporeal is to avoid their potential for erotic content, in this case for homoeroticism. When addressing the possibility of erotic content, it is important to remember that erotic feelings do not necessarily or automatically imply genital activity. These are two phenomena that may or may not be related.[28] In denying the erotic, we lose the body, the passions and the most direct connections with daily life. We also lose an opportunity to explore how homoerotic concerns arise and are addressed in Aelred's writings and how these contribute to his *theology of friendship*, which is a strategy of heteronormativity in the patterns of iterative discourses. For Aelred, Simon's death is a test and a means to develop the strength in life to face the absence of his beloved. Nonetheless, this queer reading of Aelred's writing can be complemented by the way homoeroticism is covered in his other great work, *De Spirituali Amicitia (On Spiritual Friendship)*.

De Spirituali Amicitia

The experience of losing his beloved friend did not cause Aelred to stop his life's pilgrimage towards the development of his *theology of friendship* built upon his personal experience of friendship and love within the context of Rievaulx monastery. Due to this character, a queer reading of the text attempts to address the subversive elements related to it. I turn now to Aelred's great work about friendship, *De Spirituali Amicitia*.[29] For Aelred, friendship is a combination of affection and reason, but that combination follows from an existing love of God that is experienced by both friends prior to their friendship.[30]

---

28. In taking into account the distinction between sexuality and genital sex, it is impossible to say from any of Aelred's writings that he explicitly admitted having had genital sex, but it does not mean that he never expressed his homoerotic feelings through the ways and terms he chooses for writing his works. I also understand that the case of female homoeroticism could have different aspects that are not completely contemplated in this paper. For further research on female homoeroticism in early Christianity, see Bernadette J. Brooten, *Love Between Women: Early Christian Responses to Female Homoeroticism* (Chicago, IL: University of Chicago Press, 1996). For medieval times, especially the Renaissance, see Judith C. Brown, *Immodest Acts: The Life of a Lesbian Nun in Renaissance Italy* (Oxford: Oxford University Press, 1986).

29. *De Spirituali Amicitia* (hereafter *De Spir. Am.*) is a collection of a prologue and three books under the form of dialogues about friendship. The structure is: (1) *Prologue*; (2) *Book I* What is Friendship?; (3) *Book II* The Advantages of Friendship; and (4) *Book III* The Requirements of Unbroken Friendship. (For a detailed analysis of this prologue, see James McEvoy, 'Notes on the Prologue of St Aelred of Rievaulx' *De Spirituali Amicitia*, with Translation', in *Traditio* 37 (1981): 396–411.)

30. *De Spir.Am.* III: 5, Aelred of Rievaulx, *Spiritual Friendship*. (Cistercian Fathers Series, No. 5), trans. Mary Eugenia Laker (Washington, DC: Cistercian Publications/Consortium Press, 1974), p. 92.

The ideal of friendship is not absent from descriptions of monastic life. It was developed before Aelred's time, especially in Patristic writings, as is shown in Rosemary Rader's study of Patristic monasticism:

> The rise of celibate asceticism allowed women and men to reject the designated sexual roles of society and create a social system supportive of a new way of life. Heterosexual friendship developed in response to the need for reciprocal support in realizing the mutual goals of ascetic endeavors. Literature of the period [fourth and fifth centuries] confirms that generally only those women who were dedicated to pursuing the 'angelic life' could transcend their allotted roles, to participate in other forms of ministry and a type of male/female relationship other than of marriage.[31]

With our own *(post)modern* terminology, we could read this qualitative shift introduced by Aelred as one that has the effect of transferring this ideal from its original *heteropatriarchal* context of *angelic* love into a *homoerotic* one. Aelred developed a theology that contains this homoerotic aspect after his experience of a second great friendship. However, unlike his friendship with Simon, in this case we do not know the name of the friend. John Boswell describes the circumstances of this new friendship in the following way: 'After the death of Simon, Aelred became attached to a younger monk and left a careful record of the development of their love, which, in contrast to his passion for Simon, grew slowly and cautiously.'[32] Although it is not possible to discover the name of that monk in *De Spirituali Amicitia,* Aelred does describe the process by which his love for this other monk developed:

> So love increased between us, our affection grew warmer, and our charity was strengthened until it got to the point that there was in us 'one heart and one mind, agreement in likes and dislikes', and this love was free of fear, ignorant of offence, utterly lacking in suspicion, recoiling from flattery ... after a fashion, I considered my own heart to be his, and his to be mine, and he himself felt likewise ... He was my spirit's resting place, a sweet comfort in times of grief; when I was tired with labors his loving heart received me, and his counsel refreshed me when I was sunk in sadness and lamentation. When I was stirred up he set me at ease, and when I became angry he calmed me. Whatever sadness came I took to him, so that I could bear more easily with my shoulders joined to his [the] burden I could not bear by myself. What shall I say then? Is it not a certain share of blessedness so to love and be loved, so to help and be helped, and thus to fly higher, from the sweetness of brotherly charity to that more sublime splendor of divine love, and now to ascend the ladder of charity to the embrace of Christ himself, and then to descend by the same ladder to the love of one's neighbor, where one may sweetly rest?[33]

We need to remember that this text is inscribed in the context of a writing that is about friendship. But the subversion of this context by Aelred leaves us with

---

31. Rosemary Rader, *Breaking Boundaries: Male/Female Friendship in Early Christian Communities* (New York: Paulist Press, 1983), p. 86.
32. Boswell, *Homosexuality*, p. 224.
33. *De Spir. Am.* III: 124–7.

an extraordinary homoerotic text. From the title onwards, Aelred uses a specific term to name this love towards his friend: '*amicitia*'. The connection between the concept of *amicitia* and the political patterns, as it is shown in the economic and social benefits of such friendships in the Roman Empire, is made through the ways in which male citizens developed the relationships. We may fairly infer that Aelred, by virtue of his intellectual/cultural background, uses the word *amicitia* in a Roman sense. The social meanings of the Latin word *amicitia*, which we translate as *friendship*, are important here. *Amicitia* had two different kinds of use in Roman times: one propounded by Cicero and the other by Ovid. Both usages come from Roman social conventions in which two political partners owe each other *amicitia*, that is, reciprocity and fidelity in the public field as well as in private life. The relationship also reproduces the hierarchically structured social order among Romans.[34] It is the use of this specific term that gives us the clue that Aelred's spiritual friendship was something more committed and common than it seems to be.

Amicitia was a common topic of discussion in Aelred's time, especially in light of the meaning contained in Cicero's writings. We know that Cicero wrote of *amicitia* as the intimate connection of virtue and friendship within the hierarchic priorities of the Roman aristocracy: good men could enhance each other through a friendship that was political.[35] On the other hand, we also know that Ovid valued the feelings of *amicitia* as more important than the prospect of political gain. In both cases the relationship indicated by the word *amicitia* was fundamentally rooted in a social practice that could include homoerotism, a fact not so strange in the Graeco-Roman world.[36]

---

34. Rader, *Breaking Boundaries*, p. 30.

35. Brian Patrick McGuire, *Friendship and Community: The Monastic Experience, 350–1250* (Kalamazoo, MI: Cistercian Publications, 1988), p. xxix.

36. In Greece, especially in Spartan society, homoerotic relationships were based on what is called a *pederastic* model, that is, the relation of an adult male to a younger male that includes sexual behaviour as well as training that will prepare the younger man to function well in society, especially for political and military activities. Athenian society was more ambiguous toward pederasty. But, unlike the Romans, pederasty with slaves was not tolerated among Greeks, because slaves were excluded from pedagogical formation. (See Nissinen, *Homoeroticism in the Biblical World*, p. 65.) Romans did not take pederasty as a pedagogical model for their society (ibid., p. 71). Instead, they tolerated homoeroticism of two kinds: (1) homoerotic relationships functioning in relation to social, economic and political status. It was supposed the active role would be always assumed by a citizen, while the passive role would be assumed by those of lower status: i.e. slaves. Boswell states:

> A very strong bias appears to have existed against passive sexual behavior on the part of an adult male citizen. Noncitizen adults (e.g., foreigners, slaves) could engage in such behavior without loss of status, as could Roman youths, provided the relationship was voluntary and nonmercenary. Such persons might in fact considerably improve their position in life through liaisons of this type. But if an adult citizen openly indulged in such behavior, he was viewed with scorn. Apart from general questions of gender expectations and sexual differentiation, the major cause of this prejudice appears to have been a popular association of sexual passivity with political impotence. (Boswell, *Homosexuality*, p. 74.)

In his *City of God,* Augustine takes the concept of *amicitia* as giving more weight to the Ciceronian interpretation than to the Ovidian one.[37] This Augustinian understanding regarding *Amicitia* was also the more common concept among monastic scholars in medieval times. That Aelred was uncomfortable with the Ciceronian concept of *amicitia* is explicit in his writings;[38] he preferred the Ovidian understanding.

Returning to the historical context, the connection with an understanding of *amicitia* as also including homoeroticism could be found in the probable link of Aelred with writings from the Loire School, which had begun to circulate widely among scholars and clergy in Europe around 1100 CE. Some decades before Aelred, interest in the Ovidian concept of *amicitia* appears in France in the writings of the Loire School, especially those of another abbot, Baudri of Bourgueil (*c.* 1078–1107).[39] Born to the aristocracy, Baudri rescued the concept of *amicitia* as a loving relationship between two persons of the same sex. This is the main core of his poetry. Baudri also wrote several letters to teachers from the lower classes, to priests and bishops who were mainly from the aristocracy and to other aristocrats.

---

(2) Homoerotic relationships in the context of prostitution. Although for a free citizen to become a prostitute was to lose his social position, prostitution was tolerated among noncitizens: foreigners and slaves. 'Prostitution, including male homosexual prostitution, was a common legal, and tolerated phenomenon in the Roman streets and baths. That male prostitution was legal becomes irrefutably clear from the fact that in the Augustan era male prostitutes, adult men and boys, paid taxes and were even entitled to an annual vacation day on the 26th of April' (Nissinen, *Homoeroticism in the Biblical World*, p. 70; see also Boswell, *Homosexuality*, pp. 77–80).

37. St Augustine quotes Cicero in different parts of *The City of God*, agreeing with Cicero's points of view. Especially in Book XII: 20, Augustine wonders about the possibility of loving somebody as a friend while realizing one might be destined to become their enemy. In doing this, he quotes the same question of Cicero in his *De Amicitia*, 16 (see Saint Augustine, *The City of God*, trans. Marcus Dods [New York: The Modern Library, 1950], p. 403). When St Augustine come to the section on friendship (Book XIX: 8–9) he states that human friendship is at risk of corruption due to human nature, death being the only possibility of overcoming this situation. Therefore, St Augustine affirms:

> Although, then, our present life is afflicted, sometimes in a milder, sometimes in a more painful degree, by the death of those very dear to us, and especially of useful public men, yet we would prefer to hear that such men were dead rather than to hear or perceive that they had fallen from the faith, or from virtue – in other words, that they were spiritually dead ... And hence we enjoy some gratification when our good friends die; for though their death leaves us in sorrow, we have the consolatory assurance that they are beyond the ills by which in this life even the best of men are broken down or corrupted, or are in danger of both results. (Ibid., pp. 684–5.)

38. See Charles Dumont. 'Aelred of Rievaulx's Spiritual Friendship', in *Cistercian Ideals*, p. 187.

39. Boswell situates Baudri between 1046 and 1130. Baudri was the abbot of the French Benedictine monastery of Saint Peter and later archbishop of Dol. Boswell also quotes Otto Schumann, who in his 'Baudri von Bourgueil als Dichter' [in *Studien zur lateinischen Dichtung des Mittelalters: Ehrengabe für Karl Strecker* (Dresden, 1931)] 'believed that Baudri's poems to men were insincere imitations of the writings of his model, Ovid, and cited as evidence of this his *Confessio poenitentialis* (184)' (Boswell, *Homosexuality*, p. 244, n. 1.)

In all of the letters, the homoerotic passion for the beloved friend is noteworthy. These writings were unknown outside France until around 1100 CE.[40]

As an abbot, writer and intellectual, Aelred would have probably known about Baudri's writings. Aelred expresses his rejection of the Ciceronian concept of *amicitia*,[41] while his use of the Ovidian understanding of *amicitia* is evident. As is demonstrated below, Aelred's concept of friendship and love is related to this latter understanding of *amicitia* within a monastic framework that protected it from the increasingly repressive conditions of society.

Society and sexuality

Like all of us, Aelred was moulded by his time. He could not escape it. He thought and acted according to his social conditioning. But Aelred was also part of a minority within society, one that did not entertain the same priorities as most communities within that social order. Homoeroticism, such as that expressed in his relationships with his beloved friends, was not a norm within medieval society as it was in non-Christian Roman society.

The way society is structured moulds human relations, sexual roles and attitudes. These are reflected especially in attitudes towards the body. In other words, society's intimate relationship with body and sexuality is manifested through the moral and social order. Two authors can help us to understand this relationship. Maurice Godelier, in *The Making of Great Men*[42] and Peter Brown in his *Body and Society*[43] state that there is an intimate relationship between the way body and sexuality are both moulded and the way society is structured by heteropatriarchy. Godelier in his conclusion 'The Ventriloquist's Dummy' clearly points out an interesting explanation for the arising of heteropatriarchy:

> There is no single cause, nor even an ultimate cause, of the diverse forms of male dominance encountered in history. I see rather a series of causes, which are not intentional at bottom, and which arrange themselves into a sort of hierarchy because certain ones play a more important role in the mechanism by which their efforts are combined into an outcome that is never the same from one society to another, or from one era to another. The assumption of unintentional reasons for the existence of male dominance would be sufficient to refute any conspiracy theory, but it should in no way be taken to mean that men, finding themselves in a socially advantageous position for unintentional reasons (which though meaningful obey no teleological imperative) have not worked intentionally and collectively to reproduce and widen this advantage.[44]

In taking into account this advantage of males over body and society we can start investigating the way in which the case of Aelred is inscribed in his religious and

---

40. See Gerald A. Bond, '"Iocus Amoris": The Poetry of Baudri of Bourgueil and the Formation of the Ovidian Subculture', in *Traditio* 42 (1986): 143–93.

41. Dumont, *Cisterian Ideals*, p. 187.

42. See Maurice Godelier, *The Making of Great Men: Male Domination and Power among the New Guinea Baruya*, trans. Rupert Swyer (Cambridge: Cambridge University Press, 1986).

43. Peter Brown, *The Body and Society. Men, Women and Sexual Renunciation in Early Christianity* (New York: Columbia University Press, 1988).

44. Godelier, *The Making of Great Men*, p. 231.

social context. Monasteries were still a place within society, and Western medieval society was shaped by Christianity. Therefore the way in which monasteries and society were organized resembles their understanding of body and sexuality. In the same direction, Brown points out in his studies for late antiquity:

> A thing of the natural world, the body was expected to speak of its own needs in an ancient, authoritative voice. It was only prudent to listen at times. The tolerance that was extended to the body in late classical times was based on a sense that the antithesis to the animal world, the city, was so strong that, once made, the claims of the city were inexorable. The family and the city determined the degree to which the results of the body's connection with the natural world was acceptable in organized society.[45]

As in our present time, Aelred's society was structured as other urban societies of his time. Rievaulx monastery was expected to follow this structure. According to that structure, there were roles and attitudes expected of the women and men within the social order, and people were under pressure to show fidelity to that order. Defying such a structured internalized order would imply defying the whole existence of humanity.[46]

Those persons with homoerotic feelings, those we today call *gay, lesbian, bisexual, transgender* and *intersex* people, may have been tolerated in some societies, but they were rarely fully integrated as part of society.[47] Medieval European women and men who were involved in homoerotic activities *disrupted* through their performance of gender and sexuality the social order – a fact of which those involved in *sodomy* practices (*vitium sodomitucum*) were completely unaware.[48] What underlies the punishment of individuals engaged in homoerotic practices

---

45. Brown, *The Body and Society*, p. 28.
46. Godelier noticed this in relation to the Baruyas:

> When language about the body becomes the language of the body there is nothing more to be said about society and the universe. All that remains is to experience a social and cosmic order to which the body has already submitted, beyond conscious and deliberate discourse. It is in the body rather than in consciously argued thought that 'intimate conviction' finds fulfilment and completes the demonstration that thought requires ... In fact, what is clear is that in any society, over and beyond personal relationships between individuals of either sex ... sexuality is subordinate to the conditions of reproduction of social relations. (Godelier, *The Making of Great Men*, p. 233.)

47. While Greek and Roman societies were more tolerant of homoeroticism, Western Christianity was especially intolerant to it, especially in medieval times. Boswell points out: 'Between 1250 and 1300, homosexual activity passed from being completely legal in most of Europe to incurring the death penalty in all but a few contemporary legal compilations.' (Boswell, *Homosexuality*, p. 293; see also R.I. Moore, *The Formation of a Persecuting Society: Power and Deviance in Western Europe, 950–1250* [Oxford: Blackwell, 1990], pp. 91–4.) It is not until the eighteenth and nineteenth centuries, according to Foucault, that people with homoerotic feelings or practices became a group in society with their own *identity* (ibid., p. 116).

48. *Sodomy* was a social construction that Christianity in medieval times took into account through reading biblical texts (especially from the Hebrew Bible) and Patristic writings in exclusive relation to homoeroticism. 'Peter Comestor (d. 1197) was the first influential scholar and teacher to interpret biblical injunctions against sodomy as referring specifically to homosexual

is the Augustinian conception of the body, which was seen as something related to sin and a dangerous thing, especially when in regard to sexual activity.[49] As in our present time, medieval society also conceived of the body as something to be strictly ruled by society.

We see in medieval Europe a growing process through which gender roles became more and more restricted. If, in the early medieval period, homoeroticism was tolerated, by late medieval times, it had became progressively less tolerated.[50] Two events accelerated this process: the circulation of Peter Damian's *Liber Gomorrhianus*,[51] and the deliberations of the Fourth Lateran Council.

Peter Damian, a Christian writer of the eleventh century, wrote a widely circulated work called *Liber Gomorrhianus* (c. 1048–54). In it he ignored the

---

intercourse.' (Moore, *The Formation of a Persecuting Society*, p. 92.) Mark Jordan states that this reading could be a textual abuse or misreading. He takes the example of Thomas Aquinas misreading a passage from St. Augustine's *Confessions* when interpreting *flagitia contra naturam* as *homoeroticism*. (Jordan, 'Homosexuality', in Lochrie, *Medieval Sexuality*, p. 29; see also the case-study of Joan Cadden, 'Sciences/Silences: The Natures and Languages of "Sodomy" in Peter of Abano's *Problemata* Commentary', ibid., pp. 40–57).

49. Augustine brings us to a new stage in early Christian thinking about the erotic ... Augustine introduces a note of profound sadness into the discussion by claiming that original sin is passed on to a child at the moment of conception. Even a 'natural', procreative sexual act between a subordinate wife and a husband who rules over her is deeply disturbed and characterized by sin, since humans cannot totally submit their sexual urges to their will. By asserting that sin imbues even a 'natural' sexual act within the legal confines of marriage, Augustine subtly banishes 'unnatural' sexual acts even further outside the realm of holiness (Brooten, *Love Between Women*, p. 355).

50. This progressive intolerance of homoeroticism can be seen in the records of inquisitorial tribunals. For example, Michael Rocke offers us an extensive research on homo-oriented males in Renaissance Florence judged over a period of 70 years by the Officers of the Night, an inquisitorial police in charge of the prosecution and punishment of males involved in *sodomy*. This specialized police only prosecuted severe cases of *sodomy* due to the extended practice in the Florentine male population – a fact that defied the regulations of Church and society. It was in the early fifteenth century that persecution became more severe due to political pressure. Rocke states:

> the agitation over sodomy was related in only a limited or an indirect way to this sexual practice in itself. In Florence, at least, other social and political factors played a decisive role in shaping the new repressive orientation in the early fifteenth century. Florence society in this period was undergoing a series of crises and transformations that, on the one hand, led to broad changes in administration of justice and, on the other, induced a stronger preoccupation about regulating many aspects of public morality, especially sexuality. (Michael Rocke, *Forbidden Friendships: Homosexuality and Male Culture in Renaissance Florence* [Oxford: Oxford University Press, 1996], p. 27.)

51. Peter Damian defines homoerotism as a *sin against nature* that can be performed in four categories:

> Four types of this form of criminal wickedness can be distinguished in an effort to show you the totality of the whole matter in an orderly way: (a) some sin with themselves alone; (b) some commit mutual masturbation; (c) some commit femoral fornication; and (d) finally, others commit the complete act against nature. The

ancient focus on hospitality, and defined homoerotic activities as that which brought the punishment of God on Sodom and Gomorrah. This was the first time that Sodom and Gomorrah, homoeroticism and sin were connected so strongly. As a result of the acceptance of Peter Damian's work – especially his later influence on the work of Peter Comestor, homoerotic desire was defined as a *sin*. Two important facts have to be mentioned in relation to this book. First, Peter Damian's book is written against those among the clergy who commit homoerotic acts; and second, although homoerotic practices have been forbidden and punished through *confession* as early as the sixth century when Ireland developed the auricular confession, Peter Damian's is the first systematic opposition to homoerotism, probably following Burchard of Worms, who made the most exhaustive collection of canonical penitential laws in 1002.[52]

This idea of *confession* is radically continued by the Fourth Lateran Council, which marks the beginning of what R.I. Moore calls *a persecuting society*.[53] The Council's decree of November 1215 established a more restrictive definition of Christian behaviour and, at the same time, positioned Christianity as the main requirement for all persons who were to be recognized as citizens of Western European lands for the next three centuries. The Council Fathers decided that

> All the faithful of both sexes shall, after they have reached the age of discretion, faithfully confess all their sins at least once a year to their own priest, and perform to the best of their ability the penance imposed, receiving reverently, at least at Easter, the sacrament of the Eucharist, unless perchance at the advice of their own priest they may for a good reason abstain for a time from its reception; otherwise they shall be cut off from the Church during life, and deprived of Christian burial in death.[54]

Confession was no longer a personal decision but a requirement of the law. Christians with homoerotic feelings or behaviour were faced with impossible choices. They could avoid confession, be cut off from their community and denied a Christian burial. They could be seen and treated as unrepentant sinners and a source of contagion like lepers. They could lie to the priest during confession thereby, by medieval standards, damning their own souls. Even more, they could turn their bodies and lives into a lie just by forcing themselves to feel and behave in a heteroerotic manner that would be alien to them. (This last was also a damning for their souls due to the prohibition on bearing false witness in the Ten Commandments.)

After this decree, to be Christian was the law, taking away all possibility of plurality. Thereafter, society began a more systematic persecution of Jews,

---

ascending gradation among these is such that the last mentioned are judged to be more serious than the preceding. (Peter Damian, *Book of Gomorrah*, trans. Pierre J. Payer [Waterloo, Ontario: Wilfrid Laurier University Press, 1982], p. 29.)

52. See Moore, *The Formation of a Persecuting Society*, p. 24.

53. See also Michel Foucault, *History of Sexuality* (New York: Vintage Books, 1990), p. 116.

54. E. Peters, *Heresy and Authority in the Middle Ages* (London, 1980), p. 177 (quoted by Moore, *The Formation of a Persecuting Society*, p. 6).

Muslims, prostitutes, lepers, and of those persons who engaged in homoerotic acts – all such persons were the victims of systematic persecution.[55] These groups did not fit into the stronger definitions of Christian social and sexual order. They *disrupted* the social order, putting at risk the homogenizing process that the Christian Church had chosen for society as its response to the catastrophes of those times. They also *disrupted* the sexual order, especially persons who engaged in homoerotic acts, and prostitutes, through the *macula* of impurity that labelled them. In other words, persons from these groups produced social fear because of the idea that social punishment was the result of an *angry God*. This was an age of epidemics and environmental fragility, which were seen as punishments from God.[56] These punishments were institutionalized and became the justification for the newly punitive attitudes and hatred towards persons that did not fit into the world as defined by Western Christian society.[57]

Michel Foucault, in analysing this idea of confession, also identifies the Fourth Lateran Council decree as the understanding of confession as a *ritual* for the *production of truth*. He points out that the codification of the sacrament of confession made by this council resulted in the

> development of the confessional techniques, the declining importance of accusatory procedures in criminal justice, the abandonment of tests of guilt (sworn statements, duels, judgments of God) and the development of methods of interrogation and inquest, the increased participation of the royal administration in the prosecution of infractions, at the expense of proceedings leading to private settlements, the setting up of tribunal of Inquisition: all this helped to give the confession a central role in the order of civil and religious powers.[58]

As Foucault well describes, these technologies of confession produced a new kind of understanding of the role of confession in a Christian society. One fact should be noted: the arrival of this new understanding of confession is not something which developed in a couple of years but was rather the result of decades of different

---

55. Although the persecution of Jews was not something new, systematic anti-Semitism in the Middle Ages begins with an attack on several Jewish communities in southwestern France in 1063. The lives of Jews were, from that moment on, constantly at risk. See Moore, *The Formation of a Persecuting Society*, p. 29.

56. The policing of sodomy was only a single facet of a broad effort to manage sexuality and public morality, all part of a more concentrated and efficient program of social control. Other social concerns, interwoven with these developments, heightened a sense of urgency about controlling sodomy. In particular, the demographic catastrophes linked to recurring plague, and related insecurities about marriage, children, and family life, nourished perceptions that the nonprocreative sins 'against nature' posed a threat to the very foundations of human society. The cultural resonance of this continent-wide demographic crisis may go some way toward explaining similar shifts in attitudes toward sodomy and in efforts to control it that occurred at roughly the same time in numerous Italian and European cities. (Rocke, *Forbidden Friendships*, p. 28.)

57. It is very interesting that the word used for the institutionalization of hatred in late-medieval society was '*inimicitia*'. See Daniel Lord Smail, 'Hatred as a Social Institution in Late-Medieval Society', *Speculum* 76.1 (2001): 90–126.

58. Foucault, *History of Sexuality*, Vol. 1, p. 58.

decisions until the final step taken by the Fourth Lateran Council. Aelred's case situates in the middle of this process, and because of that he is the witness of some of these processes. Furthermore, he participates, as a member of a powerful religious order, in the development of these notions. Although, as we could see in the analysis of his life and *theology of friendship*, he relaxed some of these processes in the context of his monastery, which resulted in the gaining of some admirers as well as of some detractors.

We can conclude in this section that Aelred's life fell historically between the social and ecclesiastical acceptance of Damian's *Liber Gomorrhianus* and the decrees of the Fourth Lateran Council. As can be expected, the former contributed to the structure of roles, feelings and behaviours within which all women and men of Aelred's time were expected to fit, as well as the movement towards the repressiveness of the Lateran decrees. Aelred, like others of his time, did not fit within the given structure of that social order, and his *theology of friendship* can be seen as representing a movement to counter the repressive tendencies of his time. Taking into account that this option could produce a *disruption* of the given social order, we certainly could call it a *queer movement*.

Although, as indicated above, society was already moving towards the more rigid priorities that led to the decrees of the Fourth Lateran Council, Aelred was still able to feel intense love for his male friends *and* consider himself deeply Christian. Feelings like his were not yet proscribed, as they would be after the decrees of the Lateran Council. Aelred's theology, as well as his friendships as a monk, was an acceptable alternative within the given order of his society and a way to live a different kind of life inside that order. However, it was also the product of a resignification of heteropatriarchal order and norms in the micro-context of Rievaulx. Aelred managed to *disrupt*/subvert the order by reapplying those norms in a different way to their context. In this respect, Butler's analysis on gender and sexual performativity of drag-queens could help us to explain this process in Rievaulx: '[N]orms are continually haunted by their own inefficacy; hence, the anxiously repeated effort to install and augment their jurisdiction. The resignification of norms is thus a function of their inefficacy, and so the question of subversion, of working the weakness in the norm, becomes a matter of inhabiting the practices of its rearticulation.'[59]

Monasticism and sexuality

Monasteries were expected to be models of social order. Their fidelity to the dictum of a well-ordered society can be seen in the hierarchical way in which they were organized. In order to overcome the temptations and dangerous activities of the body, monasteries were also places where passions and feelings needed to be more fully controlled than elsewhere, and Cistercian monasteries could not escape from this reality. At the same time, monasteries, as well as certain neighbourhoods in medieval cities where males engaged in homoerotic practices gathered, were places in which alternatives could be explored for overcoming the burdens of a

59. Butler, *Bodies that Matter*, p. 237.

heavy and adverse social order. In other words, there was room for a plurality of human feelings, and there were respectful and respectable ways to live within both the order and the plurality.

Aelred found a positive way to *disrupt* the social order inside his monastery. He allowed monks to express their feelings without guilt. He interpreted these experiences as a valuable resource that helped to build a different sense of community at Rievaulx monastery. Thus he took away the onus of sinfulness that had been imposed on the body and sexuality, as well as on human love and passion. He himself had to deal with his own feelings first: 'I was still glad to have found a kind of principle for friendship, according to which I would be able to control my wandering loves and attachments.'[60]

Aelred never questioned explicitly the existing social order in any of his writings: a situation that is understandable if we take into account the special position of Cistercian monasteries under papal control, which was something to treat with care. Nonetheless, Aelred's need 'to love and to be loved' caused him to express the feeling of love in many different ways. To Aelred these feelings were not a disconnection from his theology but rather vehicles through which to enter more deeply into the fullness of the monastic life. And he did not confine the privilege of using these vehicles to himself or to a chosen few. Aelred's biographer, Walter Daniel, tells us that Aelred allowed his monks to hold hands, even though this degree of intimacy was not the norm in Cistercian or other monasteries during the twelfth century.[61]

As a place in which the demonstration of human affection between monks was valued, Rievaulx became very unusual as a monastery. Thus, in his restructuring of Rievaulx, Aelred demonstrated the possibility of a viable alternative to the growing use of Christianity as a tool of repression. In doing this he succeeded in (re)constructing the dominant heteropatriarchal ideology of his society – one that restricted the roles of all women and men – through the offering of his *theology of friendship* as an alternative to hegemonic heteronormativity. This is similar to what Judith Butler calls *gender performances*. For researchers like Godelier and Brown, among others, the body is a *sign/symbol* of society, and, in *disrupting* the boundaries of the body, a distortion of social boundaries is produced. This is what Aelred did with his liberating *theology of friendship*.

Aelred's main concern was to address the place of human persons within the whole of his community. This constituted the base for his *theology of friendship*. His understanding of the human person included body, love, history and purpose, as well as soul, spirit and reason. Brian McGuire writes of Aelred's concern for the humanity of his monks in the following way:

> How does the individual with his or her special background, traumas of growth, talents, and inheritance in good and evil fit into the larger entity of society? How can he or she move from the biological family, with all its wounding experiences, into some kind of viable social family? How can one choose any exclusive community without shutting out the pressing fact of our all belonging

60. *De Spir. Am.* Prologue: 3.
61. Walter Daniel, *Life of Aelred*, p. 40; quoted in Russell, 'Aelred, the Gay Abbot', p. 58.

to a world community? Aelred found his answer in the love of the brethren at Rievaulx. He became brother and lover and so found his life: brother to all in community life, lover to some in his friendships.[62]

In doing this, Aelred *disrupted* the then traditional view of harmony and asceticism within monasteries through renewing processes towards a deep theology that allows all individuals to develop and express themselves freely as humans within the monastic community.[63]

For Aelred, personal movement towards deep monastic spiritual life required opportunities for monks to express themselves fully within the context of the monastery. Only by doing this could human beings be allowed to renew their humanity and discover in their neighbour a subject of love. For Aelred, love of one's neighbour was the way to find God who, as St John says, is the source of love. At the end of *Speculum Caritatis*, Aelred wrote about these friendships between men in the manner of those who speak of their beloved:

> It is no mean consolation in this life to have someone with whom you can be united by an intimate attachment and the embrace of very holy love, to have someone in whom your spirit may rest, to whom you can pour out your soul; to whose gracious conversation you may flee for refuge amid sadness, as to consoling songs; or to the most generous bosom of whose friendship you may approach in safety amid the many troubles of this world; to whose most loving breast you may without hesitation confide all your inmost thoughts, as to yourself; by whose spiritual kisses as by medicinal ointments you may sweat out of yourself the weariness of agitating cares. Someone who will weep with you in anxiety, rejoice with you in prosperity; seek with you in doubts; someone you can let into the secret chamber of your mind by the bonds of love, so that even when absent in body he is present in spirit. There, you alone may converse with him alone, all the more sweetly because more secretly. Alone, you may speak with him alone, and once the noise of the world is hushed, in the sleep of peace, you alone may repose with him alone in the embrace of charity, the kiss of unity, with the sweetness of the Holy Spirit flowing between you. Still more, you may be so united to him and approach him so closely and so mingle your spirit with his, that the two become one.[64]

---

62. McGuire, *Friendship and Community*, p. 147.
63. The monastic life (and genuine spirituality) is truly renewed when the ancient values and practices of the monastic life, in their perennial truth and lucidity, are pursued in a contemporary setting, with the deepest respect for the personal and harmonious development of the individual. Such an environment facilitates rather than impedes the development and exercise of the monks' freedom; it provides an atmosphere of cordial sustaining, fraternal warmth and spiritual enlightenment, conducive to the attainment of true liberty and the full flowering of the human personality in the Holy Spirit. (Raphael Simon, 'Human Aspects of the Monastic Life', in *Chapter Papers: 1971* [N/P: Order of Cistercians, 1971:50].)
See also Esther de Waal, *The Way of Simplicity: The Cistercian Tradition* (New York: Orbis Books, 1998), pp. 100–26); Andre Louf, *The Cistercian Way*, trans. Nivard Kinsella *et al.* (Kalamazoo, MI: Cistercian Publications, 1983), pp. 61, 128–9; and Louis Boyer, *The Cistercian Heritage*, trans. E. Livingstone (Westminster MD: Newman, 1958), pp. 125–60).
64. *Spec. Car.* III.39: 109.

In this way Aelred colours the spirituality of monastic life and human love with an understanding of friendship that was common in his own context. As Elizabeth Stuart rightly concludes on Aelred: 'I do not think it a coincidence that this medieval monk wrestled with feelings which we would today label "homosexual" ... Aelred does not seem to have surrendered his own experience of love through friendship to the body – fearing the suspicious climate of the Church of his day.'[65] As we can see, the case of Aelred of Rievaulx shows how the *disruption* of heteronormativities can be done in the context of small communities that honour human beings and respect their different expressions of sexuality and gender performances. Aelred's *theology of friendship* today has to acknowledge the ways through which *compulsory heterosexuality* operates all over the world, punishing those people who do not fit into its matrix. A *theology of friendship* will find, through the building of *inclusive* communities, spaces of resistance to challenge heterosupremacy and to *disrupt* its colonialism. I call these communities: *clusters of resistance and disruption* amidst the heteronormativity that operates in *Western* societies, something that could be seen in the case of Aelred and his community at Rievaulx monastery.

Aelred's *De Spirituali Amicitia* 'represents a high-point of medieval monastic writing of friendship'.[66] When we compare this first-hand witness of friendship with the writings of Peter Damian and the effects of the Fourth Lateran Council, the ways in which a hegemonic heteronormativity of society regarding sexuality is reproduced or criticized, especially in relation to the body, become more visible.

Analysis of the life and work of Aelred of Rievaulx and his monastic context shows us how homoerotic feelings can serve a positive function within a problematic issue. Most of the times the problem of homoeroticism remains an unresolved issue. In his *theology of friendship*, Aelred shows how sexuality, especially homoeroticism, was connected to Christian faith within a monastic context in which love is used as the bond of every relationship.

The works of Maurice Godelier and Peter Brown on the dominant ideology in society as expressed in the way the body is conceptualized and its relation to society is also demonstrated here, but in Aelred's case an alternative is offered from a homoerotic perspective. It is impossible to disconnect monasteries from the whole of the society that is their context. Disconnecting monasteries from the rest of their world makes it difficult to see how social patterns regarding sexuality, especially those that produce homoerotic feelings, can be integrated into a community. Even in societies where homoerotic feelings are rejected, these feelings are likely to arise within any *cluster* community such as a monastery. Aelred's contribution to the enrichment of theology is based on uniting sexuality and spirituality as one of the processes for deepening Christian faith. In doing this he succeeded in (re)constructing the dominant heteronormativity of his society, one

65. Elizabeth Stuart, *Just Good Friends: Towards a Lesbian and Gay Theology of Relationships* (London: Mowbrays, 1995), p. 98.
66. Mark F. Williams, *Aelred of Rievaulx's Spiritual Friendship: A New Translation.* (Scranton, PA/London: University of Scranton Press/Associated University Presses, 1994), Introduction, p. 9.

that restricted the roles and feelings of all women and men, through the offering of his *theology of friendship* as an alternative to hegemonic heteropatriarchy. This produced a *disruption* of the social order inside the Rievaulx monastery, giving space for different *performances* in the interaction of friendship and homoeroticism.

The fact that the Fourth Lateran Council promulgated a law about confession, which as we have seen is a mechanism of power and truth, could be a sign for the previous dissemination of practices that threatened the social order, especially those relating to homoeroticism. If it was necessary for the council to rule society by a mechanism such as confession, homoeroticism must have been a well-established practice in society as well as in monastic environments. Related to this, the work of Peter Damian, *Liber Gomorrhianus*, could be analysed in a similar way. In the case of Aelred and his community at Rievaulx, we could conclude that the possibility of homoerotic feelings within the context of a monastery, already a *disruption* of the heterosocial order, is not only possible but also a valuable part of a *spiritually liberating process*. The life of Aelred of Rievaulx, and his work connecting faith, spirituality, sexuality and love in the framework of friendship is a unique case inside the matrix of heteropatriarchy that rules the *performance* of gender and sexualities in Christian religion. The sanctity of Aelred is fully based on the expression of his *theology of friendship*. It defies our present times to explore ways through which alternative voices could be raised within our own social and cultural system, both in religious and secular contexts. It compels us to *disrupt* positively the ways through which gender and sexuality are moulded in our times. Bringing in Butler once again, the queering of Aelred and his community at Rievaulx lays on us the responsibility of thinking how this queering can help us in our present time not to reiterate the hegemonic heteronormativity but rather to create *clusters of resistance and friendship* that are bonded by friendship and love.

3

Fucking Straight and the Gospel of Radical Equality

Lisa Isherwood

> Therefore I must be intimate with you and lie in your bed with you. Daughter, you greatly desire to see me, and you may boldly, when you are in bed, take me to you as your wedded husband, as your dear darling, and as your sweet son, for I want to be loved as a son should be loved by the mother, and I want you to love me daughter, as a good wife ought to love her husband.
>
> (Margery Kempe)[1]

These words of Margery Kempe propel us into a strange world if we dare to take them at face value, which I believe she did. She is describing a conversation with Jesus; it is perhaps misleading to call it a vision since it was the outcome of affective piety, a form of meditation greatly encouraged in the fourteenth century. It was a form of devotion favoured by Franciscans and others where the pious were encouraged to visualize scenes from the Holy Life and to see themselves as part of the scene. Margery was most skilled in this way of devotion and tells us that she attended the Virgin during her pregnancy and birth, holding her hand, assisting the baby into the world and giving the exhausted mother mulled wine.[2] She was there too at the crucifixion, consoling, questioning and being acknowledged by those at the cross.[3] Margery would not have been alone in all these rather 'standard' devotional scenarios: where she parts company with others is in the physical intimacy of many of her 'conversations' and the impact they had on her life – she was propelled down queer street!

Margery married God! They exchanged the traditional vows but God promised to be more obedient to her than any child ever was to his mother. This is extraordinary theology, and more is to come. As they lay in bed God speaks to Margery, 'take me to thee as thy wedded husband, as thy dearworthy darling ... kiss my mouth, my head and my feet as sweetly as thou wilt'.[4] This is not the mystic marriage of the soul experienced by many monks,[5] Margery engages in sexual play with her God and finds it more satisfying than with her husband and sire of her fourteen pregnancies. Her communion with the divine allowed her to

---

1.   B.A. Windeatt (trans.), *The Book of Margery Kempe* (London: Penguin Classics, 1985), Chapter 36, pp. 126–7.
2.   Ibid., Chapter 34.
3.   Ibid., Chapter 80.
4.   Ibid., Chapter 36.
5.   Although new light is being thrown on just how mystical these marriages were with such work as Richard Rambuss, *Closet Devotions* (London: Duke University Press, 1997).

take a walk on the wild side and touch the transgressive. Her transgression was not only through sexual acts of what one may call theoerotica but also by placing herself at the centre of the witness of angels, saints and the Son of God himself, she was focused on and adored as the spouse of God. Indeed, God promised to be an obedient spouse in a childlike manner. Not content to stop there we see from the quotation at the beginning of this chapter that Jesus himself wished to go to her bed as both son and husband. What kind of Trinitarian theology does this give rise to, let alone what kind of ethical world does it place before us as holy?

If we theologians dare to take Margery seriously we have to face some very tough and disquieting questions. For many it has been easier to dismiss Margery altogether as a mad woman, a hysteric and most certainly not a mystic. Of course, even when she has been acknowledged as a mystic there have been any number of restrictions placed upon the 'true nature' of her mysticism. As Grace Jantzen has pointed out so eloquently, mysticism is a gendered act and as such women mystics have more trouble being acknowledged as such than do their male counterparts.[6] However, in the case of Margery even some women have trouble accepting her particular visions as befitting. Evelyn Underhill, for instance, declared that there is little in Margery's experience that can be called mystical, while Dean Inge, quite unconscious of our contemporary usage, concluded that she was 'certainly queer, even in a queer age'[7] and thus dismissed her. With the advent of Freudian analysis of religious matters, Margery was relegated to the outer darkness, along with all the other sexual inadequates.

Rather than being a repressed person Margery comes over as very much in touch with her feelings. In addition to her explicit sexual encounters with God and Jesus she 'feels' their beauty and their pain, which results in uncontrollable weeping. This was not unusual among those who practised affective piety, but the lengths to which Margery went made her extremely unusual and thus suspicious in the eyes of those in power. She was on more than one occasion accused of heresy and brought before courts, but her desire for intimacy with the divine drove her on and she remained true to her visions. Margery, more than most, illuminates Heyward's assertion that 'our sensuality is the foundation of our authority'.[8] Despite her fears – and they were many – fearing demon possession on the one hand and rape on the other, she had an embodied sensual knowledge that sustained her through her many trials in life. She had tasted, touched and been loved by God himself and his son – she had experienced this on her skin and in her heart.

Of course, Margery did not simply inhabit an ethereal world, and her closeness with the divine had practical consequences for her. She wished to be released from sexual obligations with her husband John and to travel throughout Christendom visiting holy sites and engaging in theological debate with religious people. She got her wish after fourteen pregnancies and she did indeed become a great traveller

6.   See Grace Jantzen, *Power, Gender and Christian Mysticism* (Cambridge: Cambridge University Press, 1995).

7.   Quoted in Sandra McEntire, *Margery Kempe: A Book of Essays* (London: Garland, 1992), p. x.

8.   Carter Heyward, *Touching Our Strength. The Erotic as Power and the Love of God* (San Francisco, CA: HarperCollins, 1989), p. 93.

and theological conversationalist, challenging clerics whenever she got the chance. She became free and she remained wild.

Why she has caused upset in the world of those who study mysticism is beyond the scope of this chapter but we can perhaps surmise that she was too earthy for the 'pure mystics' who understood their path as leading them beyond the physical and not more fully into it. She was certainly emotional, and once again this would not suit the dominant understanding of mysticism as detached and serenely pious. As Jantzen reminds us, the gendered construction of mysticism means that it also has social implications, and behaviour is viewed as becoming depending on one's gender and one's place in the patriarchal hierarchy. Margery, as the married mother who experienced fourteen pregnancies and still saw and touched God, would be rather a shock to the establishment. She places before us an embodied struggle and not a neat and tidy cloistered life; she opens the way for those who could be beyond clerical power to claim access to the divine. It is not beyond the bounds of possibility that she travelled so much and had so many confessors as a deliberate strategy to undermine clerical power in her life. She did after all challenge clerical power, taking as her teacher Christ himself and thus engaging in another neat trick of subversion, taking no credit for the challenge but rather conveying it as a message from Christ. She was not the first woman to do such a thing and it did seem to work, in that it often protected the women themselves from clerical punishment.

It would be quite wrong to suggest that Margery managed to negotiate equality through her actions alone and it has to be acknowledged that she freed herself from John, not through his goodwill and sense of mutuality but because she was well off enough to pay his debts. However, she did create a space for a married medieval woman that was quite extraordinary, and she got her life recorded in a book, ironically probably written by clerics. How she did this is of great interest to me as a body theologian. How through the expression of physical/sexual visions/ enactments with the divine and through weeping, and thus boldly inhabiting public space, this housewife expanded her life and the way she was able to move in the world is fascinating to me as a queer theologian.

Bodies and boundaries

As a theologian trained and immersed in the Christian tradition I take very seriously the idea of incarnation. By incarnation I do not mean the once and for all Son of God who saved the world through his death but rather the glorious abandonment of the divine into flesh and the passionate dance of the human/divine that ensues. And the purpose of this is *life* – life in abundance, liberated and embracing radical embodied equality. As a feminist I also take very seriously the understanding that how one's body manifests in the world affects how one is perceived, treated and the access one has to institutions as well as power over one's own life. For me, Margery Kempe both affirms and disrupts the body discourse of feminist liberation theology, and as such she is a fascinating figure for those who move in queer theology.

By now we are all familiar with the arguments for the pervasive nature of heteropatriarchy and the way in which it begins through acts of intimacy, be they childrearing or love-making[9]. We are bred into it and our bodies encouraged to enact it and more, to find it attractive and attracting. We are encouraged to become willing victims of a dominance/submission discourse that does not allow for full flourishing. We know from our liberation colleagues that the oppressor is no more in touch with a free and flourishing life than the oppressed, even if the materiality is more abundant. The unequal nature of this enfleshed contract was encouraged by the Church Fathers who understood woman as the inferior creation and the one to be kept down for the good of the world. It was generally understood that her rebellion would be sexual in nature and so the control of her was also embedded in sexual relations and sexuality.

Feminist theologians have pointed out how the control of women has taken the form of cloistered lives to Christian marriage, all neatly tied up so that women are reduced to the private and contained worlds that are seen as fit for them. Even within marriage female sexuality has been heavily edited and understood largely in a passive and reproductive manner. In some fundamentalist circles today missionary-position intercourse is the only form of sexual activity advocated, as it clearly enacts the place of women within the marriage and the community: laid out, barely mobile, pinned down and on the receiving end of phallic meaning.[10] In addition it is a frequent reminder that duty/service and not pleasure is the female lot, since it is the least likely position in which a woman will orgasm. In this world that overplays the liberating power of sex we should not forget that still 80 per cent of women report that they do not orgasm through intercourse, yet intercourse is still understood as 'real sex' – who is liberated, who is celebrated and, as importantly, what is the political agenda? It is the contention of many feminist scholars from a variety of disciplines that liberation is not the purpose even of so-called liberated sexuality[11] but rather the enfleshed enactment of women's place within a bigger and male-dominated system. Women are on the receiving end of phallic meaning, they are a void that needs to be filled, an absence that needs the presence of a signifier in order to be whole. While this language may be that of the academy, even in the twenty-first century, what it signifies is found everywhere in the world and still carries with it the restricting expectations that such a mindset places on the 'other'.

If we are in doubt we just have to take a look at the fundamentalist coalitions that are making political waves in the USA and Europe. Those who would normally have very little to say to each other, Muslims, fundamentalist Protestants and fundamentalist Roman Catholics find much to agree on over the place of women and children. The Christian Right in the USA has a firm ally in the shape of George Bush, and this is beginning to show in international as well as domestic policy. Religious fundamentalism is built on the backs of women who are confined to the home to rear children and serve men by divine decree. It is no wonder then

---

9. See Lisa Isherwood, *The Good News of the Body* (Sheffield: Sheffield Academic Press, 2000) or Alice Miller, *The Drama of Being a Child* (London: Virago, 1987).

10. Lacan reminds us that women are empty holes that need to be filled with the phallus in order to be given any meaning and worth.

11. See for example, Sheila Jeffreys, *Anticlimax. A Feminist Perspective on the Sexual Revolution* (London: Women's Press, 1990).

that this religious/political Right is concerned about the United Nations (UN) and its liberal policy-making[12] – that is to say its concern for the rights of women and children. Within this very narrow religious understanding women and children have no rights, and indeed no role other than that assigned to them by men. In short, their meaning in life is defined by men, just as Lacan suggested. The Christian Right believes that children's rights undermine parental authority and the Convention for the Elimination of Discrimination against Women undermines and indeed destroys family life. What kind of religion is this that sees the dignity and equality of women and children as capable of undermining all that it holds holy – that is the family and the advanced capitalist system that rides it. George Bush is coming more and more in line with the Christian Right and so it may be no accident that he has in recent days declared that the UN is outdated and has outlived its usefulness.

On the home front Bush has ensured that the judiciary is packed with anti-choice judges, and he has closed the office on Women's Initiatives and Outreach. He continues to only support 'abstinence only' programmes, even in HIV/AIDS programmes, and he has reimposed the global gag on non-governmental organizations (NGOs) who receive US money providing abortion counselling. No NGO that receives funding from the USA can have programmes related to reproductive health. He sent Christian Right representatives to the Asian/Pacific conference on Population and Development in 2002, where they attempted to ban condom use for HIV/AIDS prevention and to dismantle sex education programmes. In addition he cut $3 million to the World Health Organization to prevent research on an early abortion pill and cut $2 million for women's reproductive and maternal health programmes in Afghanistan. This sexual/reproductive control of women is of course social control beyond the bed/birthing room. It reduces women's sphere to that of the home and leaves them vulnerable economically and legally. Let's not forget it is a Christian Right agenda! Unless one believes that freedom is in chains and that God herself made men and women socially different and with different mental and emotional capacities then a problem raises it head, one that those who embrace and celebrate the glorious diversity and flourishing of incarnation need to address. There is no desire here to devalue motherhood, or indeed underplay relationships, but rather to assert yet again, as though women have not said it enough, that women are more than mothers and we flourish best when in mutual relation and not in the service of men and children. In order that we may dance with our incarnation we need basic bodily and social freedoms. That women should be in danger of losing these rights hundreds of years after Margery gained hers is almost unbelievable – indeed, many who pursue this agenda probably bank on the person in the street finding it so unbelievable that they pay little attention to the erosion of rights that come in almost daily.

That a Christian movement should be behind the curtailing of women's rights is still shocking even though we know that much of Christian history and many Christian doctrines have demonstrated just how anti-woman Christian interpret-

---

12. See Doris Buss and Didi Herman, *Globalising Family Values. The Christian Right in International Politics* (Minneapolis, MN: University of Minnesota Press, 2003).

ations have been. Somehow one expects that the modern world will have exerted its influence on the Christian community and it can be understood that woman is not inferior to man. Of course this is not the case and so dubious biblical inter-pretation and limited readings of tradition lead to declarations about the roles of men and women that come more from Aristotle than from Christ. Roles by which women are contained as sexual beings with marriage and when there their sexual and reproductive rights are highly prescribed by male authority. These issues are further complicated by the way in which traditional families have come to underpin the economic system of the West, and it is no accident that many fundamentalist groups proclaim that those who live in traditional families will flourish financially as well as spiritually. The combination of nuclear family, the limited role of women, religion and economics is a well-established one, and it plays a large part in the political agenda of the Christian Right. For this reason then, it would seem, those who are into queering theology will also have to open themselves to the queering of heteropatriarchy and the traditional family. Fucking straight and the gospel of radical equality are shown to be incompatible.[13]

Margery Kempe gives us a graphic example of a woman who in her lifetime moved from the traditional to the very queer, changing economic and social circumstances as she went. From the confines of her birthing bed, on which she nearly lost her mind, she engaged with the person of Christ as a handsome and sexually desirable young man who spoke words of comfort and hope to her. This embodied encounter was the beginning of her revolution. It was the first of many intimate moments Margery would share with Jesus and God, each leading to a greater assertion of her own being and bringing her closer to a full and free life. So, quite unlike the intimacy that so many women experience with men where they are drawn more and more into a giving away of themselves in the service of male needs and desires, these divine enfleshed encounters propelled Margery towards her own 'godding'.[14] Her sexual intimacy with the divine did not limit her life – she was even free to lust after others – rather it set her understanding of her self within a bigger picture. We will never know if this divine sex affected the way she felt about sex with her husband: she had been passionate about him when they met, but she certainly declares that God is a better lover. Why? Is it purely the fulfilment of autoeroticism that makes her declare this, or is it much more: is it the space and sense of fullness that these divine encounters spurred her on to embody? By truly queering her marriage and the nature of her relationship with the divine – having sex with father and son – she moved into a space that she could hardly believe possible, one in which she was both satisfied and free. This is far removed from the Christian Right agenda for women which, through the control of women's bodies, wishes to bring into being the return of Christ. Which is it to be? The two are mutually exclusive despite our best efforts at liberalism! If incarnation is to flourish rather than a constructed and controlling Christ then women have to be

---

13. I hope I have made it clear that fucking straight is a system and not just a description about actions and sexed bodies.

14. This is a phrase used by Carter Heyward to refer to the way in which we, through mutual relation, come to embody the divine within and between us.

free, have to have control over themselves and to make space for the children they choose to bear. Fucking straight or fucking queer questions our entire theology and the world we dare to hope for and live towards. In a real sense private acts of intimacy create our world – they draw us into the social and the politics embedded in it. As Christians we are called to live in the world but not of it; this does not stop at the bedroom door, it permeates all aspects of our lives. Fucking queer is a Christian commitment that changes the world.

> *'I'm a "professional lesbian" ... and yet on some deeper level,*
> *I was fucking* straight'[15]

Would it have been easier for Margery to become a lesbian, to abandon husband and home in the pursuit of self and God in the arms of a woman? Many women have thought so. However, these words at the head of this section, spoken by a 'convert' from butch-femme relationships illustrate just how confusing the pursuit of radical equality in relationship and through the skin can be. After years of being in butch-femme relationships Heather Findlay realized that she was not living in the kinds of freedoms and alternate reality that she had believed would be for her as a lesbian. Her life was to a degree laid out before her in terms of expected norms of behaviour and her desires were to an extent also mediated by an external and half-acknowledged set of assumptions. In being a wonderful femme she had never quite overcome the male in the head and had to a certain degree projected that on to her women partners, who enacted it for her.

Many will be familiar with the old adage that feminism is the theory and lesbianism is the practice, but we see that lesbianism alone may not ensure that the inequalities graphed into heteropatriarchy are avoided. It all has to be much queerer than that! Nothing it seems is challenged if we simply graph the binary oppositions of gender on to differently sexed bodies – we still end up fucking straight! This as we have seen is no small matter since it means we play out in our skin a dominant–submissive agenda which hinders the flourishing of incarnation.

Liberal agendas have to some degree meant that we can all too easily overlook the subtler points of patriarchy in the name of inclusion and acceptance. As Sheila Jeffreys[16] has pointed out, much that is labelled transgressive and that liberals are encouraged to accept is in fact just as exploitative of others as the so-called patriarchal norm. This is because many of the practices require that we make an 'other' to act upon or to desire. Feminists have always challenged this other status, but have often fallen silent when being asked to comment on public sex, SM or butch-femme relations. Can there be liberation and radical equality when we are enacting 'otherness' between us?

There is no doubt that women have become freer to understand and pursue their own desires. As we are constantly reminded, women are moving from being purely objects of desire to subjects of our own desire and this is extremely healthy.

---

15. Heather Findlay, 'Losing Susan', in Sally Munt (ed.), *Butch/Femme. Inside Lesbian Gender* (London: Cassell, 1998), pp. 133–46 (see esp. p. 145).

16. See Sheila Jeffreys, *Unpacking Queer Politics* (Cambridge: Polity Press, 2003).

Through this knowledge we are able to make choices that are really ours and in so doing affirm more of our humanness.[17] As an incarnational theologian I have to applaud this move and affirm that incarnational theology requires more humanness and less abstraction of the self. However, there is a nagging doubt and I think this is to do more with ends than means.

I am a member of a church that has for generations encouraged people to beat themselves and others for the pleasure of God and Christ. This kind of spiritual SM has not, in most cases, led to a greater affirmation of the self but rather an abjuration of self that is damaging for both the individual and the community that would thrive best with self-loving and affirming people within it. This then is my concern: that if SM for example becomes the end in itself and not a means to exploring and expressing different aspects of one's self, which when understood can be integrated into a greater whole, we may be in danger of simply reaffirming many of the negative aspects of our theology and our culture that we have struggled for decades to overcome. I have heard it argued that SM between women is quite different from that between the sexes, many feminists being unwilling to take part in the latter and enthusiastic about the former. The difference: power, even in such a power-layered situation. The argument goes that between men and women SM is simply an enactment of patriarchal gender relations, even if the tables are turned. Whereas between women it is an exercise in total trust and exploring edges. It also has to be added that the argument goes on that it can give women a sense of embodied power that most heteropatriarchal sexual enactment denies. (This is power and not empowerment – an issue that feminists have historically had difficulty with.) I think the time is right for an investigation of these issues in the light of queer theology, and we may be surprised by the results.

My concerns are in the same areas around butch-femme relationships. While I am aware of and accept the testimony of those who have lived this that although appearing to mimic heteropatriarchy it never does and has no desire to do so, I am not sure how binary opposites are overcome when roles are very limited.[18] Once again I find myself affirming the means and questioning the ends, if we have a set of practices that enable the exploration of our desires and a freeing of some part of ourselves then this is to be welcomed. However, by fixing these identities, do we move the revolution further? Do we more deeply embody radical incarnation? I am reminded that the 'master's tools will never dismantle the master's house' (no pun intended!) since one does not overcome oppression by permanently taking on the role of oppressor.

Judith Butler, who is butch and into SM, has reassured us that gender is nothing but a performance. But what is being performed and does it run the risk of becoming fixed? It is not usual to hear of a butch becoming a femme or vice versa. Further, is it really possible to go beyond the binary opposition of gender through performance alone? Masculinity is a system not simply a performance, that is to

17. See Polly Young–Eisendrath, *Women and Desire. Beyond Wanting to be Wanted* (London: Piatkas, 1999).

18. I am delighted to say that we hope to publish a book in this series which deals with butch-femme relationships and explores them as a form of spiritual practice.

say it does not end when the individual ceases the performance, and its construction under patriarchy has weighed heavy on women and men. Is performance then a queer enough perspective; can we push enough boundaries with it? Dare we ask if desire itself requires the creation of 'otherness' to find fulfilment? These are disturbing questions and like all things that move and disturb they are theological questions too.

Western Christianity has depended on the otherness of God for both the love and devotion that such a God requires and the social control that such a God generates. Also, as we have seen, the influence of Christianity has found its way into social and emotional relationships, and so otherness plays a central role in the workings of our lives. Both the theology of the West and social and personal relationships are underpinned by a kind of romantic masochism which in my opinion has worked against us on all levels. However, feminist theology has for many years now been removing the otherness of the divine and locating it within and between people. Theologians like Heyward have located the divine within the erotic, the raw energy and power that lies within and between us, the force that draws us out, attracting us to each other and the world in a dance of justice-seeking.[19] Although Heyward does not wish to do away with a part of the divine that exists separately from us, her theology does make it difficult to see where this separate existence may be – the result of this is that God is never wholly, if at all, other. In the reverse we are never 'other' to the divine. This is a relationship of mutuality, co-creation and, although Heyward does not say it, co-resurrection.

In truth we have heard this language before in one way or another, and still the world and the churches remain unashamedly committed to the perpetuation of 'otherness', having spiritualized their theology to such a degree that one need hardly notice that things should be different. In some ethereal realm there is no otherness and all is well! Hearing then is obviously not enough.

Margery Kempe places before us the embodiment of moving beyond otherness. She weds God but this is still the Godhead who for her is father, son and spirit [who we should understand as female] with a very important addition – Margery herself. We are boldly told that God himself declared to her 'and God is in you and you are in him'.[20] And further that she is wedded to 'the Godhead'.[21] This is a very extraordinary marriage, one that crosses all kinds of boundaries and opens up all kinds of possibilities. Everything is thrown into disarray, as we have seen, but what emerges is a relationality based on radical subjectivity. Why radical? Well, because this is subjectivity with no persona, with no hidden corners but rather a raw and gaping laid bareness of the self in relation to the self and the not-self with total absence of otherness. Margery shows how a desire for the other/God moves on and develops into an erotic engagement with the divine/self and not-self and most importantly how this changes things dramatically. There can remain no otherness and I believe her weeping demonstrates this – Margery does not simply observe the

---

19. Carter Heyward, *The Redemption of God. A Theology of Mutual Relation* (Washington, DC: University of America Press, 1982).

20. *The Book of Margery Kempe*, Chapter 35, p. 124.

21. Ibid., p. 122.

beauty or suffering of others, Jesus, Mary, saints or people in the street, she *is* the beauty and the pain. She embodies it all and demonstrates that through her reactions. She graphically illustrates that movement beyond otherness which heightens all experience as it is based in the core of our being, that place where all is one and all is connected. That place beyond otherness.

The beyondness that it becomes possible to think about when we dare to take Margery's story seriously is not the otherworldliness of much Christian theology. It is not a moving beyond in that spatial and temporal sense but rather a destabilizing of identity while also affirming it – a type of nomadic subjectivity. Margery's self becomes so much bigger when she is both wedded to and an integral part of the Godhead, her edges are expanded but at the same time she moves around her own core in a dance of autoerotic/erotic self-discovery. The nomad in her is experiencing Margery the father, Margery the son, Margery the spirit at the same time as embracing father, son and spirit (female) as wedded lover. Of course, in this mutual subjectivity father, son and spirit all experience their divinity through Margery. Now we are talking queer!!! Subjectivity is heightened the more identity becomes nomadic, but this is no mere gender performance – father, son and spirit are all interchangeable and as such go beyond gender categories and into animal, mineral, ether, bread, wine, presence and absence, and so much more.

This is a subjectivity with no edges, a contradiction, a boundarylessness that gives meaning but fixes nothing. Through not losing her identity, but rather cosmically affirming it, Margery moves her world and places before us endless possibilities.

Dancing with the wild woman

So what does Margery offer us as queer theologians? If we take her seriously she places transgression at the heart of our theology – real and at times shocking transgression. Not simply because she speaks of sex with God but because of the tangled web of divine/human relationships that she embodies as the holy path. Her embodiment connects her erotically to the core of the divine unfolding, divine cleansing flows in her tears, redemption and salvation run through her veins and resurrection throbs in the intimacy of her relationality.

This changes everything – in the language of queer theology, she changes the object of her discourse (devotion) and thus her own subjectivity. Margery is released into a fuller life through changing 'the subject' and she expands the boundaries of theology by being so liberated. It has long been the contention of feminist liberation theologians that the divine is not complete but is in process just as we, and the whole of the cosmos, are. Margery demonstrates this through her sexual union with all aspects of the Godhead. It is my belief that an insistence on static boundaries and perfected gods that has led Christianity down a sterile path and has severely inhibited its potential to bring about world-transforming change. Margery appeared to be without boundaries, she moved beyond fucking straight, this is perhaps her gift to us as individuals and her challenge to us as queer theologians. She propels us to explore limitless embodiment and radical subjectivity, and in so doing truly to incarnate the gospel of radical equality.

While we allow the enactment of fixed binary opposites, stable and unequal categories on our bodies through sexual stereotyping and sexual intimacy we fail to open to the diverse/surprising wonder of radical incarnation. Fucking straight has no part in the embodiment of a gospel of radical equality.

Elizabeth Stuart

Act I

Mary stood weeping outside the tomb. An icon of melancholy, of love unknown and stolen from her. To see inside the tomb she has to bend and there she is confronted by presence and absence mischievously combined. Angels greet her with a performance which the cloud of her melancholy does not allow her to 'get'. The tableau they create is of the ark of the covenant, and in particular its mercy-seat. God promised to meet his people 'from between the two cherubim' which edged the mercy-seat (Exodus 25.22). Cherubim are engaged in the queer act of guarding something which is present and absent at the same time. Any clear distinction between presence and absence dissolves between their wings. The woman approaches them blind to their significance, wrapped in her performance of grief. They tease her, 'Woman, why are you weeping?' The question is designed to pierce through her performance, to make her see them, to feel their presence and his absence which is also his presence. But she cannot, she turns away from them and towards a stranger who also asks her the same teasing question 'Woman, why are you weeping? Whom are you looking for?' But still it bounces off her grief. She still seeks the one she could not have. It is only when the stranger calls her name that she feels the presence. And what does she do? Remember the many images produced of this moment in Western art, *'Noli me tangere'*, Mary reaching out to the risen Christ who backs away, remember and then think again because the author of the Gospel of John tells us that when she heard her name Mary 'turned herself'. She had already turned to him when she emerged from the tomb, so now she turns away. She speaks not to his presence but to his absence. In a reversal of the divine encounter with Moses, the woman turns her back on her God who has himself been hidden in the rock (Exodus 33.17–23). Perhaps her gaze is refocused on the cherubim who guard the absent presence and who wink back with glee at her sudden understanding. The male-female gaze is broken and this is reinforced by the words of Jesus, 'Stop clinging to me.' All clinging is ended. Genesis 2.24: 'Therefore a man leaves his father and his mother and clings to his wife, and they become one flesh' – is shattered with death and resurrection.

The resurrection of Christ is the archetypal, primordial queer moment. If J.B.S. Haldane was right when he said, 'Now, my suspicion is that the *universe* is not only queerer than we suppose, but queerer than we *can* suppose ... I suspect that there are more things in heaven and earth than are dreamed of, in any philosophy',[1] it is because of this moment. This is Derrida's 'impossible', the missing piece of the jigsaw of signification. But, as Rowan Williams has noted, the missing piece brings anything but closure, because it is all about the ungraspable nature of God in Christ. The divine cannot be owned, cannot be tied down, but can only be received as a gift and born witness to.[2] The resurrection can only be laid hold of through re-enactment, and that includes performance of the space between the cherubim. It is a perpetually open sign, this last piece in the jigsaw that renders all meaningful. The meaning is not to be grasped but to be given.

St John's account of the resurrection connects more clearly than any other of the canonical gospels the end of death and the end of sex/gender. The scene repeats with critical difference the creation of male and female and the bonds of marriage in Eden. Here in a different garden, the man does not return to dust but returns from dust to life, here male and female do not cleave unto one another but let go of one another. Here in the rush of resurrection the gaze that has been historically hardened into the structures of heterosexuality is broken.

Act II

The Church gathers for its annual Easter vigil. It gathers in darkness and absence. Cut off from the life of the Eucharist, the Church huddles in death while its God rampages through the streets of hell. No one feels the darkness of the soul more than the priest whose very self is dissolved in the absence of sacrament. Into this darkness thick with absence and death comes the light, turning night into day, the pillar of fire signalling the divine presence burst from the bonds of death. This is the night in which light penetrates darkness and the waters of death transforming them into the womb of life. In the old rites of the Catholic Church the blessing of the baptismal waters involved, among other gestures, the celebrant dividing the waters in the form of a cross and saying the following:

> Who by a secret mixture of His power renders fruitful this water prepared for the regeneration of men [*sic*], so that those who have been sanctified in the pure womb of this divine font, and born again as new creatures, may come forth a heavenly offspring; and that all who are distinguished either by sex in body or by age in time, may be brought forth to the same infancy by grace, their mother.

Into the chaos of death are the baptized plunged taking with them their distinguishing marks, their sex and age, to be reborn 'to the same infancy' by grace. Baptism repeats the scene in the cemetery garden, the turn, the breaking of the gaze. This is why Paul, widely believed to be citing a baptismal formula, could declare: 'There is no longer Jew or Greek, there is no longer slave or free, there is no longer male and female; for you are all one in Christ Jesus' (Galatians 3.28). The cleaving is now not between male or female but the soul/Church and God. This is the primordial marriage, the leaving behind of the life of constructed

---

1. J.B.S. Haldane, *Possible Worlds and Other Essays* (London: Chatto & Windus, 1927).
2. Rowan Williams, *On Christian Theology* (Oxford: Blackwell, 2000), pp. 184–96.

identities for a new type of belonging determined only by God. Stephen Moore has recently explored the queering of the Song of Songs in early Christianity as theologians like Origen, and later Bernard of Clairvaux, read the text as an allegory of the soul's relationship with the divine.[3] Marriage is de-sexed in the radiance of the resurrection and its repetition in baptism. Resurrection repetition in baptism and in the annual renewal of the baptismal vows enables the coming into being of resurrected life, at least in theory. In practice, of course, Christianity has clung to gender as to dear life, and more recently has sold its soul to contemporary constructions of sexuality and gender and found itself out of step with its foundational rhythm of death and resurrection. The prayer referred to above was cut when the liturgy was reformed. Queer theory nudges the Church back to its tradition and itself calls out for resurrection realization.

Grief

Judith Butler has argued that in dominant contemporary Western culture at least gender is 'a kind of melancholy'.[4] From Freud she takes the notion that melancholia is unfinished grief, indeed grief that cannot be completed or resolved. The connection between gender and melancholia lies in the construction of the subject in contemporary Western culture. For Butler the subject is constructed upon loss, 'a certain foreclosure of love becomes the possibility for social existence'.[5] To be, then, demands the loss of certain types of love which are not named and not mourned. To be is to be heterosexual, the alternative is not to be, the alternative is death. Social death certainly, but AIDS helped to earth homosexuality in corporeal death. Heterosexuality is haunted by the love it may and cannot mourn; maleness is disturbed by femaleness and vice versa. Gay and lesbian people may have embraced the place of death as a place of life, but they too, while resisting the melancholic heterosexual subject, are nevertheless constituted by it and their own subjectivity is dependent upon it. Homosexuality no less than heterosexuality is constituted by unacknowledged grief for impossible love. The contemporary subject is therefore grounded in grief, in loss. For Butler a key element in the subjection of subjectivity is the turn. The turn of the subject to or on itself, the response to being hailed, the embrace of irresolvable loss is an essential movement in the production of the subject.

The figure of Mary Magdalene at the tomb of Jesus is a melancholic figure. She mourns for love that is impossible, the unresolved grief upon which gender depends and the impossible love for Christ which is further compounded by the absence of his body. The cherubim and then Christ himself both draw attention to and offer the possibility of escape from the melancholia of gender through the appellation, 'woman' and the question 'why are you weeping?' In her turn towards the man she believes to be the gardener Mary repeats the turn towards a subject-

---

3. Stephen D. Moore, *God's Beauty Parlour and Other Queer Spaces in and around the Bible* (Stanford, CA: Stanford University Press, 2001), pp. 21–89.

4. Judith Butler, *The Psychic Life of Power: Theories in Subjection* (Stanford, CA: Stanford University Press, 1997).

5. Ibid., p. 24.

ivity grounded in melancholy reinscribing it upon her body. But the calling of her name awakens her to the reality of resurrection and her second turning disperses the subjectivity of subjection, dissolves melancholy and ends gender. She addresses her teacher not face to face but in the space between the cherubim, and he breaks the bonds of gender.

Sarah Coakley has argued that Butler's project of causing 'gender trouble', disrupting the performance of gender by repeating those performances with critical differences so as to reveal their nature as performances, has much in common with the ancient ascetic tradition within Christianity.[6] Furthermore, she argues that Butler's focus on the loss and unacknowledged yearning that underpins desire, coupled with her belief that it is possible to transcend the limits of gender through unconventional performances, suggests an unconscious reach towards the eschatological which could release Butler from the never-ceasing round of parodic performance which is the only catalyst for change she envisages. Coakley brings Butler into dialogue with the early Church theologian Gregory of Nyssa, who also sought to transcend the contemporary constructions of gender. Gregory envisaged the resurrected body as non-sexed and the progress towards it involving a series of 'gender switches and reversals' which Gregory plays out in his *Commentary on the Song of Songs*.[7] For Gregory, of course, the goal of this process is union with the divine, and the necessary threshold to such union is death. However, death in Gregory's theology is not a terrifying threshold into the unknown because the ascetic life is an anticipatory performance of life beyond it, and so is the Eucharist.[8] Nevertheless, death is the threshold onto the life beyond gender, the life of resurrection. Butler is not at all concerned with death or what might lie beyond it. This is something she has in common with much contemporary Christian discourse. It was the genius of the late Michael Vasey to realize the connection between the contemporary Church's embrace of modern constructions of gender identity and a loss of eschatological imagination.[9] The absence of an afterlife deprives the Christian mind of a space beyond heterosexuality and homosexuality. It leads to, or at least allows, the identification of discipleship with heterosexual relationships and family life in dominant ecclesial discourse (and homosexual relationships in the reverse resistant discourse) and with such identification comes the collapse of the religious life and the celibate vocation which challenges it. There is a great forgetting of the Church's 'queer' tradition when death is evaded. Death is essential to the queer project.

Camping around the crem.

Butler has always been careful to recognize that even though gender might be a matter of performance, it is impossible to live outside of the gender scripts which repetition writes upon our bodies, 'the task is not whether to repeat, but

6. Sarah Coakley, *Powers and Submissions: Spirituality, Philosophy and Gender* (Oxford: Blackwell, 2002), p. 159.
7. Ibid., p. 165.
8. Ibid., p. 163.
9. Michael Vasey, *Strangers and Friends: A New Exploration of Homosexuality and the Bible* (London: Hodder & Stoughton, 1995).

how to repeat or, indeed, to repeat and, through a radical proliferation of gender, to displace the very gender norms that enable the repetition itself'.[10] Repetition with difference, critical difference, is the key to exposing gender as a matter of performance and offering the possibility of ultimate transcendence. Camp can be understood as repetition with critical difference, difference which unravels or at least literally teases apart the tapestry of gender.

No one can avoid death. This is a repetition into which humanity is locked as long as history lasts. We are born, we live and we die. Sometimes this whole process can take but a few minutes, sometimes it can take a century or more, but whatever our lifespan the process of decay begins the minute we are born and will reach its end. Death shadows our life, eventually overtaking our steps. We all participate in the dance of life and death, repeating the rhythm in our own bodies, acting out the script of death. And yet the Christian performance of death is positively camp in Butler's terms.

Christians die along with the rest of humanity, but not in the same way. For the Christian, life and death are queered, indeed this is at the heart of Christian praxis. Mary Magdalene at the tomb encounters the defeat of death. God has embraced death and thereby defeated it. Hell is harrowed into nonexistence. As St John Chrysostom put it:

> Hell was in an uproar because it was done away with.
> It was in an uproar because it is mocked.
> It was in an uproar, for it is destroyed.
> It is in an uproar, for it is annihilated.
> It is in an uproar, for it is now made captive.
>
> Hell took a body, and discovered God.
> It took earth, and encountered Heaven.
> It took what it saw, and was overcome by what it did not see.[11]

Whatever death now involves it does not herald the absence of God, the source of life, for there is now no place where God is not. Death is not in dualistic relationship to life any more than male is to female; in fact both death and life are deconstructed in the blaze of resurrection. In the resurrection God overwhelms death with life, but he does so as a mortal human being. We all know that there is something about death that is sticky, the death of one recalls the death of another and as we move through life the ball of grief gets larger, a heavy weight upon our souls. To Christ attached the stickiness of all human death, grief and sin. It was not just that God defeated death but that God did so in human flesh, and this has profound implications for flesh itself. It bursts from the tomb, the same but different: a flesh no longer meant for cleaving nor for oblivion. Christians die, their bodies wear out or fall vulnerable to disease or violence, but a Christian death is a death with critical difference. For the Christian, death no longer promises or threatens oblivion, the absence of God. It does not even threaten the end of bodiliness, but

---

10. Judith Butler, *Gender Trouble: Feminism and the Subversion of Identity* (New York: Routledge, 1995), p. 148.
11. St John Chrysostom, Easter Sermon.

rather becomes a physical experience/encounter with the divine. For Ladislaus Boros, death is profoundly sacramental: 'Death should be looked on ... as a "basic sacrament", mysteriously present in the other sacraments ... As the supreme, most decisive, clearest and most intimate encounter with Christ ... death summarises all other encounters.'[12] The sacramental nature of death is lost in most contemporary British funeral rites and practices where the mourner has replaced the deceased as the locus of attention and the sense that the congregation is there to pray for and witness an encounter between God and the dead, as they witness the sacrament of marriage or baptism, is absent. In some crematoria, for example, the dead are even sidelined, positioned to one side of the podium. Many Protestant funeral rites, of course, steadfastly avoid prayer for the dead. The dead can often be an awkward presence at their own funeral, to be acknowledged only through remembrance, through a recollection of a life, constructed as a story now ended. An embrace of death as sacramental, as a passage into a profound encounter with Christ, would involve some changes in the contemporary dominant Christian culture of death in Britain. The deceased would become the absolute focus of the funeral liturgy, as she or he is, for example, in the funeral rites of the Orthodox Church, and the congregation would construct themselves less as mourners ('why are you weeping?') than as witnesses and as advocates as they are at weddings, filled with awe, love and some sadness but not hopeless grief, as they pray for the person on their pilgrimage beyond this life. We would also have to relearn to perform death, to prepare for death as we would for a baptism, confession, confirmation or an ordination. The dying (and that includes us all) would be encouraged to look forward to our death, to reflect upon it so that it can be embraced when it comes. We need an *ars moriendi* for our time in which we queer cultural constructions of death to reveal the sacramental nature of dying. Christians must learn to perform 'death' badly from a cultural point of view. We die, but we are not consumed by death. We die to live and to live more fully than we do now. Our dead are not lost to us but remain part of the Church. Their story continues. This is the tradition of the Church, but it needs to be constantly performed through practice.

But death is not simply something a Christian encounters at the end of her or his life. There is a sense in which Christians have already died and gone to heaven, and those theologians who have conceded to others the argument that a focus on death and beyond leads to a pie in the sky theology which bolsters rather than challenges social injustice have missed the point of baptism.

Through baptism Christians are sacramentally united with Christ and the performance of his death and resurrection is repeated upon their own bodies, the stickiness of Christ's nature is realized. Death and resurrection are written on the bodies of Christians, their very characters are shaped by this drama (a fact symbolized in the wearing of a cross and in the act of making the sign of the cross) because they are part of the ongoing performance of it. The last things are also the first things for Christians, the defining movements of their characters and lives. Christians queer death by embracing it and experiencing it as soon as they

12. Ladislaus Boros, *The Moment of Truth: Mysterium Mortis* (London: Burns & Oates, 1962), p. 165.

can and by living through it. The radical discontinuity wrought by baptism has traditionally been symbolized by the assuming of a new name and garment and the opening up of the body through word '*ephphatha*' and anointing. Those who are baptized share in the new humanity of the resurrected, but they live out this humanity in a world still in the process of being redeemed, still clinging to an old humanity. This is the tension of the Christian life, as Pannenberg noted: 'Baptism is there all our lives. The need to appropriate it afresh each day goes along with this present perfect, for in the sign of baptism our baptismally based new identity as Christians is set 'outside' the old humanity but is lived out physically in it, so that our lives are determined to be absorbed by the new identity and transformed into it'.[13] Christians imitate the present absence/absent presence of the tomb. They live within and are shaped by culture, but there is also a sense in which they are absent from it, orientated towards and in receipt of another world, an alternative reality. Similarly, though absent in death, those who have died continue to live and to be present to those united with Christ.

The nature of the performance required of the baptized is always going to be a complex issue, but two things are clear: first, that the ontological change affected by baptism in which selfhood is grounded in Christ requires a performance of humanness critically different; second, that there is no room in the baptized soul for melancholia. Death is dead. Grief is not part of the Christian performance.

Act III: The comedy

Ironically, Christians seem to have traditionally been much more comfortable with tears than with laughter. The early Church inherited from the dominant cultures in which it lived a distrust of laughter and associated it with lack of control and sophistication, cruelty and certain fertility and gnostic cults.[14] Early monastic rules are full of warnings of the dangers of laughter and punishments for those who succumb to it. Weeping, on the other hand, was approved of because it was considered to be an appropriate reaction to sin and the redemptive suffering and death of Jesus. John Chrysostom argued that Jesus never laughed but he is recorded as having wept and declared that those who mourn are blessed.[15] This is because those who mourn are fully conscious of their own sin and that of the world: sin for which Christ had to undergo terrible suffering.

And yet laughter could not be silenced completely. After all, the New Testament rings out joy to the world and promises laughter in the kingdom of heaven (Luke 6.22). In the Eastern Church, holy fools clowned around, defying all the religious and social conventions of the day in imitation of St Paul's desire to be a fool for Christ. St Symeon of Emesa for example would aim walnuts at people in Church, eat on fast days and carouse with prostitutes. Holy folly and laughter came to be

---

13. Wolfhart Pannenberg, *Systematic Theology*, Vol. 3 (Edinburgh: T & T Clark, 1998), p. 253.

14. Ingvild Sælid Gilhus, *Laughing Gods, Weeping Virgins: Laughter in the History of Religion* (London and New York: Routledge, 1997), p. 5.

15. John Chrysostom, *Homilies on the Gospel of Matthew*, VI.5–6.

regarded as a sign of how close that person had come in both body and soul to the state of resurrection.[16]

In the Middle Ages, both the Church and the universities focused their minds on *homo risibilis*. Conscious of Aristotle's claim that laughter is a distinguishing feature of human nature, theologians had to wrestle with the problem that Jesus, the model human being, who during this period became an object for imitation as well as worship, never laughed. Some argued that Jesus's example proved that laughter was alien to our God-given nature; others, starting with Aristotle, argued that Jesus had been capable of laughter, as all human beings are, and therefore the absence of it in his life must be significant. The significance might lie in the fact that true laughter was only to be found in God and hence ought to be postponed until the next life. This eschatological dimension to laughter is prominent in premodern Christianity. Attitudes to laughter were largely determined by the ambivalent attitudes to the body that dominated Christianity during the premodern period. Never falling into dualism, theologians wanted to affirm the body as a site of redemption and knowledge of God, whilst at the same time wrestling with bodily passions and behaviour that appeared to overcome the spirit. The medieval Church encouraged some controlled expressions of laughter, and this must be understood in the context of a growing emphasis upon embodiment. The relics of the saints were honoured and Christ was understood to make himself really present in the form of the sacraments. The feast of Corpus Christi inspired the performance of the English mystery plays which pulsate with humour, much of it very earthy and much of it focused on the inability of some to grasp the nature and significance of the incarnation.

During the Feast of Fools, celebrated on 1 January in medieval Europe, clergy parodied the liturgy, dressed up as women or as animals, rampaged around churches and mocked their superiors.[17] This was undoubtedly a feast which allowed the tension inherent in a tightly structured, hierarchicalized Church to be released and contained. However, there was more to it than that. The feast took place during the feast of Christmas when the Church had enacted once again the story of God assuming human flesh, casting the mighty from their thrones and raising the lowly. The Feast of Fools was also an irruption of incarnational energy and a protest against the Church's failure to realize that energy within its own life.[18]

Laughter was also a feature of the feast of Easter in some parts of medieval Europe. The *risus paschalis* (Easter Laughter) involved preachers using earthy humour to the delight of their congregations.[19] The humour encapsulated the joy at the resurrection and the end of death. Patrick Kavanagh has described the resurrection as 'a laugh freed for ever and for ever',[20] and the Easter laughter echoes

16. Gilhus, *Laughing Gods, Weeping Virgins*, p. 69.

17. E.K. Chambers, *The Mediæval Stage*, Vol. 1 (London: Oxford University Press, 1954).

18. Gilhus, *Laughing Gods, Weeping Virgins*, pp. 78–88.

19. Karl-Josef Kuschel, *Laughter: A Theological Reflection* (London: SCM Press, 1994), pp. 83–7.

20. Patrick Kavanagh, 'Lough Derg', cited in Daniel W. Hardy and David F. Ford, *Jubilate* (London: Darton Longman & Todd, 1984), p. 73.

this. Monastic rules warned of the dangers of laughter which disrupted the controlled body, but monasticism also produced a *risus monasticus*, a counter-culture of humour which included the *joca monacorum* collections which date from the eighth century.[21]

The Renaissance was also a time in which theologians laughed. All of Erasmus's works are soaked in humour, including his *Annotations on the New Testament*. His great hero was Socrates, who had died with humour as well as hemlock on his lips, and his great inspiration was Lucian, whose work he translated and whose satirical deconstruction of the religious traditions and practices of his day provided a model. For Erasmus, the human state was quite mad. The fool laughs at the Christian, who is a fool in the eyes of the world, but the Christian laughs at the fool, for the Christian has insight which reveals the world of the fool to be one of vanity.[22]

With the Reformation and Enlightenment came a renewed distrust of laughter as an enemy of reason, but there have always been those who found epistemological value in laughter. Kierkegaard saw in both the comic and the tragic 'the discrepancy, the contradiction, between the infinity and the finite, the eternal and that which becomes'.[23] The idea that laughter emerges from an experience of incongruity which is also in some sense an experience of transcendence also characterizes the work of Henri Bergson, who saw the comic as lying above all in the incongruity between mind and body and most often evident in the breaking through of physicality into human pretensions of disembodied reasonableness.[24]

Somewhere along the line holy laughter was silenced and unremitting grief was allowed to cloud the face of the Church. Laughter-lines were replaced by the paleness of melancholy as the Church simultaneously lost confidence in the reality of the resurrection and uncritically bought into modern constructions of gender and sexuality. There can be no doubt of this connection between gender/sexuality and resurrection. The Gospel of John makes it plain and so does Gregory of Nyssa. It is evident in Jesus's teaching on marriage, 'For in the resurrection they neither marry nor are given in marriage, but are like the angels in heaven' (Matthew 22.30). Karl Barth said of angels:

> We know nothing of their essential being and its particular nature. We know nothing of their mutual relationship and distinction. We know nothing of the way in which they are a totality yet distinct. But we do know that even in the mystery of their being, they exist in and with the kingdom of God coming and revealed to us ... They are in the service of God.[25]

21. Jacques Le Goff, 'Laughter in the Middle Ages', in Jan Bremmer and Herman Roodenburg, *A Cultural History of Humour: From Antiquity to the Present Day* (Cambridge: Polity Press, 1997), pp. 40–53.

22. M.A. Screech, *Laughter at the Foot of the Cross* (London: Allen Lane, 1997).

23. Johannes Climacus, *Concluding Unscientific Postscript* (Princeton, NJ: Princeton University Press, 1941), p. 459.

24. Henri Bergson, *Laughter: An Essay on the Meaning of the Comic*, in W. Sypher (ed.), *Comedy* (Baltimore, MD: Johns Hopkins University Press, 1980).

25. Karl Barth, *Church Dogmatics*, 3.3, ed. G.W. Bromiley and T.F. Torrance (Edinburgh: T & T Clark, 1960), p. 451.

Angels are beings whose attention is fixed only upon God and who exist to do God's will. The turn of Mary Magdalene is a turn towards an angelic state, a re-orientation of desire to its ultimate end, the divine and with that angelic turn, notions of gender and sexuality are fractured, displaced and rendered non-ultimate. It is a turn away from melancholia towards laughter (hence the teasing of the angels and the Christ).

The Church needs to recover its sense of humour. It needs to recover its parodic rhythm. Repetition with critical difference is how the Church performs. It is how it interacts with culture, it is how it keeps itself open to the renewal of the Holy Spirit. And this performance begins in death. Christians die, but that is all they do for death; they are not consumed by death, they die to enter life. Hence the baffling longing of figures such as Ignatius of Antioch and countless martyrs through the ages for death. In embracing death, martyrs queered it, performing it subversively in order to point to its defeat. This queer performance begins at the resurrection and reverberates across the cosmos. With the end of the dualism between life and death comes the end of the dualisms of gender and sexual orientation, the dualisms of race and class. The Church is mandated as the body of Christ to live out this new reality in the midst of a world still being born into it. The Church is mandated to laugh in the midst of a world misted in melancholia, thereby disrupting it. Michel Foucault, writing of the soul in his study of discipline and punishment, said: 'It would be wrong to say that the soul is an illusion, or an ideological effect. On the contrary, it exists, it has a reality, it is produced permanently around, on, within, the body by the functioning of a power that is exercised on those that are punished.'[26]

The social construction of the soul which writes itself on the body is one of the defining concepts of queer theory. Foucault believed that the best means of resistance to such a function of power lay in self-scrutiny and renunciation, and here he was influenced by the example of early Christian ascetics. Self-scrutiny and renunciation, however, are necessary not just as a form of resistance but also as a means of creating a space to receive an alternative identity, a gift of sheer grace, given in baptism: the identity given by God. This is the identity which cannot be destroyed by death because it is a resurrection-identity, an identity forged in the white heat of Christ's rising and an identity which mirrors that rising. It is an identity that is given at baptism and renewed in the Eucharist.

Act IV: The Eucharist

I once went to a Robbie Williams concert. When the time came for him to sing his popular hit 'Angels', he sang the first line and then sat down while the audience sang the song for him. It was a transcendent moment. The song had transcended the singer/songwriter, the audience transcended their atomistic selves and became one voice and the process was one of sheer joy. The spiritual nature of the experience was enhanced first by the song, which is of course about angels, and by Williams

---

26. Michel Foucault, *Discipline and Punish: The Birth of the Prison* (New York: Vintage Books, 1979), p. 29.

himself who introduced it by saying, 'Pick up your hymn-sheets and sing along.' The joyous transcendence of community singing reaches its peak in the Eucharist where mortals join their voices to angels and archangels, cherubim and seraphim and the whole company of heaven, not just in the Sanctus but also in the whole act of Eucharist. For in the Eucharist the shadow of death disappears altogether and earth and heaven are united in the marriage of the Lamb. The power of the Eucharist lies not in its dramatic rehearsal of the last supper, nor in its anticipation of a reality to come; the power of the Eucharist lies in the rent veil between God and humanity, heaven and earth, death and life. This 'eschatological thrust' has been highlighted by Pope John Paul II in his encyclical, *Ecclesia de Eucharista*:

> in celebrating the sacrifice of the Lamb, we are united to the heavenly 'liturgy' and become part of that great multitude which cries out: 'Salvation belongs to our God who sits upon the throne, and to the Lamb!' (Rev. 7:10). The Eucharist is truly a glimpse of heaven appearing on earth. It is a glorious ray of the heavenly Jerusalem which pierces the clouds of our history and lights up our journey.[27]

Scott Hahn has drawn attention to the close connection between the book of Revelation and the Eucharist, the Eucharist reflecting the heavenly worship described in the Apocalypse.[28] From the fact that it takes place on a Sunday, through to the presence of priests, altars, vestments, incense, bread and the reading of Scripture, the making of penance, the sign of the cross, the singing of glorias, allelulias and the sanctus, the presence of angels, saints and Mary and, of course, the Lamb of God, the Eucharist reflects the heavenly liturgy described in Revelation. The Eucharist *is* heaven. In the Eucharist the participants experience the defeat of death and the reality to which they move. For a long time only the baptized could participate in the consecration because only they had been through death and marked with the sign of the cross, the sign of victory over death. They enter heaven and engage in the activity for which they have been made: the praise of God. Now Eucharists tend to be open to all, for all of the liturgy and this testifies to primordial baptism of the cross by which all are saved. There is a sense in which the whole of creation has a place at the Eucharist.

In the Eucharist worshippers repeat the resurrection scene at the tomb. The priests leads the people in a turn away from a world of melancholic grief ('Death will be no more, mourning and crying and pain will be no more' Revelation 20.12), a world of gender towards the new creation.

The worshippers gaze upon an altar in imitation of Mary's gaze at the tomb. In some traditions the altar is literally a tomb containing the relics of martyrs in a sepulchre set into the stone (again this imitates the presence of martyrs under the altar in John's vision [Revelation 6.9]. But the altar does not remain empty. The critical difference of this repetition is that the Lamb takes its throne upon the altar in the form of bread and wine. Christ has ascended to his Father. We may not cling to his gender but we can now taste, see and smell his presence. Presence is realized

---

27. John Paul II, *Ecclesia de Eucharista* (Rome: Vatican, 2003), para. 19.
28. Scott Hahn, *The Lamb's Supper: The Mass as Heaven on Earth* (New York: Doubleday, 1999).

but gender is still rendered absent. And not just two angels, but the whole court of heaven, saints, martyrs and the dead gather to join in the feast. It is in the Eucharist that the Church laughs because it is in the Eucharist that the Church encounters resurrection. Michael Vasey noted that 'The biblical and traditional images of heaven are so preoccupied with style and public celebration as to be almost camp. While relentlessly political, they have more in common with a Gay Pride event than with the sobriety of English political life or the leisurewear informality of evangelical Christian life.'[29]

In the Eucharist the Church camps it up along with the angels. The surfeit of heaven reaches earth and pushes aside space and time; death has no sway; all identities save that given by God are rendered non-ultimate. It is in the Eucharist that we learn what our ultimate destiny is. We learn that our gaze is orientated to the Lamb, to the altar/sepulchre surrounded by angels; this is the end and fulfilment of all desire. Here the space outside the Eucharist is exposed as a place of want and lack, a place of endless repetition, of yearning, of desire that can only be repeated, never fulfilled. In the Eucharist baptismal identity is renewed and fulfilled. In the Eucharist death is transcended and angels and mortals become one in activity, intention and desire. In the Eucharist we are as angels in heaven. In the Eucharist the primordial marriage between Christ and soul, the Lamb and the Church is celebrated, to be reflected and anticipated in love between persons of any gender.

Epilogue

A queer death is at the heart of the Christian gospel. The resurrection rolls in the end of death and the end of gender-based identities all in one. After the resurrection those incorporated into it by virtue of their baptism are simultaneously released from the bonds of death and the bonds of constructed identities. They have to die and they have to live out the scripts that are written on their bodies, but those scripts are overwritten by the baptismal identity given as sheer gift from God. So that when the baptized die they should die subversively as people who regard dying as not a passing over into the realm of death but into the great heavenly liturgy, and when they live they should live subversively as people freed from the melancholia of gender, living in the laughter of the resurrection. Throughout Christian history the destruction of death has been linked with the subversion of gender. It can be no mere coincidence that as the Church in the West, bound by its slavery to post-Enlightenment rationalistic world-views, lost sight of heaven, one consequence of which is the reduction of the Eucharist even in the Roman Catholic Church in Western Christianity to a family meal, it also bought into modern constructions of gender and sexual orientation, baptizing them. Having now deprived itself of an eschatological space from which to view the world, it runs the risk of being lost in melancholia, able only to endorse the status quo, unable to offer any hope, damning humanity to the endless repetitions of unfulfillable desires.

The Christian story is a comedic drama: every act involving a dance with death; every act resounding with the laughter of resurrection; every act orientating

29. Vasey, *Strangers and Friends*, p. 248.

us beyond our constructed identities, beyond our sexual desires, beyond death towards a life which is not strange to us but experienced in every Eucharist. It is all very queer.

5

On the Politics of Embodiment and the Mystery of All
Flesh

Graham Ward

In this essay I wish to raise a question concerning the organization of an enquiry, any
enquiry. My enquiry here is into the body of Jesus Christ. Two different analyses are
fundamental not only to the nature and findings of the enquiry but to the constitution
of the enquiry itself. The first set of analyses concerns the why which drives this
enquiry; and the second set of analyses concerns the how, the way of proceeding
with the enquiry. The first set of analyses concerns desire, attraction and the relationship between the enquirer and the object of the enquiry. With the second set of
analyses one can distinguish immediately between metholodogical questions (why
type of enquiry is undertaken) and those elements and relations which organize the
space of the methodology – perhaps even lend significance to why this methodology
is chosen rather than any other. It is the latter with which I am most concerned here.
That is, the assumed knowledges governing the enquiry itself.[1] I will treat the first
set of analyses cursorily at this point because I wish to return to it more fully having
dealt with what is assumed in order for the enquiry to take place at all.

Why enquire?

It should be no surprise to find throughout the tradition of Christian thinking on
the body of Jesus Christ that sexual language is frequently employed. Therefore, it
should come as no surprise to find a number of contemporary Patristic and medieval scholars from Virgina Burrus, Kate Cooper and Elizabeth Clark to Caroline
Walker Bynum and Mark Jordan drawing attention to this language.[2] The work

1.   As Michel Foucault points out, 'The fundamental codes of a culture – those governing its
language, its schemas of perception, its exchanges, its techniques, its values, the hierarchy of its
practices – establish for every man, from the very first, the empirical orders with which he will
be dealing and within which he will be at home' (*The Order of Things: An Archaeology of the
Human Sciences* [London: Tavistock Publications, 1970]). My second set of analyses might be
termed an archaeology of the 'fundamental codes of a culture'.

2.   See Virginia Burrus, *Begotten Not Made: Conceiving Manhood in Late Antiquity*
(Stanford, CA: Stanford University Press, 2000); Kate Cooper, *The Virgin and the Bride:
Idealized Womanhood in Late Antiquity* (Cambridge, MA: Harvard University Press, 1998);
Elizabeth A. Clark, *Reading and Renunciation: Asceticism and Scripture in Early Christianity*
(Princeton, NJ: Priceton University Press, 1999); Caroline Walker Bynum, *Jesus as Mother:
Studies in Spirituality in the High Middles Ages* (Berkeley, CA: University of California Press,
1982); Mark Jordan, *The Invention of Sodom* (Chicago, IL: University of Chicago Press, 1998).

of queer theorists and the new attention to the different historical and cultural understandings of embodiment has only returned a number of scholars of early Christianity to their treasured texts in an effort to point out that modernity's commitment to the twin-headed heterosexual difference and homophobia is a blip in the history of Western civilization. The language of sexuality and queer relations frequently found in accounts of the body of Christ issue from a fundamental erotics driving the enquiry itself. This has always been so. In the past the enquiry into the body of Christ was governed by a calling, a discipleship, a formation, a participation, a desire, an anticipation and relation. The enquiry is conducted within an encompassing affectivity. The telos, for example, of enquiries such as Tertullian's in *De Carno Christi* or Gregory of Nyssa's in his commentary on the *Song of Songs* is identification with the object of the enquiry: to be made one with Christ. The same is true about current enquiries and this present enquiry; for the point is that neither the object nor the enquiring subject has a place outside an affective or erotic economy that gives rise to the enquiry. I enquire into the nature of this body or into those places (the Scriptures, the Church, the Sacraments) where this body may be found, because I am drawn to it – it is the object of my longing.

There is introduced with this erotic affectivity a gendering of relations, opening questions concerning the constitution of the maleness of Jesus Christ and the relationships of this maleness to the economy of salvation. The erotic relations transcend the dimorphism of heterosexuality/homosexuality, as they deepen the nature of sexuality itself. The erotic is excessive to the sexual, bearing as it does upon that *caritas* which is the mode of God's own activity. It is not that our longing to understand Jesus Christ, to embrace and be embraced by that body which is given so completely for us, negates the sexual. The sexual is the very mark of embodiment itself; a mode of intense relation such that the body experiences itself as such. But desire reorders the sexual as a deeper mystery of embodiment unfolds. Divine embodiment moves us to affirm our own embodiment in a new way – as a temple of the Spirit, to use the Pauline term, as holy, as graced, as transcending our understanding. The gendered relations as set up by the erotic affectivity within which the enquiry into the body of Jesus Christ takes place *are* queered. For they render unstable the categories of sexual difference that might attempt to describe those relations or the performance of the enquirer with respect to the gendered body of Jesus Christ. It is not that gender disappears. Gender is not transcended. It is rather rendered part of a more profound mystery; the mystery of relation itself between God and human beings. I am found in God most myself, my sexual, gendered and gendering self – but I have to be taught what it means to be such a self by the Christ who draws me into a relationship with him. It is then the very male specificity of the body of Jesus Christ that comes to determine how I understand my own embodiment.

How an enquiry proceeds

So much then for my first analysis of what pertains to the purpose of the enquiry. Let me turn now to a more detailed analysis of the assumed knowledges which the enquiry demands, having already shown how the affectivity circumscribing the enquiry raises, as it queers, some of the categories involved. While so engaged let me also emphasize that these knowledges may indeed, should indeed, undergo revisions and repudiations as well as affirmations as the enquiry proceeds. Knowledges are never stable. But in order to engage in such enquiry, in order to raise questions such as 'how do we give an account of this body of Jesus Christ?' we have to assume that we have some knowledge of what a body is. We assume that we know what being human is and even what being 'God' is, in so far as this differs from being human. We assume knowledge of what being male is, what it means, how it can be read with respect to this body. Several recent sociohistorical and anthropological studies have pointed out how each culture figures and understands the body differently. After Foucault, Pierre Manent has called into question our knowledges about being human,[3] and, by implication, our knowledges about being divine. And how do we read the Jewish maleness of Jesus Christ when we neither have the body itself nor a body of writing by this Jewish messianic figure such that we can engage with reading the signs? Several sets of cultural assumptions then inform any investigation into the body of Jesus Christ – even when that investigation is a strictly theological one which roots itself in rehearsing the tradition and reframing the creeds (of Nicea or Chalcedon). For example, the nineteenth-century investigations into the historical Jesus, and the kenotic Christologies that followed from that investigation, occur at a time of the increasing medicalization of the body and increasing confidence (following various declarations of rights) about what it is to be human. In this medicalization, the body is profoundly secularized. As Michel Foucault was one of the first to show, in both of these events, the human body becomes a localized site of certain immanent operations. Reduced to what is observable and explicable, the body becomes an organic machine.[4] It takes on a disenchanted opacity; it becomes an identifiable substance. The nineteenth century was also a time when the new muscular masculinities, sketched by the likes of Winkelmann, from Greek statues, were being formed in the German gymnasia and the English public school.[5] So the theological investigations work along with the cultural assumptions that bodies and being human are physiological givens, that they are sexually differentiated on biological grounds and that being manly is to be strong, forthright and self-controlled. These gendered bodies are constituted of brute data that can be empirically tabulated and positivistically analysed. Gendered human bodies are objects that can be catalogued. So questions of their meaning and the construction of their gender, questions about the cultural specificity of the scientific interpretations of them, are rendered invisible. As such there is little difference between a live and a dead body; and yet what difference there is *is* what being human is all about. The nineteenth-century theologians assumed certain knowledges about Jesus's Jewish embodiment, humanity and sex and, on the basis of such assumptions, it followed

3. See Pierre Manent, *The City of Man*, trans. Marc A. LePain (Princeton, NJ: Princeton University Press, 1998).

4. For the *episteme* of the gaze which respect to the body see *Birth of a Clinic: An Archaeology of Medical Perception*, trans. A.M. Sheridan (London: Routledge, 1989).

5. See George Mosse, *The Image of Man: The Creation of Modern Masculinity* (Oxford: Oxford University Press, 1996).

that his historical existence could be sketched, his biography written and his psychological profile drawn, while throughout his masculinity rendered invisible questions concerning sexuality and gender.[6]

For several decades the social sciences have been learning how to quarry and question their own assumptions and thereby reopen debates once thought to be closed and rethink issues once thought to be settled. Theology too needs to understand how time-conditioned is its language and thought; how what it assumes it knows needs to be critically assessed. It needs to understand also the kinds of bodies its own discourse has been implicated in producing. History shows how Christian theology shaped the anorexic body of the Middle Ages and the heterosexual body of the nineteenth century. Christian theology was profoundly involved in biopolitics – it still is. Recently, Daniel Boyarin has demonstrated how Jewish theology also played its part in the rise of heterosexuality and the development of Jewish male (and by implication female) bodies.[7] By taking just one of those three assumptions – knowledges of specifically ethnic bodies, being human and sex – for enquiring into the Jewish body of Jesus Christ, we can begin that critical reflection and think through its theological significance. But we can also begin to ask what kind of bodies theological discourse is implicated in today.

Philosophically, questions about the meaning, interpretation, presentation and representation of the body do not arise until late developments in phenomenology such as those of Merleau-Ponty.[8] After Merleau-Ponty bodies are not just there. Embodiment can be rethought.[9] The investigations that have been conducted into the body over the last 20 or 30 years in the wake of phenomenological essays by Merleau-Ponty such as 'The Chiasmus' have taught us something of the complex politics of bodies.[10] In the work of Michel Foucault, Jean-Luc Nancy and Luce Irigaray – all explicitly indebted to Merleau-Ponty – bodies are no longer simply givens. Nor are they *tabulae rasae* that receive cultural inscriptions. A new perspective arises that emphasizes that we have no immediate access to what is most intimate to us.

Let me be clear at this point: I am not suggesting that contemporary accounts of the body are any more true or more faithful to the truth of embodiment than the accounts emerging from the Renaissance onwards of the body's facticity. Contemporary accounts are figurations and the scientific accounts remain significantly institutionalized – by medicine and governments. The point I am making is double-bound: we cannot just assume that we know what a body is; and yet

---

6. For a further and more detailed example of how sociocultural conditions mediate our Christologies see Stephen D. Moore, *God's Beauty Parlour and other Queer Spaces in and around the Bible* (Stanford, CA: Stanford University Press, 2001), pp. 90–130.

7. See *Unheroic Conduct: The Rise of Heterosexuality and the Invention of the Jewish Man* (Berkeley, CA: University of California Press, 1997).

8. All of Merleau-Ponty's work treats embodiment, but the most influential writings concerning the sexual body are found in *Phenomenology of Perception*, trans. Colin Smith (London: Routledge, 1989), pp. 67–365.

9. For a truly interesting and significant account of theological embodiment in Christ see Michel Henry, *Incarnation* (Paris: Seuil, 2000).

10. Maurice Merleau-Ponty, *The Visible and the Invisible*, trans. Alphonso Lingis (Evanston, IL: Northwestern University Press, 1969).

not to assume, not to have any notion of embodiment, would stymie any enquiry before it had been undertaken. And so when I came to write my own account of transcorporeality and the body of Christ in my contribution to the volume *Radical Orthodoxy* and in *Cities of God*[11] I was working with narratives of the unbounded body of Irigaray, the imaginary body of Lacan, the performed body of Butler and weaving these notions of the body back into older theological accounts of embodiment evident in Tertullian, Augustine and Gregory of Nyssa. Furthermore, I wished to emphasize that the composition of an argument was not an innocent strategy. I was doing no more than offering a Christological interpretation of some continental views of embodiment. Although I related this interpretation directly to the Scriptures, I was not, by doing that, trying to lend my interpretation a transcendental or ecclesial legitimacy. I was not saying 'This is the nature of Jesus Christ's body and all embodiment' (given that in Christian theology the nature of the world is read in terms of the one through whom and by whom that world was created). I was telling the story of the body of Jesus Christ in another way. Any enquiry into the body of Jesus Christ assumes a knowledge of the nature of embodiment, assumes an account of substance – I was assuming the knowledges of the body that have been fashioned since the phenomenological turn to the body over 40 years ago.

This suggests a profound and a productive agnosticism or, more theologically, mystery, concerning the body itself, to which I will return in the final part of this chapter. All we have is a variety of opinions and beliefs that we necessarily assume are true in order to form the basis for the enquiry at all. What we have when we begin the enquiry are cultural models (frequently internalized) that allow and enable us to make the necessary assumptions. Thus a certain politics is not only evident but inevitable. It is the politics that interest me in this essay – not the interpretation of the body of Jesus Christ as such. I wish to investigate these politics in what follows to demonstrate: (a) how they can be understood and (b) how they might be employed in part of a larger history of cultural change and transmission – one that demands we ask why are we interested in the body of Jesus Christ today and what kind of interest is it. What does this very enquiry say about where we stand now ? Finally, (c) I wish also to offer a theological account of both these politics and the history of cultural change and transmission in which they figure. I am aware that this composes a double movement – investigating the cultural politics of the theological representation and then theologically representing the cultural politics themselves. I open myself to the criticism of circularity. But then I would argue that the criticism of hermeneutic circularity belongs to an ahistorical logic. We never step into the same river twice. Similarly, we are never in the same position having turned through the reflexive circle. Temporally and contextually we are always elsewhere. In confronting the cultural politics within theological reflection and then embracing those politics as something theologically positive, what I am attempting to develop is new methodology for theological enquiry. This

11. 'The Displaced Body of Jesus Christ' in John Milbank, Catherine Pickstock and Graham Ward (eds), *Radical Orthodoxy: A New Theology* (London: Routledge, 1999), pp. 163–81; Graham Ward, *Cities of God* (London: Routledge, 2000), pp. 97–116.

methodology would tender a much more public and responsible theology than we are used to.[12] I hope, finally, to spell out more of what I mean by 'public'.

To render my investigation into the politics of the Jewish, male body of Jesus Christ manageable and also specific I will examine the question of circumcision in two representations divided from each both culturally and historically. I chose circumcision for three pertinent reasons. First, it has always been not only a physiological but a political action, since it marks a boundary of inclusion and exclusion. While the act (the removal of the foreskin from around the penile helmet) has remained the same, the way that act is understood and evaluated shifts continually. The technology for accomplishing the act of circumcision, the context in which it is done and the persons involved in its execution have also changed. Now it is performed in hospitals by the laity, by qualified medical staff. This is mainly because the foreskin is viewed as a potential harbourer of certain infections. The politics implicated in circumcision change with each cultural context. Secondly, circumcision has recently formed a focus of interest in accounts of the Jewish male body by Elliot R. Wolfson[13] and Daniel Boyarin.[14] These accounts detail the theologies of circumcision. They represent the weaving of theological discourse into our present cultural preoccupations with embodiment. Thirdly, circumcision is also viewed in Christian theology as *the* mark of incarnation. That is, the parentage of Jesus of Nazareth may be ambivalent but his circumcision has traditionally been seen as evidence of the humanity of Christ, a fact which has been pointed out by Leo Steinberg.[15] Circumcision is the first indication of the gendered corporeality of the Christ – for Steinberg this explains the unusual but frequent emphasis in medieval and Renaissance art on Jesus's penis. In my two examples I wish to investigate the different cultural politics in which the circumcision of Jesus is implicated.

Luke's gospel

My first example is the account of the circumcision itself in Luke's gospel, and my first question about this account concerns why it occurs only in Luke's gospel. What does it signify? Mark's gospel has no infancy narrative, and so the lack of any reference to Jesus's circumcision is readily explicable. John's gospel contains one reference to circumcision (John 7.22–3), but not an account of Jesus's own. Of course, it could be argued that since there is, at best, only a veiled reference to the birth of Jesus in the prologue to John's gospel (John 1.14), as with Mark's gospel there is no narrative necessity for mentioning the circumcision. Though since both gospels are often taken by scholars to have been written with the Gentile world in mind, and given the controversies St Paul records in his letters about whether Christians as inheritors of a Jewish messianic tradition should be circumcized or

12. This project is developed further in Graham Ward, *Cultural Hermeneutics and Christian Poetics* (Cambridge: Cambridge University Press, forthcoming).

13. Elliot R. Wolfson, *Circle in the Square: Studies in the Use of Gender in Kabbalistic Mysticism* (New York: SUNY, 1995).

14. Daniel Boyarin, *Carnal Israel* (Berkeley: University of California Press, 1993).

15. Leo Steinberg, *The Sexuality of Jesus Christ in Renaissance Art and Modern Oblivion* (Chicago, IL: University of Chicago Press, 1996).

not, it is significant that they are silent on the issue. But of *what* is that silence significant? The question is unanswerable, but perhaps the very absence of any mention of Jesus's circumcision signals a politics we cannot access now. It is possibly a politics that needs to be taken into account especially when interpreting the silence in Matthew's gospel. For most New Testament scholars concur that Matthew's gospel has an implied Jewish readership. It is also a gospel with an infancy narrative and a concern to show not only that Jesus is the *fulfilment* of the Jewish law and prophecy, but that Jesus is the *continuation* of the Jewish tradition. Luke's gospel, on the other hand, has an implied Graeco-Roman reader, being addressed to Gentile converts with little or no background knowledge in Judaism but with some Hellenistic education. Various studies have argued that the Greek of Luke's gospel is more rhetorically conscious, the vocabulary more sophisticated. So when the circumcision ought to appear in Matthew's gospel to show that Jesus of Nazareth really did live out the letter of the Jewish law, it doesn't. It appears in a gospel addressed to Gentile outsiders. Why is this? Or more accurately, why might this be?

Let me suggest that what is missing, present or elaborated in any of the gospel accounts of the life of Jesus, is governed not simply by a theological project but also by a cultural politics. If we view every culture as a set of interrelated symbolic systems, establishing values here, legitimating certain forms of activity there, denigrating other, opposing values, criminalizing forms of activity inconsistent with the lifestyle being advocated, then with the overlapping of those symbolic codes certain symbols are given more priority than others. Certain symbols are key symbols, or foregrounded symbols, which are used to interpret or order other less valued symbols. Each person internalizes this priority, and its hierarchies, often without reflection. In this way specific cultural ideologies become normative. Each person then reproduces, modifies, even possibly critiques such priorities and hierarchies in the various practices that make up everyday living within any particular cultural context. I suggest Luke is doing the same with respect to circumcision; that circumcision becomes not exactly the organizing or key symbol but one that, in the milieu in which Luke's gospel was composed, took on a certain weight, a significance that it may or may not have had in the Johannine community, for example, or the cultural contexts in which both Mark and Matthew were writing. The circumcision is an important foregrounded action for Luke because of its significance to the people he was addressing – and I want to examine why. I wish to access the cultural politics, the movement of social energies which leads Luke to be concerned with the body of Jesus in this way.

It is a scene given a certain rhetorical prominence. For not only does it parallel and repeat (albeit differently) the circumcision and naming of John the Baptist (Luke 1.59) – where the Baptist foreshadows the perfections of Christ – but it acts as a tiny bridge between two large pericopes, the nativity (Luke 2.1-20; where narrative attention is drawn to the pastoral framing and that which Mary kept pondering in her heart) and the presentation in the Temple (Luke 2.22-40; where Simeon prophesies the piercing of Mary's soul in the context of sacrifice). The circumcision links salvation to naming, weaving a complex relation between Mary's body and Christ's. For the cutting Jesus undergoes Mary herself will undergo when 'a sword will pierce through your soul *also*' (*de*; Luke 2.35). The present event of circumcision dissolves into the future prophecy while it floats upon a past resonant with connotations of shepherds, kings and sacrificial lambs. Time is being governed; an explicit sense of providence is performed through certain symmetries: John and Jesus; Mary and Jesus. The brief action takes on a symbolic weight, a diaphanous quality – as if when held up to the sunlight of eternal truth that watermark of what has been and what will come permeates the present significance of the act. The action is weighted with mystery in the process of which the circumcision is theologized. We need to understand what occurs to the event itself in such a theologizing.

I am unconvinced by those who might suggest this inclusion of the circumcision in Luke's gospel was an early example of what we have come to term Orientalism:[16] a Western European employing Western European views of Eastern practices in order to add a bit of local colour or novelistic realism. That is not Luke's cultural context. It is the context of nineteenth-century thinkers and narrators such as Holman Hunt. The circumcision forms one of several references by Luke to Jesus's conformity to the Jewish Law. That is its theological *raison d'être*. But I want to get behind that gesture and think through why it becomes a theological *raison d'être* at all. What I am suggesting is that it is at the same time an event with specific cultural resonance of which we today register the reverberations, but concerning which we know not clearly how to proceed. What does it mean to portray the removal of the foreskin from the penis of Jesus the incarnate God? What did it mean for Gentile Christians? What did it signify to those who read the Gospel according to Luke? We know from the book of Acts (thought by most to have been written by the writer of Luke's gospel) and the Pauline epistles what difficulties circumcision raised in the Gentile world. Furthermore, as Daniel Boyarin argues, 'For the Jews of late Antiquity, I claim, the rite of circumcision became the most contested site ... precisely because of the way that it concentrates in one moment representations of the significance of sexuality, genealogy and ethnic specificity in bodily practice.'[17] So what kind of politics was this account of circumcision implicated in?

The circumcision of Jesus in Luke is associated textually with naming, sacrifice and salvation. These themes were taken up and developed by the early Church Fathers such as Ambrose and Augustine in their allegorical readings of the circumcision. As such, circumcision was related to three sets of issues. First, it was connected with a set of moral dispositions to be imitated by followers of Christ: kenotic obedience, self-denial, a disciplining of the sensual flesh. Second, it was linked to a set of soteriological criteria and a particular model for the operation of atonement: the bloodletting was a down payment for the redemption to follow, a token of the sacrifice on the cross. Third, it was related to a set of eschatological values: the eighth day on which the liturgy took place was symbolically associated with the final resurrection (the eighth being the day following the last day in the cosmic calendar). From the early sixth century, 1 January became the Feast

---

16. See Edward Said, *Orientalism* (London: Routledge, 1980).
17. Boyarin, *Carnal Israel*, p. 7.

of the Circumcision in the Christian Church. It was the great feast (no doubt to replace pagan feasting) between Christmas and Epiphany. And most of the material we have on the theology of the circumcision is found in sermons and homilies preached on this feast day. This allegorizing of the surgical event was a continuation of Jewish hermeneutical method. Circumcision was already being employed metaphorically to refer to hearts and ears in the Old Testament, and no less than Philo in his essay *The Migration of Abraham* proclaimed: 'It is true that receiving the circumcision does indeed portray the excision of pleasure and all the passions, and the putting away of the impious conceit, under which the mind supposed that it was capable of begetting by its own power.'

Now all this is very erudite, but we need to note what occurs in this allegorical move (and, more generally, in the tendering of a 'theological interpretation' to a concrete event). An episode in a narrative is opaque. Its brute factuality interrupts the smooth flow of events such that it draws attention to itself and raises the question about how we are to understand its inclusion. In the face of that opacity we accredit not artistic or creative integrity, but, since we are treating a sacred or revelatory text, we accredit it with theological value. That is, we deem its opacity not to be a case of bad writing, nor aesthetic pragmatism (some local colour to make the account more believable), nor the chronicler's addition of another bit of biographical information. We deem the opacity to be theologically significant. However, though we deem it significant, we do not quite know of *what* it is significant. By wheeling in the allegorical interpretations of the Philos, the Origens and the Gregory the Greats, we are weighting the episode down with symbolic suggestiveness. In other words, we are legitimating its significance by an appeal to the way it encodes transhistorical and eternal verities. To employ good Hellenistic vocabulary, we are translating *historia* into *theoria*. By this move we both transfigure the material – which has been made to render its true form – and displace the act itself. The body begins to disappear, so that in the hermeneutical shift towards moral dispositions, soteriology and eschatology we are no longer talking about the handling and the mutilation of sexual organs. We are treating the preparation of the heart or soul for receiving the divine. We are not talking about the cutting of male flesh, an incision into masculinity itself. In this theologizing we both bypass the way circumcision is a political act implicated in issues of gender, genealogy and ethnicity and we bypass the metaphorics of the theological discourse that has transfigured the event. For concerns with the production of moral dispositions, moral subjects, soteriological models of redemption that revolve around an exchange mechanism between two asymmetrical powers, and eschatological dreams of new forms of embodiment, new liberational *jouissances*, are both freighted with political implications.

I want to suggest that the circumcision of Jesus – the attention to the body of this man – was important for Luke. It was making a cultural and political statement. It said something about embodiment, about Jewish masculinity (and by implication femininity), something about the way certain figurations of the body are invested with cultural status, something about the politics of embodiment. For the body, until its medicalization and dissection in the late Renaissance and early seventeenth century, was not a discrete entity. It was not only malleable; it was mapped onto and composed other bodies larger than itself – social and political bodies. Furthermore, the body established a hierarchical system of values in which the physical was related intimately to the cosmic. The perfection of the physical was an aspiration towards the realization of political harmony and cosmic beauty. What then does the circumcized body mean when it is conceived as figuring the social and political body, or as an analogue of the cosmic or divine body – not simply a physical (or even spiritual) one?

Circumcision in late medieval and Renaissance culture

Let us move now to the second example of the cultural politics of the circumcision of Jesus and its representation/interpretation. This brings us closer to home (historically and geographically) and rescues me from the troubled waters of New Testament exegesis and the sharks within those waters ready to take lumps out of unwitting theologians who wander in there untrained, unlettered. The circumcision of Jesus, as already mentioned, has been celebrated by the Church since the sixth century, but it enjoyed a certain cultic fashion in the fourteenth, fifteenth and early sixteenth centuries in particular. Suddenly, additional to the regular sermons still preached all over Christendom at the opening of the year, collections of orations delivered in the Vatican by aspiring theologians like Campano (in his *De circumcisione*), Carvajal (in his *Oratio in die circumcisionis*), Cardulus (in his *Oratio de circumcisione*) and Lollio (in his *Oratio circumcisionis*) were published. A study of them has been made by the historian of rhetoric John O'Malley.[18] This was a time when Catherine of Siena claimed a betrothal to Christ that was mystically figured as the wearing of her Lord's foreskin as a ring. Paintings represented this mystical exchange, while several churches claimed to have the prepuce of Christ – most notably St John Lateran. Steinberg has examined how several painters in this period depicted the visitation of the Magi as an inspection of the circumcized genitalia of Jesus. This inspection can be observed, for example, in Botticelli's *Adoration of the Magi* (1470) and in Pieter Bruegel's *Adoration of the Magi* (1564).

Now part of what we are witnessing here is a cultural shift from the medieval period towards a new valorization of the material, expressed in a new emphasis upon the incarnation. Christ was humanized. No longer portrayed as king and victor, he is shown as the vulnerable human victim. Christ is brother and friend. He was to be lived out in the world, as St Francis preached and practised. Bernardino Carvajal (preaching before Sextus IV) proclaimed: 'By circumcision he showed himself to be truly incarnate in human flesh.' But despite this new turn to embodiment, there was a continuation of the tradition of allegorizing the circumcision, emphasizing its relation, in the new covenant, to baptism, self-sacrifice and the glorified resurrected body.

This revaluation of the circumcision was not simply a Christian phenomena. Elliot Wolfson has demonstrated the way in which kabbalists developed what the

---

18. John O'Malley, *Praise and Blame in Renaissance Rome: Rhetoric, Doctrine and Reform in the Sacred Orators of the Papal Courts, c. 1450–1521* (Durham, NC: Duke University Press, 1979).

Old Testament and Mishnah employed as a trope into the mystical symbol. In the *Zohar* circumcision is associated with the ability to see the *Shekhinah*, the divine presence. The circumcision, as an inscription in the flesh of the Hebrew letter *yod* (the first letter of the tetragrammaton) 'represents the divine imprint on the body'.[19] The physical opening, therefore, in the seal that, in its symbolic valence, corresponds to an ontological opening in God. Furthermore, entering the *Shekinah* is an erotic experience of penetrating the divine feminine. The kabbalists, in Wolfson's account, related the eye and the penis in an expression of how the initiated had the ability to see mystically and understand. They also related the phallus to the mouth, 'the covenant of the foreskin and the covenant of the tongue'.[20] A secret wisdom is imparted such that 'the process of circumcision, the removal of the foreskin and the uncovering of the corona, is a disclosure of the secret. In the disclosure of the phallus, through the double act of circumcision, the union of the masculine and feminine aspects of God is assured.'[21]

Yet despite all this cultural attention to circumcision, whenever the naked member of Jesus was displayed pictorially or in sculpture, it is never a circumcized penis that is revealed. Steinberg lists a number of paintings of the naked baby Jesus by Cariani, dal Colle, Perugino, Conegliano, Corregio and others, in all of which Jesus seems to be well over eight days old and yet never is the penis circumcized. Perhaps more striking are the sculptures of Michelangelo, especially the Risen Christ and his famous David. These bodies are not Jewish bodies and neither of them shows a circumcized penis. Now why, in a culture that found great significance in the circumcision and the humanity of Christ, is the circumcision itself not physically portrayed, even when the genitals of Jesus are carefully delineated? Why is circumcision orally and textually proclaimed and physically and visibly masked? What is organizing the denial here, just as, in the account in Luke's gospel, what is organizing the avowal there?

Let me remind you that it is the politics not the interpretation as such I wish to focus on here. Politically I am struck by the rejection of the Jewish body in both the Graeco-Roman period and in Renaissance culture. This rejection gave rise in both periods to persecution and pogroms. Youths being educated in the Hellenistic schools exercised naked and it is recorded that some Hellenized Jews who attended such schools underwent surgery to replace the foreskin (see 1 Macc. 1.15; Josephus, *Antiquities* 12.241; 1 Cor. 7.18). In the Renaissance period circumcision was mainly associated with Muslims (who were slaves) or with Jews, who were associated with the greedy and covetous sides of nascent capitalism. In both cultures the circumcized body is a socially and aesthetically (and therefore also cosmically) inferior body. In both cultures the circumcized body was a mutilated and wounded body; not the kind of body that could function as a microcosm of cosmic and political harmony. Why should the resurrected body of Christ have its foreskin restored?

19. Wolfson, *Circle in the Square*, p. 30.
20. Ibid., p. 42.
21. Ibid., p. 45.

The politics of embodiment

Let me suggest that what we witness with respect to Luke's inclusion of an account of the circumcision of Jesus (coy as it is on details) and the attention to a spiritual reading of circumcision, rather that its physical inscription, in the fourteenth to six-teenth centuries are political gestures (of different, maybe opposite, kinds). They are accounts of the body of Christ that are grounded upon certain cultural a priori about embodiment. Luke appears to be making a gesture of resistance to a cultural hegemony. The Christology outlined is one in which Christ is a counter-cultural figure: an ally of the poor, the sick, the destitute – all who are socially margin-alized. Michelangelo, on the other hand, is inflecting a cultural hegemony in a different manner (after all the marble bodies of neither David nor the resurrected Christ are Italian, they are Platonic). His Christology is one that emphasized Christ as the perfect form of human being. The cultural resources for envisaging such perfection were classical figurations of the young, athletic body. As classical statues were being excavated, rediscovered and collected, so, in what might be termed an historicist move, Michelangelo returns to figurations of the body evident in the time of Jesus himself. In this inflection the Jewish body is rendered socially, politically, aesthetically and finally theologically invisible. A different cultural politics, a different cultural negotiation, is involved in both accounts of the body of Jesus Christ. Different theological statements emerge in different times, under different circumstances.

The accounts themselves issue from cultural assumptions about the nature, function, even telos of the human body. As I said at the beginning of this essay, these politics of embodiment are inevitable. But let me take this further. If the politics are inevitable, how does theology handle the pragmatics of its own dis-course? To clarify the issue: the recognition of the politics of interpretation must accept that knowledges are local. The body of Jesus Christ (or the Virgin Mary), for example, will be differently conceived and differently theologized in different cultures and in different times. How then does Christian theology retain its com-mitment in faith to the one Logos? It seems to me that two answers are possible, but I can only accept one *for theological reasons*. In the first answer, theology accepts a broadly nominalist and later Kantian metaphysics. That is, it accepts that God is totally unknowable, absolutely transcendent, the wholly other, and that therefore all any of us trade in is symbolic exchanges. I would reject that answer for numerous reasons. The most pertinent of these are:

(a) The nominalist dualism (later the dualism of noumenal and phenomenal) cannot treat embodiment at all. The body in such a metaphysics is at best a machine activated by a mind.

(b) The nature of incarnation is such that God does not remain absolutely tran-scendent, wholly other. The body of Jesus Christ understood theologically is, to use Derrida's term, a 'quasi-transcendent' and, to use Irigaray's term, a 'sensible transcendent'.

(c) There is a subtle imperialism at play with the enunciating position of this metaphysics. Whence can the claim be made that God is wholly other and human beings traffic merely in symbols for a transcendent reality which may or may not correspond with that reality?

This first answer to the problem of theology's production of local knowledges avoids the politics involved in construction, the violence that is ineradicable in rhetoric, by shifting attention to the universal on the other side of the particular.

The second answer, the one I would wish to develop, is to embrace the inevitability of being implicated in a cultural politics; to accept that theological discourses on the body of Jesus Christ, for example, produce local knowledges. They are specific negotiations within specific sociohistorical contexts. Both relativism and universalism can be avoided by developing a Christology that takes time and embodiment seriously.

This Christology would emphasize, on the one hand, the continual displacement or expansion of the body of Christ as it is inflected in this place and that, by this church and that, even by this atheist and that. By these means the Christ-effect is disseminated endlessly, but not, I would argue, arbitrarily. To return to the analyses at the beginning of this chapter, of what drives the enquiry into the body of Jesus Christ, the dissemination is determined by an erotics, a participation, a relation. The relation holds – focusing all these disseminations back to that which has solicited and produced them: the body of Jesus Christ. As in the Eucharist but also beyond it, the body is broken and distributed by the Church.

On the other hand, one would also have to emphasize in such a Christology, how the body of Jesus Christ as it operates upon and within and as the social and poetical body, the ecclesial and sacramental body – in what I have called variously its displacement, expansion, fragmentation and dissemination – participates in the unfolding operation of the Triune God with respect to creation. The politics of interpretation, the endless figurations of the body of Christ are, then, that which constitutes the very participation of the human in the divine. So that in each historical epoch, as in each distinct geographical-cum-ethnic location, something new is expressed, revealed, produced in a divine/human cooperation about the body of Christ. We are called to make meaning in God – this is the particular commission of Christian *poeisis*. That is, Christian theologians have to render visible the operation of the Word, the body of Christ. Nicephorus, the ninth-century apologist for icons, wrote in his *Third Refutation* (3.39) that, following the resurrection, Christ's body, although it appears in a most visible and divine form (*theoeidestaton*), remains a body. It does not change itself into the divine essence (*ousia theotetos*). The fact that Christ is no longer known after the flesh (2 Cor. 5.16) does not mean he has abandoned or rejected embodiment. It means he has been released from physical constraints – or physical constraints that have become viewed as such following the mathematical approach to understanding the world.[22] Theological reflection upon that embodiment is itself a participation in that extended embodiment as it moves through time and space and redeems the material. Christian *poiesis* is itself political, for the Logos is not frozen; orthodoxy is not a frozen Logos. The Logos is person and operation. Christology is not a

22. See Foucault, *The Order of Things*, pp. 46–77.

timeless holy grail handed down from fathers to sons in the purity of its form. No doctrine is. A constant shaping takes place in the interstices between human making and *theopoiesis*. What issues from the accumulation (Nyssa might call it *skopos*) of *paradoses* is the profound mystery of embodiment itself; not just the embodiment of Jesus Christ but the ineffable nature of each human person and all forms of embodiment. For the mystery continually exceeds our local constructions of what it presents. What we discern, and the early Church Fathers discerned, about the body of Jesus Christ becomes a meditation on the human person created *imago dei* and *as such* being the priest of the created order around them. As priest, the human vocation is then voicing the mystery, which becomes a doxology, of materiality itself.

Such a Christology and theological anthropology do not get theologians themselves off the hook for producing racist or sexist bodies of Jesus Christ. The reflexivity involved in embracing the cultural politics implicated in every discursive production requires a moral responsibility (and a humility on the part of the theologian) that is sensitive to how others might receive what has been produced. Some conflict is inevitable, as some violence is inevitable, in all rhetorics of persuasion. But in accepting, as Augustine once taught in *De Civitate Dei* (*The City of God*), that it is both necessary to make judgements and equally necessary (pending the last and final judgement) to admit ignorance, then all accounts of the body of Jesus Christ remain open for correction, critique and supplementation. None of them are beyond contestation.

To conclude, then, by returning to what I set out at the beginning of this essay. What both Luke's account of Jesus's circumcision and the Renaissance theologies of the circumcision reveal is how theological discourse is part of a much wider cultural politics. Accounts of the body of Jesus Christ draw upon assumptions about both the nature of embodiment and what is valued and/or denigrated with respect to the representation of that embodiment. This involvement in a cultural politics renders theology public in the sense that it cannot ever (logically) simply talk to the insiders about the nature of what is believed. The language of theology and the categories for its thinking extend its discursive practices far beyond its own sectarian interests. Theological discourse is implicated in the production of bodies, in the biopolitics of such a production. The realization of this must make theologians responsible to the wider contexts of their productions, more reflexive about the politics and rhetorics of their accounts and claims. Furthermore, there are good theological reasons for this reflexivity – to wit, being so implicated is to participate in the unfolding of the Godhead with respect to creation. To accept, reflect upon and work within the cultural politics of any one time and place is an incarnational act itself, the constitution then of the body of Christ. As such theologians reflecting upon the embodiment of Jesus Christ help to raise the question of the politics of embodiment itself. In doing this those politics become not simply a cultural but a theological issue. There is a politics of faith.

Coda

I realize I leave two significant questions hanging from those raised in the earlier part of this chapter. These questions are related: why there has been increasing attention to the nature of Jesus Christ's embodiment since, say, Tom Driver's short but influential article 'Jesus and Sexuality' in 1965 and what kind of body is Christian theology implicated in producing today? The answers I give are more speculative because the evidence upon which I am relying is more disparate than the rich texts of the ancient or Renaissance pasts. I would suggest the attention to the nature of Jesus Christ's embodiment is part of a wider cultural obsession in affluent locations around the world with the body. This wider obsession that desires to turn the body into the most finely balanced sensorium so that it might experience its own joys and pains to the full, is, I suggest, a response to the fear of the body's disappearance. While the call goes out for new incarnationalisms (from critical theorists like Irigaray, Cixous, Kristeva and Butler), while in the UK new health and sports clubs open every week, while cooking and celebrity chefs daily take up more media time, while high-street fashions populate the pages of every glossy magazine and film-stars parade their designer labels, while films like *Hannibal* are produced reflecting the fears for and fascinations with the consumer body and while the genome project publishes its regular breakthroughs, the deepening of cyberspace and the multiplication of mobile phones is making gnostics of us all. Our working is becoming more and more disembodied. A profound invisibility is the cost of our spectacle society. And the invisibility most affects bodies: the bodies of workers in countries and continents that do not appear on maps of global operations; the bodies of the disenfranchized within our own societies; and our own bodies too. As I said, this is speculative because the evidence as you can see is disparate.

So what kind of bodies is theological discourse – in its very reflections upon, interpretations of and participations within the body of Christ – producing today? The court is out on this one for the moment. Though what seems evident to me is a new malleability, ambiguity, porousness, hybridity and mixing of the organic and the mechanistic. The cyborg and the angels are figures for new bodily perfections, and we theologians are busily inventing queer Christologies that somehow offer Christian models for an incarnationalism or that turn to an embodiment which is culturally more pervasive. Perhaps theology is doing no more that reproducing the bodies that are culturally in fashion. But if so, then theology really has lost its critical way, and needs to return to the wounded and violated body of Christ: the body as always in some sense circumcized and in need of circumcision. What knowledge issues not only from the gendered body and about the gendered body, but from the wounded body about the wounded gendered body? Teresa de Lauretis once wrote of gender as trauma.[23] Perhaps there would be another place to begin again.

23. Teresa de Lauretis, *Technologies of Gender: Essays on Theory, Film and Fiction* (Basingstoke: Macmillan, 1987), p. 3.

6

SEX AFTER NATURAL LAW[1]

Gerard Loughlin

For many people, sex has become the defining issue for the identity of the Christian Church in our time, at the beginning of the twenty-first century. The issue of sex is thought to define the Church, both in itself and in its relationship to the contemporary world in which it participates. But for some people, the Church's discussion of sexuality is indicative of how far it is already unduly influenced by the wider world's obsession with sex. Such people think that the Church now thinks too much about sex because the world does. To think that the identity of the Church is tied up with its attitude to sex is to mimic the world, which seeks to find in sex the truth about itself.

But if sex is not the single defining issue for the identity of the Church in our time, it is certainly one of them. Moreover, sex has become the focus of divisions within the Church, in all its denominations, and many fear that these divisions will grow deeper and wider, leading to further splits and separations. If the Church has been captivated by a worldly obsession with sex, it is an obsession it cannot simply seek to ignore, since sexual issues threaten its integrity and whatever remains of its fragile unity.

However, while it would be hard to deny that the world is obsessed with sex, it is misleading to suggest that the Church has merely fallen prey to this obsession, and this for at least two reasons. First, it can be argued that the world's obsession is not the cause but the effect of the Church's own, preceding obsession. And second, it can be argued that because the Church is a body it also is sexed, and that therefore there is a truth to be known about its sex, which will also be the truth about our own sex, individual and social. Owning up to the issue of sexuality should thus be viewed as a positive opportunity for the Church. For it is good that the Church can learn to say that she has sex.

Sexing the Church

It was the French historian-philosopher Michel Foucault (1926–84) who argued that in the nineteenth century there emerged a particularly modern attempt to

1. This chapter is in part based on a talk on the Church and sexuality that I gave at the University of Durham in October 2000. It was one in a series of Millennium Lectures on the Church and Society, organized by the Revd Samuel Randall and the Very Revd Nicholas Coulton.

'tell the truth of sex', using scientific and bureaucratic methods of record and analysis to produce medical discourses about sex. But telling the truth of sex was already the concern of two preceding endeavours, the *ars erotica* and the *scientia sexualis*.[2] The former – which Foucault finds in numerous ancient societies – is an esoteric knowledge of the erotic arts, that does not confer social power but instead control of the body for the production of pleasure. *Scientia sexualis*, on the other hand, Foucault finds to be uniquely Western, concerned with establishing social power through the production of knowledge, a knowledge that is above all solicited through the practices of Christian confession and its secular derivatives. From the thirteenth century onwards, penitential techniques turned Western men and women into confessing animals, and a privileged theme of their confessions was sex. Thus the Western world experienced what Foucault describes as the 'transformation of sex into discourse', first the discourse of the penitent to the confessor, and then of the pupil to the pedagogue, and of the patient to the psychiatrist.[3]

> It is no longer a question simply of saying what was done – the sexual act – and how it was done; but of reconstructing, in and around the act, the thoughts that recapitulated it, the obsessions that accompanied it, the images, desires, modulations, and quality of the pleasure that animated it. For the first time no doubt, a society has taken upon itself to solicit and hear the imparting of individual pleasures.[4]

There is thus a fine irony in thinking that the truth of the Church now depends on the telling of its own sex, like a patient in the psychiatrist's chair, or a guest on the Jerry Springer Show. For it is the result of the Church's own putting of sex into discourse, its own production of 'sexuality', when the latter is understood as that latent desire which must be solicited in order to be known. The irony is also terrifying, because just as Foucault thinks that we demand that 'sex speak the truth' in order that it 'tell us our truth',[5] so today we demand that the Church tell us about its sex in order that we might know the truth about the Church. And that truth has proved to be terrible. The Church has confessed to being misogynistic and homophobic, and, as we have been hearing more recently, paedophiliac. The Church has not always confessed to these misdemeanours with public apologies, issued by Church authorities with all due ceremony, as has been fashionable with regard to some past failings. The confessions are made more quietly, in other arenas and through other modes of discourse; in discussions such as this essay, which are heard by very few.[6]

2. Michel Foucault, *The History of Sexuality*, Vol. 1 (Introduction), trans. Robert Hurley (Harmondsworth: Penguin Books [1976], 1984), pp. 57–8.

3. Ibid., pp. 61–3. See also Pierre J. Payer, *Sex and the Penitentials: The Development of a Sexual Code 550–1150* (Toronto: University of Toronto Press, 1984).

4. Foucault, *History of Sexuality*, Vol. 1, p. 63.

5. Ibid., p. 69.

6. An all too rare event was the apology offered to gay and lesbian people by Bishop William Newman, an auxiliary in the diocese of Baltimore. In the Spirit of Pope John Paul II's *Tertio Millennio Adveniente*, he wished to lead the Church 'in seeking the forgiveness of God for the sins individually and collectively which the church has committed against the gay and lesbian community'. See *The Tablet* (6 January 2001): 28.

This brings us to a second reason why a discussion about the Church and sexuality is not simply a capitulation to contemporary secular obsessions with sex. On the contrary, discussion of the Church and sexuality is a proper concern of the Church with itself as a sexed body. It may seem odd to talk about the Church in this way – as a body that has sex – but it is entirely orthodox and traditional, if employing a rather more naturalistic idiom than is usual. It is an idiom that simply takes seriously the Church's own body symbolism. From the beginning, the Church has understood itself as the body of Christ, as the social body called together by Christ, in whom each is a member, and of whom Christ is the head. The Church is this body not only because called by Christ but also because fed by him, with his own flesh and blood. This is why it is in the celebration of the Eucharist that the Church is most itself, most bodily; when it is given God to eat.

At the same time, the Church has also understood itself to be the bride of Christ, called to bodily union with him, so that the sexual joining of bodies, is also part of the Church's imagination of itself, of herself, in her union with, and difference from, the divine. If we also recall that the Church is identified with Mary, who brought Christ into the world, and from whom alone he has his flesh – his 'corporeal substance'[7] – we realize that the Church is imagined in terms of the most intimate of fleshly communions: a body that is both united and differentiated within herself.

The body of the Church, which is most clearly visible in the celebration of the Eucharist, is startling. It is composed of many diverse bodies and is yet also one body, which is both human and divine, being the body of Christ. At the same time it is a maternal body, with enough sustenance for everybody; while also a nuptial body, where each is brought together through desire of the other, attracted by the beauty and allure of Christ's body. As bride and mother, the Church is properly sexed as female; but as composed of many bodies, she is also multisexed, as male and female, gay and straight, and as all other variations and dispositions. Thus part of what it is for the Church to speak her sex, is to say, for example, that she is woman, or that she is lesbian.

The Church, in the prayerful practice of her imagination, looks for the redemption of all aspects of human life, including sexual life, through its incorporation into the complex body of Christ. The Church reimagines our bodies and their sex, by placing them in a different context, a different story, within which they gain new meanings, new natures, because joined together in and with the new body of Christ.

In order to bring out the difference that the body of Christ makes for our own sexed bodies, and our own sexualities, I want to briefly sketch an alternative imagination of the body and its sex, which I think increasingly holds sway in our Western societies. For want of a better name, I am calling it the imagination of utilitarian Darwinism, or, more simply, modern nature.

7.   Thomas Aquinas, *Summa Theologiae*, I.119.2.

Darwinism and utilitarianism, procreation and pleasure

In recent years, Darwinian or evolutionary theory has been increasingly applied in disciplines other than the purely biological, such as sociology and psychology. Thus we now have sociobiology and evolutionary psychology.[8] While these discourses draw on profound advances in the biological sciences, they are also deeply committed to evolutionary theory, not just as a means for understanding natural mechanisms but also for a metaphysics that displaces all other attempts to think the meaning of human existence, whether philosophical or theological.[9] Indeed, Charles Darwin himself had such pretensions, writing in one of his notebooks: 'Origin of Man now proved – metaphysics must flourish – he who understands baboons will do more towards metaphysics than Locke.'[10] Darwin may have been right about John Locke (1632–1704), whose philosophy is part of the problem, but the metaphysical pretensions of sociobiology and evolutionary psychology far outstrip the philosophical and theological acumen of their proponents or, more importantly, the justified claims of the sciences on which they draw.

John Locke's philosophy is part of the problem because the 'traditional' account of God, against which much sociobiology and evolutionary psychology direct their polemic, goes back no further than to Locke himself. Many of these writers – whom I will simply call Darwinists – rail against forms of Christian fundamentalism that oppose evolutionary to 'creationist' theory. Of course there can be no defence of creationism, which is bad science and even worse theology, knowing nothing of the doctrine of creation (*creatio ex nihilo*).[11] But the Darwinists fail to note that the fundamentalist traditions against which they set themselves are no older than their own scientific traditions. In this regard, both evolutionist and creationist are strangely indebted to John Locke and to modern rationalism, with both seeking a similar certainty of knowledge that older traditions eschew. But this is an aside to my main interest, which is to indicate how Darwinist metaphysics imagines the human body and its sex.

Human sex, as both a means of reproduction and as an intense pleasure constantly sought by human beings, is a problem for evolutionary biology. For it would seem that asexual reproduction is a more efficient means for passing on genetic inheritance, and given sexual reproduction, it would seem more viable if it were restricted to periods of fertility alone, as in many other

8.　See E.O. Wilson, *Sociobiology: The New Synthesis* (Cambridge, MA: Harvard University Press, 1975); Jerome H. Barkow, Leda Cosmides and John Toby, *The Adapted Mind: Evolutionary Psychology and the Generation of Culture* (Oxford: Oxford University Press, 1992).

9.　Mary Midgley nicely notes how writers like Richard Dawkins and Stephen Hawking have proposed to answer the old question about the meaning of life, without first having understood the question. They suppose that people are looking for a causal explanation, when in fact they want a story, the ending of which will give the point and purpose of life. See Mary Midgley, *Science as Salvation: A Modern Myth and its Meaning* (London: Routledge, 1992), Chapter 1.

10.　Charles Darwin quoted in Steve Jones, *The Language of Genes: Biology, History and the Evolutionary Future* (London: HarperCollins, 1993), p. 78.

11.　See Kathryn Tanner, *God and Creation in Christian Theology: Tyranny or Empowerment?* (Oxford: Basil Blackwell, 1988).

animal species.[12] Darwinism cannot say that sex is pleasurable in and for itself, since Darwinism attempts to explain everything in terms of some evolutionary advantage. Thus Darwinism suggests that those animals – such as chimpanzees and humans – who engage in sex for pleasure do so because it serves the end of forming social and personal bonds that are advantageous for successful reproduction. Malcolm Potts and Roger Short, for example, argue that if early hominid females were fertile for only a few days in a three- or four-year cycle, due to gestation and three years of lactation, the evolutionary opportunity of frequent and pleasurable though infertile sex would keep male hominids interested, and bond the parents 'in the task of bringing big-brained, slow-developing children to maturity'.[13]

For Darwinism, the bottom line is reproduction, since in so far as Darwinism explains anything, it is always explained in terms of reproductive advantage. Darwinism is the creed that makes reproduction not only a physical, but a metaphysical principle, as the meaning and point of human life. Thus Potts and Short can tell us that the male gibbon, as he swings 'in great arcs from branch to branch' is 'merely a vehicle' for carrying 'testes'; and the testes are merely a vehicle for producing sperm, and sperm, of course, exists merely to make more gibbons.[14] Potts and Short conclude their study of the evolution of human sexuality by imagining a future in which men and women join together to celebrate 'the differences that ultimately make them essential to one another for the perpetuation of our species and for the fulfilment of our brief lives on this planet'.[15] But for Darwinism, the perpetuation of the species is the fulfilment of our brief lives, since we are finally only reproductive mechanisms that serve only the purpose of reproduction, and everything else is merely accidental. As Matt Ridley puts it, 'reproduction is the sole goal for which human beings are designed; everything else is a means to that end'.[16]

The Darwinist vision is actually bleaker than this suggests. For when Ridley speaks of 'design', he, like all Darwinists, means design that is the product of undesigned mechanisms, which simply operate, and which have no real goals or ends. As Richard Dawkins notes, the designs of nature are illusions, the product of 'natural selection, the blind, unconscious, automatic process which Darwin discovered', and which has 'no purpose in mind'. Natural selection 'has no mind and no mind's eye. It does not plan for the future. It has no vision, no foresight, no

12. Richard Dawkins has a ready answer to this problem, arguing that sexual species have a better chance of survival than asexual ones. See *The Blind Watchmaker* (Harmondsworth: Penguin Books [1986], 1991), p. 268. But for a more detailed, less sanguine discussion see Matt Ridley, *The Red Queen: Sex and the Evolution of Human Nature* (Harmondsworth: Penguin [1993], 1994), Chapter 2.

13. Malcolm Potts and Roger Short, *Ever Since Adam and Eve: The Evolution of Human Sexuality* (Cambridge: Cambridge University Press, 1999), p. 33. See also Jared Diamond, *Why is Sex Fun? The Evolution of Human Sexuality* (London: Phoenix [1997], 1998).

14. Potts and Short, *Ever Since Adam and Eve*, p. 25.

15. Ibid., p. 333.

16. Ridley, *The Red Queen*, p. 4. On the priority of genes and their interests see Daniel C. Dennet, *Darwin's Dangerous Idea: Evolution and the Meanings of Life* (Harmondsworth: Penguin, 1995) (pp. 328–9).

sight at all. If it can be said to play the role of watchmaker in nature, it is the *blind* watchmaker.'[17] As with Dawkins' earlier image of the 'selfish gene',[18] his 'blind watchmaker' is less well chosen than it might be, less precise than it should be, since a blind watchmaker still has a mind, a mind's eye, with foresight and even 'vision'. But Dawkins' point is clear enough. The highly anthropomorphic language that permeates Darwinist discourse – and Dawkins' discourse in particular – should not blind us to the fact that Darwinist metaphysics is ultimately nihilistic. For the Darwinist, human life emerges out of the void incomprehensibly, without reason. Moreover, in the Darwinist universe, human beings are merely machines for the transmission of genes that exist in order only to be transmitted – the one little bit of teleology that Darwinism permits itself; the barest of metaphysics.

For Darwinism, then, children are the only point of human sex, and the fact that making babies can be pleasurable and bonding is merely a happy effect, it being pleasurable not for the fun, but because by enjoying it we undertake it more often, thus increasing our chances of reproductive success. And the point of having children is that they in turn will have more children. Oddly, however, Potts and Short think that people are having too many children and they castigate the Roman Catholic Church for encouraging this.[19] These Darwinists urge a thwarting of the evolutionary mechanism, in the interest of a better quality of life for those children who are born.[20]

At this point, we can see that Darwinism, despite its metaphysical pretensions, must import other principles if it is to promote a particular morality, and unsurprisingly, it opts for some form of utilitarianism, which is the dominant morality of our age. Darwin himself read and admired John Stuart Mill's work, *Utilitarianism* (1861), and referred to it in the *Descent of Man* (1871). He notes that according to Mill 'moral feelings' are not innate but acquired, though no less natural for that. Darwin presumed to differ, and thought that Mill was much nearer the mark when he described our social feelings as the 'natural basis of sentiment for utilitarian morality'.[21] Darwin suggests that morality should aim not at the 'greatest happiness' but at the 'general good or welfare of the community', and in this way build

17. Dawkins, *The Blind Watchmaker*, p. 5.

18. Richard Dawkins, *The Selfish Gene* (Oxford: Oxford University Press, 1976). For a critique see Gabriel Dover, 'Anti-Dawkins' in *Alas, Poor Darwin: Arguments Against Evolutionary Psychology*, ed. Hilary Rose and Steven Rose (London: Jonathan Cape, 2000).

19. Potts and Short, *Ever Since Adam and Eve*, pp. 296–8. Darwin himself encouraged the multiplication of the human species, especially by the most 'highly-gifted'. 'There should be open competition for all men; and the most able should not be prevented by laws or customs from succeeding best and rearing the largest number of offspring.' Of course women would do the actual rearing. See Charles Darwin, *The Descent of Man, and Selection in Relation to Sex*, intro. John Tyler Bonner and Robert M. May (Princeton, NJ: Princeton University Press [1871], 1981), Part 2, Chapter 21, p. 403.

20. Dawkins also calls us to battle the Darwinian machine: 'We have the power to defy the selfish gene of our birth and, if necessary, the selfish memes of our indoctrination ... We are built as gene machines and cultured as meme machines, but we have the power to turn against our creators. We, alone on earth, can rebel against the tyranny of the selfish replicators' (Dawkins, *The Selfish Gene*, p. 215).

21. Darwin, *Descent of Man*, Part I, Chapter III (p. 71, n. 5).

upon our 'social instincts', which have been naturally selected for the 'general good of the community'.

> When a man risks his life to save that of a fellow-creature, it seems more appropriate to say that he acts for the general good or welfare, rather than for the general happiness of mankind. No doubt the welfare and the happiness of the individual usually coincide; and a contented, happy tribe will flourish better than one that is discontented and unhappy ... Thus the reproach of laying the foundation of the most noble part of our nature in the base principle of selfishness is removed; unless indeed the satisfaction which every animal feels when it follows its proper instincts, and the dissatisfaction felt when prevented, be called selfish.[22]

Darwin was more of a naturalist in ethics than later Darwinists, for whom nature seems less able to provide the basis of a universal morality, and he himself appears vague as to how one moves from sociability to morality. Like Darwinism and Christian fundamentalism, utilitarianism is a product of modern rationalism, when it is thought that universal human reason will supply ethical principles for rational human agents who have turned their back on those traditions of virtue that had sought the habitual formation of moral characters for final blessedness. For the utilitarian, right action is not something for which we have an instinctive knowledge, either through our natural sociability or due to the formation of our character through living within an imaginative world, framed by social practices and the telling of stories. Rather, right action has to be calculated on the basis of what will accord us the greatest happiness without diminishment of anyone else's happiness, or, what will accord the greatest happiness to the greatest number. There are of course many difficulties with this view, but utilitarianism trades upon them: the unresolved and unresolvable difference between self-interest and public interest, and the difficulty of determining the latter other than in terms of the former, as well as the difficulty of knowing and calculating the 'happiness' that will be either increased or decreased. But utilitarianism succeeds through its confusions, because they give it a flexibility that allows for the justification of many different outcomes, which don't have to be consistent within one another. The great power of utilitarianism is not that it enables us to resolve dilemmas, but that it allows us to justify the resolutions which we otherwise achieve. Thus governments can justify their policies in terms of the greater good, and individuals their actions and pleasures, when they are assured that they have not diminished the totality of human happiness.

In this way, utilitarianism has justified many laudable policies and actions, and persuaded people to them. But it can also persuade us to decisions that are otherwise unjustified. The strength and weakness of utilitarianism is its flexibility, and this makes it philosophically uncomfortable. It is malleable to almost any end, because it does not have an account of human nature, and so an account of the human telos by which to determine what makes for human flourishing and happiness. It must borrow such an account from elsewhere. Darwinism might be thought to provide this account, but because of its overriding metaphysical principle, it

---

22. Ibid., pp. 98–9.

proves to be as vacuous as utilitarianism itself. Darwinist sociobiology must deny that there is such a thing as human nature since human nature, as we know it, is but one moment in a process that evolves but is going nowhere. There is no human telos by which to determine what will make for human happiness; all one can do is to make a survey of what people find pleasurable at any given time. Darwinism merely sanctions the moral fashions of the day.

A somewhat different account, but with the same outcome, is advanced by evolutionary psychologists such as Matt Ridley, who argue that we do have a determinate human nature, but one that was formed during the Pleistocene era, a two-million-year period that came to an end with the birth of agriculture. We are essentially hunter-gatherers. Ridley knows what human nature was then like, because it was like what it is now, and so when we read his account of human nature we find that it repeats almost every imaginable sexist stereotype.[23] Darwinism, I would suggest, is inherently conservative, because it explains what is the case by imagining the primal scene in which the case first came to be – a 'just so story' – and the case is defined by the cultural assumptions of the relevant Darwinists. Darwinism can imagine what might be, but it has no basis for imagining what should be, and even less for what will be.

Remnants of natural law

The problem facing Darwinian ethics parallels that for neoscholastic natural law theory, except that the latter, in its heyday, in the nineteenth and twentieth centuries, was not afraid of committing the naturalistic fallacy. Crude natural law theory supposes that it is possible to read off from nature a series of precepts for human behaviour. Thus, in the classic example, we can tell what a man should and should not do with his penis from studying its natural functions. But in order to determine the latter we have to make sure that we only observe those men who know what they should be doing, and not those who are functioning 'unnaturally', no matter how natural it may seem to them. In short, we have to make sure that we are wearing the right spectacles before we start looking at nature.

Crude natural law theory was attractive because it promised a universal, non-contextual ethics; and it was possible when its proponents derived their authority not from their reasoning – which was interpretative – but from their cultural dominance. Though there are some who still advance such arguments, their cultural irrelevance renders their strictures ineffective. (Though Italy has one of the lowest birth-rates of any European country, no one supposes that Italians are more infertile or have less sex than other Europeans.) That nature is always conventional, the product of culture, was already apparent to the early eleventh- and twelfth-century scholastics, at least to the extent that some noted the necessity of identifying those parts of nature which should and should not be consulted. Thus the anonymous author of the *Leipzig Summa* was aware that the untutored might derive the legitimacy of fornication from the

---

23. See Ridley, *The Red Queen*, Chapter 8, esp. pp. 257–63.

observation of animals.[24] Further rational argument was required in order to determine which parts of nature were most educative for human behaviour. As Jean Porter notes, the scholastics arrived at their 'moral conclusions through a process of dialectical reflection' that moved 'between their understanding of human nature, and the specific norms and practices said to express this nature, and not through a process of deduction from a fixed idea of what is natural'.[25]

The same impasse confounds Darwinian metaphysics. Without a dialectical process between culturally specific 'norms and practices' and scientific observations – which are also culturally embedded – Darwinist ethics can hardly get off the ground. Thus the only piece of advice that Matt Ridley can proffer after his entertaining investigation of sex and the evolution of human nature is that we should dare to 'be different', since 'wit, virtuosity, inventiveness and individuality turn other people on'.[26]

Fair enough, we might think. But behind Ridley's playful injunction, we can detect the outlook of utilitarianism, that teaches us to privilege self-interest, and view other people as means to our ends. Driven by our biology to have sex for the purpose of its reproduction, we can go along for the ride, and either thwart its results, the having of babies, or have the babies if doing so will give us pleasure and satisfaction. In recent years, various politicians and others have sought to draw a line between selecting an embryo in order to save the life of an existing child, and doing the same in order to ensure the sex of a future one. The distinction trades on a nice sentiment, but in a utilitarian society it makes little sense. If a boy will give you more pleasure or prestige than a girl, you surely have a right to him. For to deny you would be to decrease the totality of pleasure in society.

Of course one might object that Darwinism does not have to entertain utilitarianism, that it could supplement its thin metaphysics with a different moral philosophy. For indeed, one might imagine that its meagre metaphysics are already borrowed from elsewhere, perhaps from the very philosophy it thinks most distant to itself: neoscholastic natural law theory, which is about as modern as Darwinism itself. At the very least there is a curious, even pleasing, parallel between a natural law theology that sees reproduction as the point of sexual congress, and a Darwinism for which the desire to reproduce is the one little goal that sets everything in motion. We might say that just as Darwinism would hardly have got off the ground without the idea of design that it borrowed from deism, so it can hardly muster an ethic without borrowing from natural law theory. Thus Darwinism is clothed in the discarded remnants of Christian theology.

24. Quoted in Jean Porter, *Natural and Divine Law: Reclaiming the Tradition for Christian Ethics* (Grand Rapids, MI: Eerdmans, 1999), pp. 84–5.
25. Ibid., p. 79.
26. Ridley, *The Red Queen*, p. 333.

Transforming bodies

Needless to say, the Church does, or should, imagine natural bodies somewhat differently to the way that utilitarian Darwinism does. The Church seeks to live by a different vision, a different social imagination: one that, as I have already suggested, is most visible when the Church is gathered for the Eucharist. One might even say that in the liturgical celebration of the Lord's Supper, the Church participates in that creative work in which we are shown what the world could be like, what it will be like, and so, in some sense, is already, in the creation of Christ's bodily communion. For people to enter into this bodily imagination is to have their own body transformed, seeing it not as a cog in a meaningless reproductive machine, as Darwinism imagines, nor as simply a means to their own passing pleasure, as utilitarianism supposes, but as a gift that they have received, and receive again, in so far as they give it away. It is a gift that in the giving of itself creates new life and attains to a joyful existence, beyond mere pleasure.

The cutting of bodies gives rise to the desire to be *joined* with one another. Each of us was once intimately united with another body, far more intimately than with any other body. There was a time when we were each dependent upon, but yet different from, our mother's body, who was and was not one with us. It is because the relationship of mother and unborn child is one of primordial union and difference, that Sr Mary Timothy Prokes has described it as an experience of profound and elemental sexuality, in the sense that at 'no time in later life will there be the same capacity to *reside – to live within another physically* or to share flesh and blood with such an enduring immediacy'.[27]

In the union of mother and child the self of both is given and received in a fully bodily way. Following Prokes, one might suggest that the placental relationship between mother and child is paradigmatic for all later intimate physical unions, when, as we say today, bodily fluids are exchanged. It is also, for her, an image of union with Christ. 'Womb-life is a prelude to the mature capacity of living within one another in the manner that Christ prayed for in his Last Discourse: "May they be one in us, as you are in me and I am in you, so that the world may believe it was you who sent me"[28] (John 17.21).'

The cutting of the physical union between mother and child can be understood as the birth of sexuality in each one of us, when sexuality is understood as the desire not to undo the cut but to experience again the giving and receiving of the self in and through the union of bodies. Sexuality cannot seek to unsever the cutting of mother and child, since it is that severance which gives rise to sexual desire, the desire to be different from, yet united to, another body, and in that differential union experience both the loss and return of the self. And a more fully theological rendering of this would suggest that the giving and receiving of self, the loss and return of self, that can be experienced in sexual union, is an incarnated analogy for the giving and receiving of God's life in the divine Trinity.

27. Mary Timothy Prokes, *Towards a Theology of the Body* (Edinburgh: T & T Clark, 1996), p. x.
28. Ibid., p. 97.

Thus to refigure the body within Christ's body is to reimagine sexual union, not as merely reproductive, producing more of the same; nor as merely pleasurable, an orgasmic dissolution of the self that must nevertheless return with the passing of sexual excitement, remaining the same as before; but as an intimate participation in the union of Christ with his bride, the Church, which is a union taken up into the very life of the one but differentiated God. And this mystical union is possible because it is undertaken within the Church's symbolic practices, which are practices of mutual dispossession and fidelity, and which traditionally go under the name and form of 'marriage'.

The point of sex, it is often said, is reproduction and pleasure. Reproduction, in particular, has been thought by many in the Church to be the point of sex, so that sex undertaken for any other reason was judged to be illegitimate, sinful. It is not immediately evident why this idea became so dominant in Christian tradition, since it is not evidently canvassed in the New Testament. St Paul, for one, urged that sex should be avoided if at all possible, but if not then it should be confined to marriage. But marriage, for Paul, was not for the proper ordering of sex in the interest of procreation, but in the interest of propriety. For Paul, the last thing that Christians should want to do is to produce little Christians. Marriage is not for the having of children, but a prophylactic against passion, a curb on concupiscence (I Corinthians 7.6). Such a perplexing view was to dominate much if not most Patristic teaching on sex. If at all possible, don't do it; but if you must, get married.

This position is perplexing, because it does not have any obvious basis in preceding Jewish traditions, though there is evidence that Jewish writers like Philo were influenced by ascetic teachings prevalent in the upper classes of the Greco-Roman world.[29] Paul's own teaching may more nearly reflect the influence of Stoic philosophy on his thought. Whatever its origins, it is impeccable Christian theology, since it follows from the belief that with the coming of Christ, human history has been fulfilled. The Church is living at the end of time, though it is a distended ending, stretched between the first and second comings of Christ. The Church lives between the times, between the time of the world, which is over but continues, and the time of the Kingdom, which is now but not yet, arriving but still to come. Living in such a time, the Church does not look for perpetuity through progeny, but for that more perfect, intense life that is the resurrection of the body in the eternity of God. For the Church, the point of life is not the having of children, but the praise of God in the company of the saints. Consequently, sex as reproduction is not really important.

How then can we understand the advent of children in the body of Christ? The answer, briefly sketched, is that in the Church's imagination, people do not 'have' children, as if they had made them themselves, but receive them, as gifts from God. The Church receives children, not in the hope of reproducing herself, so as to achieve some spurious immortality, but simply and only as the new life that burgeons from the life of Christ, who is yet to come, but is even now arriving, not

29. See David L. Balch, 'Backgrounds of I Cor. VII: Sayings of the Lord in Q, Moses as an Ascetic Theios Aner in II Cor. III', *New Testament Studies*, 18 (1971/2): 351–64.

least in the new-born child. As already hinted, this way of thinking of the matter understands children as born to the Church, and not merely to their parents. For the latter are not isolated couples, but part of the one body. This is why everyone has a responsibility for the children of the Church, symbolized in the practice of godparenting and of adoption. And it is also why not everyone in the Church has to look for the gift of children, why not every particular relationship or sexual act has to be open to the gift of children, in short, why there can be infertile straight couples and gay couples; why there can be celibates, consecrated virgins and single people. For in the imagination of the Church, children are first and foremost gifts that arrive through the nuptial union of the Church with her beloved, Jesus Christ.

Sex after natural law

It may seem unlikely that we could have learned the foregoing from nature. It is certainly not a lesson that Darwinism could teach us, which finds in reproduction the only meaning for our being. But when nature is understood starting from the story of Christ as its goal and fulfilment, then we may begin to see how his story, and the practice of waiting upon its fulfilment, is also the story of nature, and the law or *ratio* that it has to teach us. As both Jean Porter and Fergus Kerr – in his wonderful book *After Aquinas* – teach us, natural law theology was not always understood as the fallacious deduction of moral precepts from animal and human behaviours, and so need not be understood in that way now.[30] When we turn to Thomas, and in particular the *Summa Theologiae*, we find that there is only one question on natural law, set in the middle of an extended discussion of human law and the laws of the Old and New Testaments, the law of the good news concerning Christ. Moreover, law is the rule of reason within these various domains, but not the reason of later Enlightenment rationality – a self-directing autonomous reason – but the reason of the divine will, the eternal law by which all things are governed. '[H]uman and natural law, as well as divine law [the law of the Testaments] are located firmly in the context of divine providence.'[31]

God's providence is the ordering of the world toward God, toward its final beatitude in the communion of the saints. The natural law is the name for the movement of nature toward this end, as it participates in the eternal law, which is the cosmic movement of all things toward God. Thus the natural law is utterly theological, and to follow it is to be caught up into the movement of God's desire for God. Nature, for Thomas Aquinas, does not contain a universal, non-theological law. Rather there is only one law, which is the one will of the one God, and in which all participate in so far as they are under the law, and not turned away from God.

> In sum, in the *Summa Theologiae*, Thomas presents the natural law in the context of Torah and the New Law of the Holy Spirit, in the wider context of an account of the virtues (theological and cardinal) as the moral agent's journey to

30. See Fergus Kerr, *After Aquinas: Versions of Thomism* (London: Blackwell, 2002), esp. Chapters 6 and 7.
31. Ibid., p. 105.

face-to-face vision with God, all framed by the presupposition that the natural law is a participation in the eternal law which is identical with God himself.[32]

As Fergus Kerr develops his account of Thomas's theology, and the place of natural law within it, it becomes clear that everything is ordered by and toward the final beatitude, when, in union with Christ, we will see God face to face. Thus, far from thinking that Thomas had a 'divine command ethics', or even a 'virtue ethics', we should think of him as advocating an 'ethics of divine beatitude'.[33] It is then not so surprising that Thomas says so little about the natural law, and that what he does say is so vague, for its basic teaching must be that the good life is one ordered toward the good from which all life flows and to which it returns, toward the good of the beatific vision, which of its nature we now glimpse only darkly.

On this understanding, sex after nature – sex that follows the natural law – is sex that orders us toward the infinite joy of our consummation with and in God, in the fellowship of Christ and the saints. There is thus a real difference between the Church's sex and that of the secular world. It is most clearly seen in the living symbols of the Church, where her reality becomes most visible, as in the celebration of the Eucharist, and in those eucharistic practices of dispossessive union when, after Christ the bridegroom, we give ourselves over to another, in the *ascesis* of Christian partnership and marriage.[34]

If we follow Darwinism, and seek to learn from modern nature, we will think that the meaning of sex is reproduction and pleasure. But if we follow Christ, and seek to learn from natural providence – from the only law that nature speaks – we will find that sex has to do with the joy of union beyond all unions, a participation in that dispossessive desire when we receive ourselves again, in the infinity of God's *kenosis*. What is required for the world to know this difference, and indeed for the Church herself to do so, is for the Church to speak her sex, and this, as I have tried to suggest, will be both painful and joyful; for the Church, in the world is a body that lives under sin and under grace.

---

32. Ibid., p. 109.
33. Ibid., p. 133.
34. See further Eugene F. Rogers, *Sexuality and the Christian Body: Their Way into the Triune God* (Oxford: Blackwell, 1999), Chapter 3.

Marcella Althaus-Reid

> Queer politics ... requires a resistance to regimes of the normal
>
> (Jeffrey Escoffier)[1]
>
> But if one lifts one's skirt, it is to show one's self – not to show oneself naked like the truth (who can believe that the truth remains the truth when one lifts its veil?)
>
> (Baudrillard)[2]

First indecencies: lifting the skirts of God and strangers

Is theology the art of putting your hands under the skirts of God? If feminist theology is a revelatory theology, concerned with the liberative presence of God in history, and in the history of women, can we then redefine theology as, for instance, a reflection on God closely related to loving arts of intimacy with the Beloved? Can we express in this metaphor an affectionate and historically grounded reflection on God and women, at the margins of heterosexuality? How does Sophia-Wisdom fit in this loving metaphor? Can we lift her skirts?

Using sexual metaphors for theology is not a novelty; the Bible is full of them. However, the novelty (and the indecency) seems to come whenever we discentre the assumed man-woman sexual identities of the dyadic system of Christianity. The point is that discentring the subject of theology, we end discentring God too. I have no intention of producing any theological shock by saying that doing theology may be related to touching God under her skirts, but simply of making public the closeted affairs between theology and sexual ideology. In other words, to take this old alliance of theology and heterosexuality out of the sphere of domestic violence and to make it public. And this is what we are confronted with in the loving image of putting our hands under the skirts of Sophia-God, by denouncing the immateriality of theology and even feminist theology when it displaces the site of women's bodies by transcendental configurations. Unfortunately for us in theology, when transcendence enters the scene, the body leaves. The body may remain of course at a symbolic level of exchange, but the real body, that is the body which speaks of the concreteness of hunger and pleasure, gets displaced. In feminist theology, it sometimes gets displaced by desire, if desire is not properly incarnated. The point

---

1.   Cited in D. Alderson and L. Anderson (eds), *Territories of Desire in Queer Culture* (Manchester: Manchester University Press, 2000).

2.   *Guardian* (10 June 2001): 2.

is that desire may function as an abstraction, and as such, continues rehearsing the revelatory presence of what Butler would call the presence of the ubiquitous phallus.[3] It is precisely that phallus which represents the transcendental in theology – a phallus which depends on a messianic prototype, that is the prototype of the mystical penis of Christ. However, subversion is a hermeneutical space present in every interpretation. The mystical penis of Jesus can be subverted not by desire but by pleasure. It is pleasure which gives feminist theology, by the heaviness of its concrete allocation, antidotes to the unnecesary transcendence of the Father's phallus in Jesus and in God.

These antidotes in theology do not work following dyadic oppositional systems such as God-Father and God-Mother; or as in a discourse about 'the feminine side of God' (which by the way assumes that the core of God's identity is heterosexually male, and femininity is just a side or an extra point of view). The metaphor of theology as the act of putting our hands under God's skirts belongs to another frame of thought, more diverse and irreducible. God's skirts are a suitable divine metaphor for material girls in theology which help us to reflect on God in our lives beyond biological, parental metaphors or even dismantle – perhaps – the ghostly look of Sophia-Wisdom, and make of her an unreasonable, illogical God, with the kind of wisdom that patriarchal theology does not recognize.

Moreover, the image of touching God in an intimate way is not completely strange for us; as some discourses in feminist theologies have identified one of the persons of the Trinity as a lover, touching that lover under her skirt brings to the realm of theological imagination the reassurance, intimacy, fun and loving dialogue of women and God. In the same way, any metaphor of intimacy with God is a metaphor of mutuality, pleasurable activity and freedom after which neither we nor God are meant to remain the same. God is going to be enriched in the process.

Dislocations: what to preach? Sex or God?

The first indecent act of the theologian is that recognition that no matter the metaphor you use, theology has been and will remain a sexual praxis. To do theology as an act of defiance, the first rebellions usually come with the awareness that theological reflections are in struggle with heterosexual canonical law. That law is based on a sexual covenant of uniqueness, based on mono-loving activities. Theological mono-loving is carried through political and economical frames of thought, and it may be necessary to remember here the association between monotheism, monarchism and the subjection of women in marriage contracts. To that theology belongs a practice concerned with reaffirming a particular sexual understanding of the sacred, done by a systematization of theology and also by liturgical and structural repetitive traditions which have inbuilt sexual, political and economic standpoints. It may be useful to highlight here the concurrency of heterosexual ideological thinking which pervades current theological practices,

---

3.   See J. Butler, *Gender Trouble. Feminism and the Subversion of Identity* (London: Routledge, 1990), p. 13.

and can be found in liberation theologies, Vatican theology and some feminist theology alike.

As I am interested in a reflection that may lead us to a praxis of sexual dislocation of theology and ideology, I have called this type of material sexual theology indecent, and its praxis, indecent acts.[4] I called it indecent because this is a theology the main function of which is to destabilize the decent order, that is a constructed political, social and sexual order which has been ideologically sacralized, and whose moralizing objective is based on the dyadic reflection on a dyadic God. I am using here the metaphor of 'indecency' as it comes from my own Latin American context, in order to start a reflection on queer theology as a sexual and political theology with an option for the poor. Indecency is part of the dialectic of the 'decent/indecent' which regulates the individual and community lives of women in my continent by a strict codification of sexual and gender understandings. It circumscribes and supervises carefully the delimited areas of public and private lives by delimiting the territory of the proper and the improper, which unveils by default the Christian sexual construction of society and politics in my continent. The fact is that Christianity more than a theology has a sexual programme. The story of colonization shows this quite distinctively. For instance, Christianity came to Latin America with a sexual intention behind the catechisms in order to produce a conversion not so much to Christ but to the then prevalent European affective patterns of relationships. Although I need to concede that little is known of the sexual lives of people in my continent before the arrival of Christianity, it is undeniable that it was different to the Christian European sexual project. The preaching was done on sex, not on God (unless we admit the conceptual interdependency here). This can be seen in history through the struggle for the imposition of European monogamous marriage rituals against the then existent polyamorous unions, homosexual affections and cherished crossdressing practices which were later delegalized by becoming non-Christian and therefore, indecent. Yet, Christianity is a sexual project (and not just a gender project, concerned with the subjection of women). However, as we have said before, with every interpretation comes a subversion, and a popular counter-theology of heterosexuality arose in my continent.

For bigamy and God: popular theological rebellions

I find this point important, because there is a lesson from history here. Is feminist theology popular? Are queer theologies rooted in common people's experiences? I must say, yes. Queer theologians find tradition through discontinuation. Indigenous revolts, as for instance against the Jesuit missions, were sexual revolts, and as such I consider them part of the Church traditions of sexual ideological disruptions. The *chamames* (religious and political leaders of the Guaraní nation) called people not to disbelieve in the Virgin Mary and the Trinity, but to actively defend bigamy and concubinage as part of a social, political and religious rebellion against the

4. For further discussions on this point see Marcella Althaus-Reid, *Indecent Theology. Theological Perversions in Sex, Gender and Politics* (London: Routledge, 2000).

imposed colonial order. However, that act was also part of a theological struggle for a different understanding of God and sexuality, which has much to do with the way people organize themselves as society. Idolatry was homologized to dissident sexual behaviours.[5] Therefore, what we can now call a sexual discontent was in reality a discontent with Christianity, and a legal discontent against the state. Following with this example, in many countries the Jesuits had the power to hold civil and criminal courts, and their missions (called *reducciones*, literally 'reductions') had their own jails and system of punishment for sexual offences such as marrying a first cousin or having two wives. For people who have learned their ecclesiastical history through films such as *The Mission*, it may be disappointing to know how the missions separated couples (or triads) and banned otherwise happy and harmonious relations as part of a political and religious hegemonic project. As a document from a group of elders at the time says, the Christians came to destroy the indigenous nations by destroying their happiness in love.

It is important to reflect on this gesture of sexual defiance by the colonies as a challenge to Christian theology, because through it we can see how people perceived that Christian dogmas were to be destabilized by rebelling against the imposition of monogamy or heterosexual affective contracts. There is a methodological issue there, because that was the people's theology at the time, dismantling oppressive structures of the Church not by arguing about the Trinity, but by delegitimizing the Christian sexual project. However, if theology is a sexual act, to stand up for bigamy or polyamorous relationships is to stand also for a queering attitude to Christology, Mariology or the Trinity. Queering theology does not leave theology intact in its systematic structures, traditional positions or ecclesiologies, but uses its own sexual ways of knowing to question the sacred as a heterosexual assumption. That is of course, high sexual revolt in theology. If the theologian puts her hands under the skirts of God, she is establishing a different pattern of dialogue with the sacred and with herself and her community of resistance. This heralds the end of unnecessary transcendence and the beginning of sensual concretization in theology.

On queerings

Queering the theologian
Feminist theology is never neutral, nor are theologians neutral practitioners. Feminist theologians have ideological and geopolitical investments in their praxis. Christian theology interpellates theologians by making them supposedly 'free' to respond to God's appeal, which is a sexual theological appeal. Freedom, in reality, is what is lacking. The heterosexual appeal of God comes with the understanding of a given. One does not need to be a feminist theologian to participate actively in approving or disapproving the heterosexual ideology of theological methods, in the same way that one does not need to be a liberation theologian to engage in politics

---

5.   I am indebted for these comments to Merry E. Wiesner-Hanks, *Christianity and Sexuality in the Early Modern World. Regulating Desire, Reforming Practice* (London: Routledge, 2000), especially the chapter on Latin America.

in one's own theological praxis because sometimes in/difference does it. In/differentiating habits in theology do not work for neutrality but for the identity of the stronger ideology. This is the equivalent of the law of the jungle in Christianity. However, a theologian should stand in full consciousness of what she supports, or at least, any theologian working from a liberationist background (as I do) should do so. Therefore, when I say that I 'stand queer', I want to make clear that I stand in a tension: alone, with full responsibility for my discourse but also with my particular community of struggle. That community is made up of networks of aliens, or the community of strangers who cast a highly suspicious hermeneutical circle in the attempt to unveil the complexity of the sexual base lying below the construction of the Church's dogmatics and politics alike. By doing so, queer theologies also try to find the presence of the stranger God, who stands outside the classroom definitions of heterosexual thinking and is among us.

Why is it important to take a stance, and more precisely a sexual stance in doing theology? Is it not for instance enough to stand for gender equality in a neoliberal feminist agenda? If we think that we need to take a sexual stance in theology because lesbians, bisexuals or transvestites are trying to make their own contribution to the so-called theologies of story, and thus reclaiming a space of sharing the presence of God among us, that may not be the whole truth. If we think for instance that bisexuals are – and rightly so – looking for a Christology which may convince the Church that they too are children of God, that still may be a partial aspect of a queer theology. I agree that even if the pursuit of sexual equality in the Church was the only objective of queer theologies, it should be encouraged as a worthy initiative. For we know that following a contextual methodology, first we engage with critical reality and then we do theology from it as a second act. Moreover, we may also argue that as we have been using social sciences as mediatory sciences in the liberation hermeneutical circle, we have never considered heterosexuality seriously as ideology, so a different sexual theory should be welcome too. However, there is always much more to come in the work of queer theologies. For sexual theologies are concerned with structures such as the structures of love and knowledge which regulate affective and political decisions in our lives, run economic thought and may have even exiled God from churches and theology long ago. And that is why, for me, a queering theology is an encounter between strangers and a pursuit of God the stranger. God is also queer: perhaps the first queer of all.

To do feminist theology then is an act defined in relation to that sexual act of standing critically in relation to heterosexual ideology. They may be post-Christian or reformist responses; it does not matter. The important point is that our identity as theologians is shaped somehow in relation to a certain sexual response. Therefore, post-Christians may have a point in trying to break from that circle of subjection to a condition which limits exchanges and ways to do theology through the given authorized medium of expression. But so do queer theologians who have extended an alliance of different, plural sexual understanding to issues of Church tradition, ecclesiastical history and dogmatics. Moreover, the post-Christian discourse is still a much gendered position, while in queer theologies there is a deeper problematization concerning sexual and gender categories. As we all stand for something while doing theology, I like to make clear my geopolitical decisions. I stand as queer amongst queers, as I stand for the circle of hermeneutical suspicion to be taken towards new limits, and for the presence of the strangers of theology to share stories from which a new, different face of God may appear. This is a call for a body theology, but one which embodies the unknown at our gates, the strangers in theology. By encountering those strangers a different body theology occurs: a theology made with the different shapes that come from the encounter. Queering confronts the theologian's own voice and responsibility too, for as Kosofsky Sedgwick has said, the queer discourse can become so only when the 'I' is present in it.[6] It is a theology which does not essentialize. In that sense, it is the perfect example of a theology done from someone's story, and the reflection where a theologian stands up in community, in solidarity and in uniqueness. Queer we may stand, with a sense of pride and resistance which comes from the sharing of our own stories and own sufferings, and the silence of a theology which has assumed too many things about sexuality and God. This has been the theology of sexual idealization, an idealist-based theology now challenged by the materiality of our own strange communities, and the strange God who walks with them.

Queering gender-theology

It may be obvious at this point that it is not reflection on gender, that considerably new sociological category, but reflection on the sexuality of God where the possibilities of a radical theology exists. By 'sexuality of God' I am not simply saying, for instance, that God is a genderfucker, that is, a God for whom gender and sexuality are fluid categories. Neither I am saying that Jesus should be seen exchanging clothes with the Magdalene. What we are pointing at here is the sexual epistemology of salvation.

It is also clear in this context that I am saying that the sexuality of God is not given or disclosed; that it is (to use a metaphor dear to many) closeted, that is, hidden and waiting. The old theological enquiries done long ago, about Jesus's supposed femininity or God's female metaphors (curiously linked to re/production) are such a limited exercise because they never encounter strangers. If gender performances could make a difference, I for one could have started carving a statue of a transvestite, leather-clad and stockinged Christ, in the hope of liberating God from dyadic representations, as some of my sisters have done 'Christas' hanging from their crosses. And I am saying that with the understanding that Christas have been more important than many theological books. Christas made theologians become the voyeurs of a strange God by looking at her exposed nudity transgressing the cross. The presence of the woman on the cross and the richness of all sorts of theological reflections produced by that image have been extensive, but we had not reached under her skirts. Displaying the symbolics of gender, useful as it is in destabilizing theological high truths which are mere gender illusions, will not liberate. If not, I would consider myself having fulfilled my duties as a believer

6.   Eve Kosofsky Sedgwick, quoted by Linda Anderson, 'Autobiographical Travesties: The Nostalgic Self in Queer Writing', in Alderson and Anderson (eds), *Territories of Desire in Queer Culture*.

and as a theologian by simply and only crossdressing Christ as the Virgin Mary and wondered about the nature of the Messiah's relationships with married men such as Peter. The situation is more complex than that because gender performances actively repeat sexual performances (using Butler's theory), but unless we reach that core of sexual production in gender representations, our analysis will be superficial and, worse, may even reinforce the idea of sexuality as a given; that dual thinking is a given or that love-knowledge and theological knowledge are different things. Or that affective relations and economic ones have nothing in common. Or that God can be on one side of the political struggle but on the other in sexuality, and that *that* God is straight.

Thus, queer theologians are facilitators of the sexual traffic of the Church's praxis. They facilitate an encounter amongst strangers which is much more radical than gender-talk. The theological method of sharing sexual stories requires that everybody engage with honesty in a theology which takes distance from sexual ideologies. It requires that heterosexuals come out of their own closets too, in order to discuss issues such as monogamy, fidelity and family structures, because they are crucial for Christian theology and practice. Having said that, I for one recognize that when our sisters started with the gender-based enquiry into theology, the path for the improper, for indecency, to come into theology was opened. As feminist theologians opened the gates to encounter the margins, strangers and queers started to arrive, and amongst them the stranger-God came in. Elizabeth Grosz has commented that the sex of the author usually leaves traces in the text, and assumes the reader's sexuality too.[7] We may say that language and the materiality of bodies constitute the matrix of theology which leaves traces, and to find a queer, strange God in Christian theology means that we can read a different and even unlawful theology in reverse. It is us, the strangers in Christianity, who now can write the traces of a strange God among us. Why would we wish to pursue a theological reflection on a strange God? Among other things, for political reasons.

Queering colonial theology
I remember Althusser's writings on ideology, and an interesting remark made by him concerning 'fragments'. He sees fragments as carrying with them the full ideological mechanisms that the centre-totality attributes to itself. The theological fragments or 'theologies at the margins' to which we are referring here, share a colonial identity in dependency with their own colonial (or neocolonial) masters. I have argued elsewhere that a God at the margins is not a marginal God.[8] The latter would be a real God within the margins, and a God with a substantial difference from the charity models which present us with a God coming to our margins, to our borders. It is precisely that movement of coming towards the marginalized

7.   See Elizabeth Grosz, *Space, Time and Perversion. Essays on the Politics of Bodies* (London and New York: Routledge, 1995), p. 18.
8.   For further comments on this point see my article 'The Divine Exodus of God', in Werner G. Jeanrod and Christoph Theobald (eds), *God: Experience and Mystery* Concilium 289 (London: SCM Press, 2001).

which betrays that God. Where does this God belong? Which cartography of salvation has this movement towards the margins traced?

The theology at the margins that I would like to pursue as part of a queer trajectory in theology is not a neocolonial theology where an economic and affective
model of relationships needs to be either expelled from the system or incorporated by providing an understanding alien to what real margins are. Margins are
not margins except for the colonial mentality. The cultural, political and sexual
relationship of gods at the margins usually ends up ratifying colonial pacts on the
materiality of theological practices instead of unsettling them. Theirs are theological projects instead of trajectories; God is a modification of power, and there is
no sense of transgression here but of normality, with perhaps the exceptions which
constitute normality. Those are margins of gender. Those margins are not queer.

If every theology is always a sexual theology the point is how to disrupt this. A
gender-based theology does not have a chance, but neither would a sexual-based
one (heterosexual or gay), unless the instability of sex is recognized. The problem
with heterosexuality, which I consider a respectable sexual option, is heterosexual
ideology, in the Marxist sense of a dominant world-view which acts as an undis-
cussed method of understanding reality. To say that theology is and always has
been a reflection rooted in sexual practices means that there is an epistemology
which sacralizes sexual exchanges and regulations by a circle of a permanent
reconfiguration of the sacred, based on heterosexuality's symbolic structures and
value system. When it is said that theological practices do not come from heaven,
I agree. In fact, I think they come from the theologians' own bedrooms, which
also means from the theologians' own closets. What I am saying is that not only
is there an important theological contribution to the formation of heterosexual
ideologies in the history of the churches, but that that sexual ideological formation
is constitutive of the theological praxis itself. However, heterosexual ideologies
come with economic, political, racial and specific cultural understandings and
interpretation circles. Queer theology is a theology of loose alliances among
sexual dissidents which reconfigures different spaces of thinking and relating to
each other. Theologically, there are many implications in this.

The perv's handbook of feminist theological ethics

The question to ask now is, what regulatory, decent order has organized the systematic theological sexual discourse in Christianity? Which sort of classroom
ideology is behind a theological ethics which reproduces and encourages an
attitude of theological submission to one specific epistemological model such as
idealized heterosexuality in the making of systematic theology? Judith Butler
confronts us with the issue not of the constitution of gender (which in her opinion
leaves sex untheorized) but of the regulatory norms which act in the materialization of sex. That is, how sexuality is socially constructed.[9] Following from
that, we may like to use a hermeneutical suspicion to enquire how sex has been

---

9.   See Judith Butler, *Bodies that Matter. On the Discursive Limits of 'Sex'* (London:
Routledge, 1993), p. 10.

materialized through theological mechanisms. That would be asking what sort of regulatory doctrines of grace and salvation, or what Christologies, are responsible for the theological construction of sex.

Moreover, we may like to ask which are the connections between a colonial or neocolonialist theological framework of thought and those constructions of sexuality which not only gave God a penis but also regulated what that penis was supposed to do. Here we are in the area of classroom ideology which closes its frontiers with precision but also rules which categories of the indecent should remain hidden in the closets of theology and the theologians. As I have said elsewhere, if Paul Tillich was a fetishist with a penchant for SM religious symbols, I would not join Mary Daly in condemning him for that, but I would like to highlight the fact that in his theology he never addressed his own sexuality which was hidden at the core of his theological identity.[10] If Karl Barth had just paid more attention to the fact that he found marriage somehow a dull experience, we could have had a much-needed theology of mistresses long ago. That lack of engagement of theologians with their own sexual context at the moment of their reflections has kept the heterosexual roots of theology as an ideology without alternatives. But heterosexuality also has its own closets and fears, and its own ethical irresponsibility too.

I call this a *Perv's* theological ethics, because per/version is a concept that can be theologically related to alternative versions or options which it is our duty to imagine. Per/version (as a different version, or understanding) is the methodological path to take against projects of sameness.[11] Queer theologies may offer some ethical perversities to consider, as for instance:

1. Consensuality. Queer theology is a theology of alliances in agreement with their own diversity, in consensual loving dynamics. Consensuality here also means dialogic, even if code-breaking at times. A consensual relationship with the Church and with God belongs to a different order than the old hierarchical, autocratic style of organizing people and theologies to which we are accustomed.
2. We start our reflections from our own sexual stories. We lift God's skirts after having lifted our own first. In lifting our skirts we remind ourselves of our own identity at the moment of doing theology while we remain committed to theological honesty. It is from an alliance of sexual epistemologies in disagreement with heterosexual ideology and not vice versa that we reflect on grace, redemption and salvation.
3. From different sexual epistemologies we may find different ways of understanding not only the salvific project but alternative church structures too. For instance, the role of permutations has a pedagogical function: to understand the complexity of the dynamics of change in the Church.[12] The

10. See Althaus-Reid, *Indecent Theology*, p. 146.

11. For an extended commentary on the concept of theological perversions see ibid., p. 87.

12. For the use of permutation as a hermeneutical choice, see Marcella Maria Althaus-Reid, 'Sexual Salvation: The Theological Grammar of Voyeurism and Permutation', in *Literature and Theology*, 15.3 (2001), pp. 241–8.

scenes of exchanges between femmes and butches, or men in high heels and women in drag have much to teach the churches about change, the import-ance of performances and the joy of allowing plurality to be embodied in us.

From Leather groups or the community organization of poor transvestites in Buenos Aires come many lessons to teach us about the beauty of the economic and affective alliances of the excluded in the world. Feminist theologies have already discovered that pleasure (the materialization of desire) is a place to start a theology of the body which dismantles dualisms.

Volver a nuestras almas

We may be doing a theology of encountering strangers, including a stranger God and a Queer Messiah, but at the end, queering theology brings us back to ourselves, to our own lost soul. This queering trajectory is not only about destabilizing, for instance, Jesus's sexuality by finding, for instance, bisexual patterns in the Messiah's own understanding of his messianic project (which I have done as part of my indecent theological reflections), but by doing a theology for all the strangers who are entombed in us. For queering theology may have an indecent redemptive role, by inviting people to come back to themselves.

Volver a nuestras almas (To go back to our souls) is the expression Peruvian indigenous people use when they feel alienated living in the big cities of the white people and in need of encountering their true identities once more. They go back to the mountains, and they say 'I'm back in the mountains; I am back to my soul.' Strangely, queer theology also has a praxis of going back to our souls. This is a path made of ruptures and recoveries, in order to find our true selves again. For people may need to stand queer against global capitalism and understand the importance of the production of new identities at the same time, in order to practise a theology after Seattle, or after Porto Alegre. A theology which reflects the queerness of the revolution in Chiapas under Sub-comandante Marcos, where sexual understandings are changing fast as part of a new and different way of thinking politics, economics and the meaning of being human. A healing theology which dismantles false coherences and ideological scripts in theology in order to allow people to stand up as human beings against a perverse ethics and a perverse theology, which dares to take a departure from monolithic controls concerned with law and not with justice. This is the end of unnecessary transcendence and of trad-ition as industrial re-production.

As theologians, paraphrasing Elspeth Probyn's analysis on Jeanette Winterson's *Oranges Are Not The Only Fruit*,[13] we may find that the role of theological trad-ition is to disarrange what we have become as Christian women, that is, that the past shows a discontinuity with our identity as queer theologians. In a way, the

---

13. See Elspeth Probyn, *Outside Belongings* (London: Routledge, 1996), p. 112. Also from Linda Anderson's comments in 'Autobiographical Travesties. The Nostalgic Self in Queer Writing', in Alderson and Anderson (eds), *Territories of Desire in Queer Culture*, pp. 72–3.

Church traditions may show us sometimes through their closures and limitations our souls by contrast. We are what we were not supposed to be.

This means that a sort of colonial mobilization is needed when confronting traditions, and the history of the Church and the theological community. It may be that, as in the colonial experience, our Christian past negates us, but by doing so, it also affirms the production of new and multiple identities assumed in our communities. It is precisely that sense of preoccupation with the production of new identities and the role of theological imagination, more than of continuation, which is at the root of a queering theology. What we need is to remake our past, challenging the notion of established links between past and present, or between origins and identity.[14] For queer, indecent theologies are theologies of disruption which do not look for legitimization in the past or for a memory of a harmonious trajectory.

It is curious, and *queer*, to discover that, paradoxically, to come back to our souls should not be done through a path of harmony, but in diversity, dis-order and justice. We may say, using some words inspired by Pat Califia,[15] that in a theological system which has done its best to wipe out many people, even interfering with their relationship with God, our main duty is to exist. And even if queer theology is just another utopia kicking against the dogmatics of heterosexual ideology, proving that in the end not even by challenging heterosexual ideology can we transform this world, our duty is to exist. Doing theology as if touching God under her skirts is a duty of love and justice and an encounter with God among us. May we together, by the grace of God, stand always *queer* with love, courage and a passion for justice.

14. See Alderson and Anderson (eds), *Territories of Desire*, p. 72.

15. Pat Califia says that 'if you live in a society that wishes you didn't exist, anything you do to make yourself happy disrupts its attempt to wipe you out, or at the very least, to make you invisible', see Califia, *Macho Sluts. Erotic Fictions* (Boston, MA: Alyson, 1988), p. 15. I take Califia's 'to be happy' as equivalent to the right to have integrity and to write theology with sexual honesty.

QUEERING THE CANAANITE[1]

                        Ken Stone

                            I

In the contemporary religious debates over homosexuality one often encounters, especially on the part of advocates for lesbians and gay men, a rhetoric of welcome, inclusion and hospitality. And, when biblical texts are read in such rhetorical situations, the texts are both selected and interpreted accordingly. So for example the New Testament scholar Jeffrey Siker, in an interesting exercise in hermeneutics, has called attention to the early Christian controversy over the admission of Gentiles to Christian communities, as that controversy is represented in the book of Acts, in order to argue by way of parallel that heterosexual Christians should 'move beyond our marginal toleration of homosexual Christians and *welcome their full inclusion* … [L]et us *welcome* our newfound brothers and sisters in Christ and get on with the tasks to which God has called us all.'[2]

Although Siker's conclusion is gay-affirmative, his discussion is in certain respects fairly traditional, characterized for example by little interaction with the heterogeneous discourses often referred to as 'queer theory'. However, the emphasis upon 'welcome' and 'inclusion' that structures Siker's argument can also be found in more radical discussions that do take queer theory explicitly into account. A useful point of comparison in this regard is provided by Kathy Rudy's important book *Sex and the Church*. In distinction from Siker, Rudy does utilize queer theory's critical analyses of gender roles, family constructs and sexual identities; and she does so in order to challenge the ways in which Christians frequently universalize, and even ordain as Christian, certain assumptions about family, gender and sexuality that actually have their roots in the eighteenth and nineteenth

1. Earlier versions of this essay were presented to the American Theological Society in May 2001; and to the Gender, Sexuality and the Bible Consultation of the Society of Biblical Literature in Denver in November 2001. I would like to thank those members of both audiences who asked stimulating questions and made helpful suggestions. A particular word of thanks goes to Laurel Schneider, whose initial invitation encouraged me to finish a draft of the essay; to the students in my spring 2001 seminar on Lesbian and Gay Studies, at Chicago Theological Seminary, who discussed a draft of the essay with me; and to Horace Griffin for encouragement throughout the process.

2. Jeffrey Siker, 'Gentile Wheat and Homosexual Christians: New Testament Directions for the Heterosexual Church', in Robert Brawley (ed.), *Biblical Ethics and Homosexuality: Listening to Scripture* (Louisville, KY: Westminster/John Knox Press, 1996), pp. 146, 150.

centuries. Over against the tendency of both conservatives and liberals to valorize family and home as foundations for religious identity, Rudy adopts the queer practice of historicizing our current arrangements of sex, gender and kinship. Pointing out that certain New Testament texts subordinate family arrangements to Christian fellowship, Rudy suggests that Christians should not evaluate sexual activities according to contemporary notions about 'the family' at all. Rather, sexual activities should be evaluated by asking about the contribution of those sexual activities to the building of a community *wider* or *other* than that of the nuclear family. This suggestion leads Rudy to discuss sexual morality in terms of hospitality instead of, for example, monogamy. In her own words, '[r]ather than locating morality along the lines of procreation, or along the lines of complementarity, we can now measure sexual morality by determining how well our sexual encounters help us *welcome the stranger into the church* and into our life with God'.[3]

Now here we have a position that is provocative and refreshing, and a useful counterpoint to those contemporary writers who base their religious opposition to homosexuality on rigid versions of 'gender complementarity'.[4] But it is striking to note that, as with the more traditional argument of Siker, so also with the more radical argument of Rudy, the primary task resulting from the encounter between religion and contemporary reconceptualizations of gender and sexuality is understood in terms of *welcome into* the Christian community. Those who are first positioned *outside* the community must now be included *inside*. The boundary between outside and inside is not itself taken as an object of critical reflection, however, but rather reinforced by the discussion; for although Rudy appeals to queer deconstructions of such binary oppositions as 'male/female' and 'heterosexual/homosexual' to reframe our notions about Christian community, she explicitly continues to rely upon another binary opposition that structures this movement from outside to inside: the opposition between world and Church.[5]

Now I will be returning to this element of Rudy's argument at the end of this essay; but before I go further I want to make it absolutely clear that, as an openly gay man teaching in a seminary, I certainly support the goal of equal access to religious communities and institutions for lesbians, gay men, bisexuals, transgendered persons and others who may be marginalized or excluded on the basis of sexual and gender practices. It is indeed arguable that the conditions for such equal access are generated in part by rhetorical practices such as those engaged in by both Siker and Rudy, rhetorical practices which bring together biblical discourses, the language of 'welcome' and 'inclusion', and the calls for equal rights and equal participation that have emerged in the contemporary world from a range of what are sometimes referred to as the 'new social movements'. But rhetorical practices, however effective from one point of view, can also presuppose and reinscribe assumptions that, from other points of view, appear to be problematic and restrictive; and I

3. Kathy Rudy, *Sex and the Church: Gender, Homosexuality, and the Transformation of Christian Ethics* (Boston, MA: Beacon Press, 1997), p. 126.

4. For example Robert A.J. Gagnon, *The Bible and Homosexual Practice: Texts and Hermeneutics* (Nashville, TN: Abingdon Press, 2001).

5. Rudy, *Sex and the Church*, pp. 123, 126.

have increasingly come to believe that contemporary debates over religion and homosexuality too often revolve around just such a restricting set of questions and assumptions. To trope on a famous statement made by Foucault, while I certainly do not believe that a concern for 'welcoming' others 'into' religious communities is 'bad' (quite the contrary), I do believe that too much emphasis on 'welcome into' such communities can be in certain respects 'dangerous'.[6] One of the goals of this essay will be to reflect on some of the dangers.

Part of my inspiration for such a reflection comes from my reading of those writers who reject any narrow approach to sexuality and sexual identity, calling instead for attention to the interrelations of sexuality not only with gender but also with the construction of other sorts of identity, including for example racial, ethnic and national identities.[7] In the wake of such calls, I want to suggest that the identities of religious communities also need to be rethought in terms of this more complex understanding of identity; and that such a rethinking should impact upon the ways in which we speak about possible outcomes of the debates over homosexuality and religion. More specifically, in my own view, current controversies over homosexuality and religion should not be understood or articulated simply as battles for the admission of gays and lesbians into pre-existing religious communities. As Mark Jordan has suggested in relation to Catholicism, such controversies are also opportunities for learning new languages about religious lives and new ways of thinking about those lives.[8] In that spirit I want to argue here that engagement with queer theory should lead us to problematize not only assumptions about the nature of sexual and gender identities but *also assumptions about the nature of religious identities*, assumptions that seem to structure much contemporary rhetoric on the welcome and inclusion of homosexual persons into religious com-

---

6.   Cf. Michel Foucault *Ethics: Subjectivity and Truth. The Essential Works of Michel Foucault, 1954–1984*, trans. Robert Hurley (New York: The Free Press, 1997), p. 256: 'My point is not that everything is bad, but that everything is dangerous, which is not exactly the same as bad. If everything is dangerous, then we always have something else to do.'

7.   Such calls are today heard more and more frequently. Sources that have stimulated my own thinking along these lines include, among others: Kobena Mercer, *Welcome to the Jungle: New Positions in Black Cultural Studies* (New York and London: Routledge, 1994); Rudi C. Bleys, *The Geography of Perversion: Male-to-Male Sexual Behavior Outside the West and the Ethnographic Imagination, 1750–1918* (New York: New York University Press, 1995); Anne McClintock, *Imperial Leather: Race, Gender and Sexuality in the Colonial Contest* (New York and London: Routledge, 1995); and, in relation to biblical interpretation: Renita J. Weems, 'The Hebrew Women are Not Like the Egyptian Women: The Ideology of Race, Gender and Sexual Reproduction in Exodus 1', in David Jobling and Tina Pippin (eds), *Ideological Criticism of Biblical Texts. Semeia* 59 (Atlanta, GA: Scholars Press, 1992); Randall Bailey, '"They're Nothing but Incestuous Bastards": The Polemical Use of Sex and Sexuality in Hebrew Canon Narratives', in Fernando Segovia and Mary Ann Tolbert (eds), *Reading from this Place: Volume I: Social Location and Biblical Interpretation in the United States* (Minneapolis, MN: Fortress Press, 1995); Patrick S. Cheng, 'Multiplicity and Judges 19: Constructing a Queer Asian Pacific American Biblical Hermeneutic', in Tat-siong Benny Liew (ed.), *The Bible in Asian America. Semeia* 90–91 (Atlanta, GA: Society of Biblical Literature, 2002).

8.   Mark D. Jordan, *The Silence of Sodom: Homosexuality in Modern Catholicism* (Chicago, IL, and London: University of Chicago Press, 2000), pp. 237–61.

munities. I also wish to suggest that such a move might impact upon our choices about which biblical texts to read and how to read them.

In order to make and defend these points, however, I will follow in this essay a somewhat circuitous route, developing my argument through a mingling of issues normally discussed within biblical studies and issues normally discussed within queer theory. In particular I wish to consider here a sort of structural parallel between the terms 'homosexual' and 'Canaanite' as those terms are treated in the contemporary academic discourses of queer theory and biblical scholarship. Let me summarize briefly the parallel that I perceive between the recent histories of these terms, before revisiting the two sides of the parallel in more detail.

For quite a long time now the term 'homosexual' has seemed to many to have a relatively clear referent. It has served not simply as an object of interpretation but also as a lens for interpretation, framing the way other objects – for example, gender nonconformity – have themselves been interpreted. But problems have emerged in connection with the term, especially under the influence of queer theory. It has become increasingly difficult to state with certainty just what a 'homosexual' 'really is', in part because of problems involved in differentiating 'the homosexual' absolutely from its supposed opposite, 'the heterosexual'. Indeed, any rigid binary distinction between 'homosexual' and 'heterosexual' is now frequently seen as, at least in part, an effect of language, history and ideology.

So also for many readers of the Hebrew Bible the term 'Canaanite' is often imagined to have a clear ethnic or religious referent. Among scholars of the Hebrew Bible and the ancient Near East the term has frequently served not simply as an object of interpretation but also as a lens for interpretation, framing the way other objects – for example, archaeological artifacts – have themselves been interpreted. However, problems have also emerged in recent years in connection with the term 'Canaanite'. It has become increasingly difficult to achieve agreement about just what a 'Canaanite' really was, in part because of problems differentiating 'the Canaanite' absolutely from its supposed opposite, 'the Israelite'. Here, too, any rigid binary distinction between 'Canaanite' and 'Israelite' can arguably be seen today as, at least in part, an effect of language and ideology.

There is, then, a sort of structural parallel between the trajectories of the two terms 'homosexual' and 'Canaanite' in contemporary academic discourses. In the remainder of this essay I want to explore this parallel further and use it to raise questions not simply about the approach we take to religious debates over homosexuality but also about the approach we take to religious identities, and about calls for inclusion within religious communities. I will make my argument through a sort of elaboration on the two parts of my comparison, beginning with the question of the Canaanite.

II

It is probably safe to say that most Jews and most Christians have traditionally understood their religious identities to be related in some way (however complex that relation might be, and however different in the two cases of Judaism and Christianity) to the Israelites whose covenant and relations with God are represented in the Hebrew Bible. Furthermore, even many of those Jews and Christians who have only a surface familiarity with the Hebrew Bible would no doubt be able to give at least a sketchy account of the origins of the Israelites as those origins are narrated in the biblical text. After all, the large narrative complex that opens the Bible, that narrative complex found in Genesis through II Kings and sometimes referred to as a whole with the convenient label 'Primary History',[9] tells a well-known story about those origins. This story is exciting to read or hear, frequently reproduced in both religious communities and popular culture, and usefully constructed for religious identification on the part of its readers or listeners. Indeed, the structure of this narrative has throughout the centuries offered first to Jews, and then to Christians, subject positions with which to identify the position in general of the Israelites as a people and the positions in particular of specific ancestors and heroes such as Abraham, Jacob, Moses and Joshua.[10]

It is important to recognize, however, that this 'Primary History' also offers its audience a position *against* which to identify. More specifically, if the structure of many individual passages in the 'Primary History' invites readers to identify *with* the Israelites, many of those same passages invite readers to identify themselves as well over *against* the peoples who dwell in the land of Canaan prior to its conquest by Joshua and the Israelites. The distinction between the Israelites and these other peoples is stressed in numerous passages, among which Deuteronomy 7.1–6 can serve here as a convenient example:

> When Yhwh your god brings you to the land that you will enter in order to take possession of it, and he clears away many nations before you – the Hittites, the Girgashites, the Amorites, the Canaanites, the Perizzites, the Hivites, and the Jebusites, seven nations greater and more numerous than you – and Yhwh your god gives them to you and you attack them, you must completely exterminate them. Do not make a covenant with them, and do not show them mercy, and do not intermarry with them – your daughters you will not give to their sons, and their daughters you will not take for your sons. For that would cause your children to turn away from me and serve other gods, and then the anger of Yhwh will burn against you and he will destroy you quickly. This is how you will deal with them: their altars you will pull down, their sacred pillars you will smash,

---

9. Cf. David Noel Freedman, 'Canon of the OT', in Keith Crim (ed.), *The Interpreter's Dictionary of the Bible: Supplementary Volume* (Nashville, TN: Abingdon Press, 1962).

10. It will no doubt be noticed that my examples here are all male characters. This is due to my suspicion that, while the Hebrew Bible does contain a number of very interesting female characters (one of which I return to later in this essay), readers of the 'Primary History' are nevertheless frequently (albeit not always successfully) encouraged by the structure of that narrative to identify with the male characters whose stories incorporate female characters primarily in supporting roles. Of course, this fact, relevant as well to many other parts of the Bible, raises difficult issues for women readers of the Bible, some of which are helpfully sketched out by, among others, Mary Ann Tolbert, 'Protestant Feminists and the Bible: On the Horns of a Dilemma', in Alice Bach (ed.), *The Pleasure of Her Text: Feminist Readings of Biblical and Historical Texts* (Philadelphia, PA: Trinity Press International, 1990); and Renita J. Weems, 'Reading her Way through the Struggle: African-American Women and the Bible', in Cain Hope Felder (ed.), *Strong the Road We Trod: African-American Biblical Interpretation* (Minneapolis, MN: Fortress Press, 1991).

their *asherim*[11] you will cut down, and their carved images you will burn in fire. For you are a holy people to Yhwh your god. Yhwh your god chose you to be his people, a treasured possession, out of all the peoples that are on the face of the earth.[12]

In this passage and in several others (e.g. Joshua 3.10; 9.1; 24.11), the peoples in question are referred to with a list of names, only one of which is actually the name 'Canaanites'. However, this same term 'Canaanites' also seems to be used in certain biblical passages in a rather more general sense, referring to various inhabitants of the land who were understood to have lived in a number of different places and who were believed not to have been completely wiped out in the manner prescribed by Israel's god (see, e.g., Judges 1). This more general use of the term 'Canaanites', as a convenient way of referring collectively to all or many of the inhabitants of the land entered by the Israelites, inhabitants who lived in that land before or alongside the Israelites, has also been characteristic of the term's deployment in much modern biblical scholarship.[13]

Now it is possible that the average reader of the Bible imagines these Canaanites to be fairly easy to locate and describe historically. After all, much of the literature of biblical scholarship produced during the twentieth century would encourage such an assumption.[14]

It may therefore come as a surprise when the reader learns, upon picking up one of the most recent monographs on the Canaanites, that in fact 'the Israelites were themselves Canaanites, and "historical", as opposed to "literary", Israel was, in reality, a subset of Canaanite culture'.[15] Further investigation would quickly reveal that this statement, far from being an idiosyncratic opinion expressed from an isolated figure on the academic fringe, actually reflects a major recent trend in biblical and historical scholarship. All scholars recognize, of course, that the biblical narratives do often draw a sharp distinction between the Israelites and the Canaanites and locate that

11. Although I cannot discuss here the complex issues surrounding biblical and extra-biblical references to *asherim* or the *asherah*, let me note that the possibility raised by some of these references that the Israelites did sometimes worship a goddess known as Asherah, and that this goddess may even have been understood by certain Israelites as a consort of Yhwh, complicates still further the boundary constructed by the Bible and by many biblical scholars between 'Israelites' and 'Canaanites' that I am problematizing here. For further discussion see, among numerous other sources: Saul Olyan *Asherah and the Cult of Yahweh in Israel* (Atlanta, GA: Scholars Press, 1988); William G. Dever, *Recent Archaeological Discoveries and Biblical Research* (Seattle and London: University of Washington Press, 1990), pp. 121–66; Judith M. Hadley, *The Cult of Asherah in Ancient Israel and Judah: Evidence for a Hebrew Goddess* (Cambridge and New York: Cambridge University Press, 2000).

12. Except where noted, translations of biblical passages are my own.

13. Cf. Niels Peter Lemche, *The Canaanite and Their Land: The Tradition of the Canaanites* (Sheffield: Sheffield Academic Press, 1991) pp. 73–121.

14. Cf. William F. Albright, 'The Role of the Canaanites in the History of Civilization', in G. Ernest Wright (ed.), *The Bible and the Ancient Near East: Essays in Honor of William Foxwell Albright* (Garden City, NY: Doubleday, 1961); William F. Albright, *Yahweh and the Gods of Canaan: A Historical Analysis of Two Contrasting Faiths* (London: Athlone Press, 1968); J.C.L. Gibson, *Canaanite Myths and Legends* (Edinburgh: T & T Clark, 1977).

15. Jonathan N. Tubb, *Canaanites* (Norman, OK: University of Oklahoma Press, 1998), p. 16.

distinction far back in the mythical genealogies of the two sets of people (cf. Genesis 9.18–10.31). Nevertheless, most historians of Israel are inclined now to argue that the ancestors of the Israelites, rather than entering the land of Canaan as a distinct group of people and confronting there radically 'other' groups of people such as the Canaanites, were in their origins probably indigenous to that very land.

The shift in opinion is apparent, for example, even in the work of the archaeologist William Dever, a strong believer in our ability to detect and label a distinctly 'Israelite' or 'proto-Israelite' layer of material culture at a relatively early point in the archaeological record. In an address published under the title 'How to Tell a Canaanite from an Israelite', Dever, while attempting to describe the earliest evidence for the existence in Palestine of recognizable 'Israelites', nevertheless carefully notes the continuity between 'Israelite' and 'Canaanite' material remains and ultimately acknowledges that '[f]or the most part, the early Israelites were agriculturalists from the fringes of Canaanite society ... They were displaced Canaanites ... various elements of Canaanite society who decided to settle the hill-country frontier.'[16] The Israelites were not in their origins ethnically distinct from the Canaanite population, on this reading, but became distinguishable from those Canaanites only over time and through processes that are extraordinarily difficult to reconstruct. While the social and historical processes through which the Israelites emerged as a distinct group of people were complex, and the details of those processes remain greatly disputed, many scholars with otherwise divergent opinions about those processes would agree with Israel Finkelstein and Neil Silberman when they, too, conclude that '[t]he early Israelites were – irony of ironies – themselves originally Canaanites'.[17]

It is not entirely clear to all scholars, moreover, that these Canaanites from whom the early Israelites are supposed to have emerged can themselves be easily and unambiguously identified. The Danish scholar Niels Peter Lemche, far more

16. William G. Dever, 'How to Tell a Canaanite from an Israelite', in Hershel Shanks, *et al.*, *The Rise of Ancient Israel* (Washington, DC: Biblical Archaeology Society, 1992), p. 114.

17. Israel Finkelstein and Neil Asher Silberman, *The Bible Unearthed: Archaeology's New Vision of Ancient Israel and the Origin of Its Sacred Texts* (New York: The Free Press, 2001), p. 118. Cf. Niels Peter Lemche, *Early Israel: Anthropological and Historical Studies on the Israelite Society Before the Monarchy* (Leiden: E.J. Brill, 1985); Gösta W. Ahlström, *Who Were the Israelites?* (Winona Lake, IN: Eisenbrauns, 1986); Robert B. Coote and Keith W. Whitelam, *The Emergence of Israel in Historical Perspective* (Sheffield: Almond Press, 1987); Robert B. Coote, *Early Israel: A New Horizon* (Minneapolis, MN: Fortress Press, 1990); Paula McNutt, *Reconstructing the Society of Ancient Israel* (London/Louisville, KY: SPCK/John Knox Press, 1999), pp. 33–63; Keith W. Whitelam, 'Palestine During the Iron Age', in John Barton (ed.), *The Biblical World* (New York and London: Routledge, 2002).

The specialist will recognize that I am, here and in the pages that follow, quoting from scholars on both sides of a fierce argument in contemporary biblical studies – an argument sometimes referred to as a dispute between 'minimizers' and 'maximizers' – about the precise value of the Hebrew Bible as a source for the historical reconstruction of pre-exilic Israel, and about the best way of understanding the relationship between biblical literature (including biblical references to distinct groups of people such as 'Israelites' and 'Canaanites') and archaeological remains. Although it is probably true that the thrust of my own argument reveals a certain degree of sympathy for much that the so-called 'minimizers' have been suggesting, in fact I have intentionally refrained from aligning myself too neatly with either side in the contemporary dispute.

sceptical than someone like Dever about the wisdom of referring to certain very early layers of the archaeological record as 'Israelite' or 'proto-Israelite', has argued that an analysis of nonbiblical ancient Near Eastern references to 'Canaan' and 'Canaanites' actually fails to produce a consistent picture either of a clearly bounded geographical territory known to all as 'Canaan' or of a clearly recognizable group of people known to both others and themselves as 'Canaanites'. 'Canaan' does seem to have served as a general term for an area of Western Asia close to the Mediterranean Sea, and persons from that area could be and were called 'Canaanite' by others. Yet on Lemche's reading, there is relatively little evidence that more precise understandings of the term were widely shared. 'Canaanite' seems in fact to have been used most often to refer to some people other than one's own, and persons referred to *as* 'Canaanites' by others do not always seem to have understood *themselves* as 'Canaanites'. Thus, to cite one of Lemche's examples, the Phoenician king Abi-Milku included the Syrian city of Ugarit in his description of 'Canaan' in spite of the fact that the inhabitants of Ugarit do not seem to have understood *themselves* to be 'Canaanites';[18] and it is not clear that Abi-Milku understood his own Phoenician city of Tyre to be 'Canaanite' even though identifications of the Phoenicians as 'Canaanites' do seem to have been made by others.[19]

Many scholars hesitate to go as far as Lemche with such an argument. Even among scholars with quite different points of view, however, the exact nature of the boundary distinguishing the ancient 'Canaanites' from other groups of people, including the 'Israelites', often seems rather imprecise. Textual sources continue to be analysed, distinctions continue to be made among layers and types of material remains, interpretations of those remains continue to be put forward – and in all of these activities references continue to be made to 'Canaanites'. Yet the precise criteria for identifying 'Canaanites' and distinguishing those 'Canaanites' from presumably 'non-Canaanite' peoples such as 'Israelites' remain difficult if not impossible to define. The problem is in fact openly acknowledged at the beginning of Jonathan Tubb's recent monograph on the 'Canaanites':

> In the most basic terms, the Canaanites were the people who occupied the land of Canaan from time immemorial, and the land of Canaan can be defined only

---

Not only do I believe that the rhetoric of this disagreement has become unnecessarily polarized and personal; in addition I find it significant, in the context of the present argument, that even in the writings of the so-called 'maximizers' such as Dever, the precise nature of the line dividing 'Israelite' from 'Canaanite' is finally somewhat slippery and elusive. A thorough 'discourse analysis' of this dispute between 'minimizers' and 'maximizers' would, in my view, reveal much about the politics of modern biblical and archaeological scholarship. Indeed, it might even show that the processes producing representations of 'minimizers' and 'maximizers' are not altogether different from the processes producing representations of 'Canaanites' and 'Israelites'. It is important to note, however, that this dispute is *not* a dispute between critical scholarship and religious fundamentalism. Almost no participant in the debate would, for example, accept as historical the picture of Israel's origins found in the book of Joshua. For a discussion of the relevant historical and archaeological issues that helpfully refrains from identifying polemically with either side of the dispute, see the excellent treatment in McNutt, *Reconstructing the Society of Ancient Israel*.

18. Cf. Tubb, *Canaanites*, p. 16.

19. Cf. Lemche, *The Canaanites and their Land*, pp. 52, 28–49.

as the geographical area occupied by the Canaanites. This not terribly helpful circle can be broken only by first defining the land of Canaan by reference to modern political states and their boundaries. This is not a satisfactory process, since it assumes that the people contained and included within the defined area were, by reasons of their own self-perception, Canaanites. In reality, however, the identity is 'received', having been imposed by modern scholarship on the basis of socio-cultural analogies and artefactual differentiation.[20]

How, then, does Tubb get around this difficulty so as to produce a volume on the 'Canaanites'? Precisely by defining 'Canaanite' in such a fashion that the distinction between 'Canaanites' and other peoples disappears: 'Ammonites, Moabites, Israelites and Phoenicians undoubtedly achieved their own cultural identities, and yet ethnically they were all Canaanites.'[21]

But, it may be objected, surely the relevant issue here for the reader of the Bible is not ethnicity, geography or historical origins, but rather religion. Is it not on the basis of religion that the 'Canaanite' and the 'Israelite' ought to be distinguished? This solution, borrowed directly from the Bible, has indeed often been adopted by biblical scholars, as we shall see in a moment. However, in much recent scholarship the imprecision of the boundary between 'Canaanite' and 'Israelite' extends even to matters of religion. '[I]t is essential', Michael Coogan insists, 'to consider biblical religion as a subset of Israelite religion and Israelite religion as a subset of Canaanite religion'.[22] So too Dever, right in the middle of an argument for the validity of referring to the remains found at a certain archaeological level as 'Israelite' or 'proto-Israelite', acknowledges that the very few religious objects found at that level 'suggest connections with the old Canaanite cult of the male deity El ...' If Dever's archaeological 'Israelites' are to be characterized in terms of religion, that religion must be described as 'still in the tradition of' the 'older Canaanite "fertility religions"' that would have been well-suited to an agrarian lifestyle'. Even with respect to religion, then, a clear boundary separating the Israelites from the Canaanites is, outside of the Bible at least, surprisingly elusive.

Given this ambiguity in the historical sources, one may wonder whether the supposedly clear distinction between 'Israelites' and 'Canaanites' in the biblical texts, to which I have already referred, is itself as clear as it might at first appear. In fact the answer to this question does depend a bit on which biblical texts one consults. The representations of Canaanites and other non-Israelite residents of Canaan in parts of the book of Genesis, for example, stand in some tension with representations of those peoples in such biblical books as Deuteronomy and Joshua;[23] and the relatively neat picture found in the latter two books stands in some contrast,

20. Tubb, *Canaanites*, p. 13.

21. Ibid., p. 14.

22. Michael David Coogan, 'Canaanite Origins and Lineage: Reflections on the Religion of Ancient Israel', in Patrick D. Miller, Paul D. Hanson, and S. Dean McBride (eds), *Ancient Israelite Religion: Essays in Honor of Frank Moore Cross* (Philadelphia, PA: Fortress Press, 1987), p. 115.

23. Robert L. Cohn, 'Before Israel: The Canaanites as Other in Biblical Tradition', in Laurence J. Silberstein and Robert L. Cohn (eds), *The Other in Jewish Thought and History* (New York and London: New York University Press, 1994), p. 98.

again, with the more complicated picture found in the book of Judges. So too the books of Chronicles arguably take a distinct approach to the question of Israel's origins which may not assume that the Israelites entered the land of the Canaanites from the outside;[24] and, in an intriguing passage, Ezekiel is told to open an oracle to Jerusalem by saying, 'Thus says lord Yhwh to Jerusalem, "Your origin and your birth were in the land of the Canaanite. Your father was the Amorite, and your mother the Hittite"' (Ezekiel 16.3). Such differences of emphasis among the various biblical books are themselves important indicators of the instability of the boundary between 'Canaanite' and 'Israelite'.

Notwithstanding this inner-biblical heterogeneity, however, it does seem that much of the 'Primary History' deploys the word 'Canaanite' and related terms largely as a way of distinguishing the Israelites by way of contrast, especially with respect to religion. Whatever the historical realities in ancient Palestine might have been, the term 'Canaanite' is in the biblical narrative literature frequently a relational term, assuming particular meanings within specific contexts by serving as a point of contrast to something else – the 'Israelite' – which, of course, it thereby helps to define. As Lemche puts it: 'The Canaan of the Old Testament, the archetypal enemy of ancient Israel, is therefore not an enigmatic old nation that once upon a time occupied Palestine. It is more of a literary device created in order to make a distinction between the heroes of the narrative, the biblical Israelites, and the villains, the Canaanites.'[25]

Much biblical literature does seem to presuppose such a demarcation between 'Israelite' and 'Canaanite', and this opposition does continue to be used by some scholars for the interpretation of archaeological remains. Yet, as we have already seen, this demarcation is, in its binary form, surprisingly unstable when examined more carefully. Outside of the Bible (and perhaps at certain points inside it), any absolute boundary separating the Israelites from the Canaanites is shifting and elusive. Rather than being a self-evident fact of ancient Palestinian history, the absolute opposition between 'Israelite' and 'Canaanite' identities turns out to be in large part an effect of biblical discourses.

III

The biblical distinction between 'Israelites' and 'Canaanites' has not simply influenced readers of the Bible, however, but has been perpetuated by them in turn. Close attention to some of these processes of perpetuation casts a troubling light, moreover, on the dynamics by which the boundaries of identity are too often articulated with matters of sexual practice. Until fairly recently biblical and theological scholars were not content simply to accept the biblical representation of the Canaanites as a specific group of people who preceded the Israelites in the land of Canaan. They also accepted, and for that matter elaborated upon, the bib-

24. Sara Japhet, 'Conquest and Settlement in Chronicles', *Journal of Biblical Literature*, 98 (1979): 205–18.

25. Niels Peter Lemche, *The Israelites in History and Tradition* (London/Louisville, KY: SPCK/John Knox Press, 1998), p. 129.

lical representation of the Canaanites as an especially wicked lot. This elaboration can be seen, among other places, in the long tradition of writing about 'Canaanite religion' as a (for the most part vaguely defined) 'fertility religion'. Such a phrase does accurately recognize that concerns about both agricultural production and the generation of offspring seem to have been characteristic of most of the religions of the ancient Near East, and in that sense it continues to be a useful term – though a term that, properly defined, probably should be applied to Israelite religion as well. But the 'fertility religion' of the Canaanites was throughout the twentieth century further associated – or even conflated – by modern scholars with a supposed Canaanite 'sex cult'[26] leading influential scholars who focused upon the Canaanites to refer ominously in their writings to 'sexual abuses in the service of religion'.[27] Such characterizations of Canaanite religion have clearly functioned within the discourse of biblical scholarship to make not merely literary or historical but also moral distinctions between Israelite religion and Canaanite religion. As a result, these distinctions have also served to justify the harsh condemnations and violent treatment of the Canaanites within biblical literature. Drastic measures were necessary, biblical scholars have been quick to assure us, in order to combat 'the inroads of a Canaanite sexual rite into Israel'.[28] Now evidence for this supposed 'Canaanite sexual rite' is actually very murky, and is based in large part on the translation of scattered biblical references to *qedeshim* and *qedeshot* as 'cult prostitutes', 'temple prostitutes' or 'sacred prostitutes'. These references will be known to many participants in the debates over religion and homosexuality, for it has occasionally been argued that Levitical references to male homosexual intercourse are actually references to cultic anal intercourse supposedly practiced by some of these *qedeshim*. But while the *qedeshim* and *qedeshot* are certainly religious functionaries looked upon negatively by the biblical texts, their actual function is extremely ambiguous and has been the subject of much reassessment of late on the part of biblical scholars and scholars of ancient Near Eastern literature.[29] Cognate terms outside the Bible, while also somewhat obscure, do not generally support a sexual interpretation; and the occasional appearance of these figures in the Hebrew Bible in close textual proximity to prostitutes and harlots (in, e.g., Deuteronomy 23.17–18 and Hosea 4.14) is arguably not an indication of their function but a product of the rhetorical association made in a number of biblical texts between sexual promiscuity and

---

26. Hans Walter Wolff, *Hosea: A Commentary on the Book of the Prophet Hosea*, trans. Gary Stansell, ed. Paul D. Hanson (Philadelphia, PA: Fortress Press, 1974), p. 14.

27. Albright, *Yahweh and the Gods of Canaan*, p. 132.

28. Wolff, *Hosea*, p. 14.

29. The issues are rather complex but, for useful discussion, one should consult, among others, Stephen M. Hooks, 'Sacred Prostitution in Israel and the Ancient Near East', PhD dissertation, Hebrew Union College; Robert A. Oden Jr, 'Religious Identity and the Sacred Prostitution Accusation', in Robert A. Oden Jr (ed.), *The Bible Without Theology: the Theological Tradition and Alternatives to It* (San Francisco: Harper & Row, 1987); Tikva Frymer-Kensky, *In the Wake of the Goddesses: Women, Culture, and the Biblical Transformation of Pagan Myth* (New York: Free Press, 1992), pp. 199–202; and, for a different approach, Karel van der Toorn, 'Female Prostitution in Payment of Vows in Ancient Israel', *Journal of Biblical Literature* 108 (1989): 193–205.

forms of religious practice that were distasteful to the biblical writers. A more complex interpretative puzzle surrounds the use of the term *qedeshah* in the story of Tamar in Genesis 38, to which we will return below. Based on the available evidence, however, one can make a compelling argument that longstanding beliefs in Canaanite 'cultic prostitution' are without any firm scholarly foundation.[30] It is hard to disagree with Tikva Frymer-Kensky when she asserts that 'the whole idea of a sex cult – in Israel or in Canaan – is a chimera, the product of ancient and modern sexual fantasies'.[31]

But where do we find the origins of these 'sexual fantasies'? Important as it is to acknowledge the likelihood that readers have projected their own 'fantasies' onto biblical (and other) texts, it is also necessary to recognize that the biblical texts are themselves easily appropriated for the production of such fantasies, not because these texts actually speak about 'cultic' or 'sacred prostitution', but rather because the texts do already contain a polemical caricature of the sexual practices of the Canaanites. The roots of such a polemical representation appear among other places in Leviticus 18 and 20 (the only chapters in the Hebrew Bible, incidentally, in which male–male intercourse is clearly and explicitly forbidden). The rhetoric surrounding the explicit sexual prohibitions listed in these chapters sets up a sharp distinction between the Israelites and the population that, according to the biblical narratives, dwelt in the land of Canaan before the Israelites. While the proscriptions of particular sexual acts by God are assumed by the text to be relevant both to the Israelites and the other nations, these other nations are mentioned primarily because they have already been cast out of the land. They suffered this fate, according to the discourse of Leviticus, because they practised those 'abominations' – and in particular, in context, sexual abominations – that God is now forbidding to the Israelites. Thus we find in Leviticus the following passage:

> Do not defile yourselves by any of these practices, for by all these practices the nations I am casting out before you defiled themselves. And the land became defiled, and I punished it for its iniquity, and the land vomited out its inhabitants. But you will keep my statutes and my ordinances and you will not do any of these abominations, neither the citizen or the alien who resides among you. For the people of the land who were before you did all of these abominations, and the land became defiled. Do not let the land vomit you out by defiling it, as it vomited out the nations that were before you. For anyone who does any of these abominations will be cut off from their people. So watch my admonition not to do any of these statutory abominations[32] that were done before you, and not to defile yourselves by them. I am Yhwh your God. (Leviticus 18.24–30)

---

30. It has often been noted that the chief 'evidence' for Canaanite 'cultic prostitution' is found in fact neither in the Hebrew Bible nor in sources that could under almost any definition be construed as 'Canaanite', but rather in certain comments about West Asian religion found in such Greek writers as Herodotus and the Patristic writers who followed them. For analysis see especially Oden 'Religious Identity', pp. 140–7.

31. Frymer-Kensky, *In the Wake of the Goddesses,* p. 199.

32. I owe the translation 'statutory abominations' to Jacob Milgrom, *Leviticus 17–22: A New Translation and Commentary* (New York and London: Doubleday, 2000), p. 34.

A similar sort of passage occurs at the end of the list of sexual prohibitions in Leviticus 20, though here food practices are added to sex practices as marking the distinction between Israelites and other groups of people:[33]

> And you will keep all my statutes and all my ordinances, and do them, so that the land which I am causing you to enter, to dwell therein, will not vomit you out. And you will not walk according to the statutes of the nations that I am casting out before you, for they did all these things and I loathed them. But I told you that you will possess their land, and I will give it to you to possess, a land flowing with milk and honey. I am Yhwh your God who separated you from the peoples, and so you will separate the clean animal from the unclean, and the unclean bird from the clean. And you will not make yourselves detestable by animal or by bird or by anything with which the ground teems, which I separated for you to treat as unclean. You will be holy to me; for I, Yhwh, am holy, and I separated you from the peoples to be mine. (Leviticus 20.22-6)

While this chapter says nothing about *qedeshim*, any sort of 'sacred prostitutes', or any other type of 'sex cult', only a small step was necessary in my view for scholars to move from reading passages such as this one to attempting to describe the supposed sexual abominations of the Canaanites. Even if many scholars went much further in their descriptions than the evidence should have allowed, they were surely encouraged in their reconstructions by the link already forged by the biblical authors themselves between sexual abomination and the ethnic/religious Other. Indeed, these passages from Leviticus 18 and 20 arguably fit into an unfortunate pattern in the Hebrew Bible whereby, as Randall Bailey puts it, the 'use of sexuality by either innuendo or graphic detail functions literarily as part

---

33. In a longer version of this essay, to be included in a study of food, sex and biblical interpretation in a 'queer' framework, I consider further the way in which this passage articulates food and sex in order to construct a boundary between the Israelites and their non-Israelite, e.g. Canaanite, neighbours. Here I will simply note, for those unfamiliar with contemporary debates over the archaeology of ancient Palestine, that while attempts to differentiate 'Israelites' and 'Canaanites' on the basis of sexual misconduct have recently (and rightly) disappeared from much of the scholarly literature, a newer argument has emerged which suggests that ethnic distinctions between early 'Israelites' and their non-Israelite neighbours can be correlated with layers of material remains on the basis of the presence or absence in those remains of pig bones. The argument depends upon recognition of the use of food to construct ethnic boundaries. The absence of pig bones in the archaeological remains of certain sites is understood as evidence for abstinence from the eating of pork, and hence as evidence that the remains in question belong to Israelites; while the presence of pig bones in the archaeological remains of other sites is understood as evidence for the eating of pork, and hence as evidence that the remains in question belong to non-Israelites. See, e.g., Israel Finkelstein, 'Pots and Peoples Revisited: Ethnic Boundaries in the Iron Age I', in Neil Asher Silberman and David Small (eds), *The Archaeology of Israel: Constructing the Past, Interpreting the Present* (Sheffield: Sheffield Academic Press, 1997; William G. Dever, *What Did the Biblical Writers Know and When Did They Know It? What Archaeology Can Tell Us about the Reality of Ancient Israel* (Grand Rapids, MI and Cambridge, MA: Eerdmans, 2001), p. 113; Finkelstein and Silberman, *The Bible Unearthed*, pp. 118–20. How far this argument can be sustained remains to be seen. For important qualifications see the thorough discussion in Brian Hesse and Paula Wapnish, 'Can Pig Remains be Used for Ethnic Diagnosis in the Ancient Near East?' in Silberman and Small (eds), *The Archaeology of Israel*, pp. 118–20.

of an agenda of discrediting ... individuals and nations and thereby sanctioning, or sanctifying, Israelite hatred and oppression of these people'.[34] Of course as Bailey recognizes, such uses of sexual matters to make distinctions among groups of people, and to 'discredit' particular groups of people in the process, are by no means confined to biblical texts and biblical scholars. On the contrary, the tendency to define an 'inside' and an 'outside' of identity by defining the Other on the basis of the Other's supposed deviant sexual practices – and, in the process, defining oneself by way of contrast – is extremely widespread. As Sander Gilman suggests, 'For a secure definition of self, sexuality and the loss of control associated with it must be projected onto the Other.'[35] This sort of securing of the self can be understood as one part of the phenomenon that the feminist political philosopher Iris Marion Young refers to as 'border anxiety'.[36] Building in part upon Julia Kristeva's influential discussion of the 'Abject',[37] Young points out that much demonizing of the Other takes place because of the basic insecurity occasioned by the presence of that Other. This insecurity arises in part because the Other is not quite so different from oneself as one might wish to believe; hence the Other challenges the security of the boundaries of one's self. Thus 'border anxiety' arises as part of an attempt to establish those boundaries more firmly and to avoid the 'fear, nervousness and aversion'[38] that result from any fluidity in those boundaries.

Now it is certainly not difficult to imagine a scenario in which this sort of 'border anxiety' overdetermined the writing of such passages as Leviticus 18 and Leviticus 20, resulting in biblical rhetoric about the supposed sexual misconduct of Israel's 'Canaanite' predecessors. In thinking about the historical and social circumstances that produced these passages as we have them, we do well to focus on the context in which not only the book of Leviticus but also the Pentateuch and even the 'Primary History' as a whole arguably reached their present form: the post-exilic, Persian period of Israel's history. The most significant development in this context, so far as the biblical literature is concerned, was arguably the attempt by those who 'returned' to Judah from Mesopotamia to forge a distinct religious and ethnic identity in a small province on the western end of the Persian empire, and to do so in opposition to other groups of people who were already living in that province. Indeed, E. Theodore Mullen Jr has recently made a compelling argument that the production of the 'Primary History' can be understood in relation to:

> ... the formation of a distinctive Judahite ethnic identity that was recreated during the Second Temple period. During this period a variety of traditions were

---

34. Bailey, '"They're Nothing but Incestuous Bastards": The Polemical Use of Sex and Sexuality in Hebrew Canon Narratives', p. 124.

35. Sander L. Gilman, *Difference and Pathology: Stereotypes of Sexuality, Race, and Madness* (Ithaca, NY: Cornell University Press, 1985), p. 24.

36. Iris Marion Young, *Justice and the Politics of Difference* (Princeton, NJ: Princeton University Press, 1990), p. 146.

37. Cf. Julia Kristeva, *Powers of Horror: An Essay on Abjection*, trans. Leon S. Roudiez (New York: Columbia University Press, 1982).

38. Young, *Justice and the Politics of Difference*, p. 146.

reapplied to the community of the restoration in an effort to forge an enduring identity, the boundaries for which can be traced in the literature that came to be regarded as 'scripture'. The necessity of recreating and reconfirming the group's identity can be understood as a survival mechanism that is a predictable result of crisis-producing situations such as the exile and subsequent restoration.[39]

Mullen therefore concludes that 'the various materials contained in Genesis through Kings may be understood as providing a narrative foundation for the reformulation and maintenance of "Israelite" ethnic and national identity in the Second Temple period'.[40]

Thus the rhetoric of those passages in Leviticus 18 and 20 that construe sexual misconduct (and also, in Leviticus 20, the transgression of food stipulations) as the cause for a people's being 'vomited' out of the land serves several different functions simultaneously. First, such rhetoric serves to differentiate the Israelites from other nations, to assert the unwillingness of those other nations to follow the path that God wishes Israel to follow, and to justify the removal of those nations from the land that God has promised to the Israelites. By describing the sorts of sexual behaviour that the other nations are supposed to have engaged in, but which Israel's God forbids, the author of Leviticus 18 and 20 contributes to the formation and maintenance of the boundary of Israelite identity by appealing to principles that illustrate what the anthropologist Fredrik Barth, in an influential discussion of ethnic boundaries, has called 'basic value orientation: the standards of morality and excellence by which performance is judged'.[41] As Barth points out, the claim that one belongs to a particular ethnic identity group entails a willingness to be judged by the standards of behaviour considered applicable to the ethnic identity group in question. The author of Leviticus in its final form attempts to clarify who the Israelites, as well as the post-exilic Judahites who identify with them, are by specifying among other things the standards of sexual and eating behaviour to which God expects them to conform.

But as scholars have long recognized, this discourse in Leviticus 18 and 20 also serves as an explicit warning for the Judahites about possible conse-quences of future transgressions and implicitly as an after-the-fact explanation of the Babylonian exile. By stating that God had long ago told the Israelites that they would be 'vomited' out of the land if they participated in the same sorts of behaviour that had motivated the 'vomiting' out of earlier nations, the passages at least hint that insufficient attention was (understood to have been) paid to proper observance of these precepts by the pre-exilic Israelites, whose actions led to the Babylonian exile. The fact that a Judahite audience for these texts could conceivably identify with various positions – that of the ancient Canaanite who was supposed to have been, and for the most part was

---

39. E. Theodore Mullen Jr, *Ethnic Myths and Pentateuchal Foundations: A New Approach to the Formation of the Pentateuch* (Atlanta, GA: Scholars Press, 1997), pp. 11–12; cf. Mullen, *Narrative History and Ethnic Boundaries: The Deuteronomistic Historian and the Creation of Israelite National Identity* (Atlanta, GA: Scholars Press, 1993).

40. Mullen, *Ethnic Myths*, p. 327.

41. Fredrik Barth, Introduction, in Barth (ed.), *Ethnic Groups and Boundaries: The Social Organization of Culture Difference* (Boston, MA: Little, Brown, 1969), p. 14.

understood to have been, destroyed but still, paradoxically, continued to exist in the land (cf. Judges 1); that of the pre-exilic Israelite who is supposed to have known the law but was vomited out of the land anyway; that of the post-exilic Judahite who wishes to avoid the fate of both sets of previous inhabitants of the land – undoubtedly contributed to the formation of a certain sort of anxiety. To borrow the words of Robert Cohn, the biblical authors 'shaped the Canaanites as the Other whose sin justified their dispossession, but who also threatened to take Israel down the same path. As outsiders who became insiders, the Israelites ... seem never quite secure in the land. The Canaanites as the insiders who became outsiders serve as the symbol of that insecurity.'[42] The ambiguity of the boundary between 'inside' and 'outside', to which Cohn's language points, must have motivated the 'border anxiety' that both produced and was perpetuated by the harsh rhetoric of Leviticus about the supposed abominations of the Canaanites.

However, the fact that biblical scholars have often replicated, and even elaborated or exaggerated, the rhetoric that was produced out of Judahite 'border anxiety' is also in need of some explanation. Such an explanation might start with the recognition that most biblical scholars have themselves been affiliated in some way with Judaism or Christianity, and so on the basis of their own modern religious identities have tended to identify with the Israelites or Judahites rather than the Canaanites. But, of course, the boundaries of modern religious identities are as unstable as the boundaries of ancient ones; and just as border anxiety among the Israelites or Judahites produced a phantom picture of wicked and sexually deviant Canaanites in the first place, so also border anxiety among modern Jewish and Christian biblical scholars who identify with the biblical Israelites has contributed to a sensationalized picture of a depraved Canaanite culture and religion, over against which Israel's narrated extermination of its predecessors receives legitimization.

Examples of this process at work can be found, among other places, in the writings of William Foxwell Albright, one of the most influential North American biblical scholars of the twentieth century and a pioneer in the modern study of the Canaanites. As Burke Long has shown in a fascinating book,[43] Albright's impressive scholarly endeavours were inextricably tied up with his own involvement in the construction of particular sorts of identities, including that of the modernist Christian who is able to take full account of the reliable results of scientific archaeological and historical research. Albright was convinced that modern Christians could and should understand themselves to be heirs to a tradition that went back to the Israelites. In arguing for the importance of understanding thoroughly the biblical tradition, Albright was forthright about his belief that modern Christians must maintain the boundaries of the religious identity that resulted from this tradition. Not only in ancient times but also today those boundaries were in Albright's opinion under attack: 'Now again

42. Cohn, 'Before Israel', p. 77.
43. Burke O. Long, *Planting and Reaping Albright: Politics, Ideology, and Interpreting the Bible* (University Park, PA: Penn State University Press, 1997).

we see the religious world confronted by the imperious necessity of choosing between biblical theism and Eastern pantheism, which threatens to sweep away theistic faith as it is reinterpreted by neo-Gnostic religious thinkers of the contemporary West.'[44] Reading such passages in the context of Albright's work as a whole, it is difficult to avoid the conclusion that Albright's own 'border anxieties' impacted his understanding of Israelite identity and the threats that it once faced, including above all the threat of the Canaanites. And, in the discourse of Albright, as in the discourse of the biblical texts with which he identified, border anxiety resulted in the production of rhetoric about the sexual abominations of the Canaanites. This sort of rhetoric is found in passages such as the following, in which Albright attempts to justify the attempts of the Israelites to exterminate the Canaanites:

> From the impartial standpoint of a philosopher of history, it often seems necessary that a people of markedly inferior type should vanish before a people of superior potentialities, since there is a point beyond which racial mixing cannot go without disaster. When such a process takes place – as at present in Australia – there is generally little that can be done by the humanitarian – though every deed of brutality and injustice is infallibly visited upon the aggressor. It was fortunate for the future of monotheism that the Israelites of the Conquest were a wild folk, endowed with primitive energy and ruthless will to exist, since the resulting decimation of the Canaanites prevented the complete fusion of the two kindred folk which would almost inevitably have depressed Yahwistic standards to a point where recovery was impossible. Thus the Canaanites, with their orgiastic nature-worship, their cult of fertility in the form of serpent symbols and sensuous nudity, and their gross mythology, were replaced by Israel, with its pastoral simplicity and purity of life, its lofty monotheism, and its severe code of ethics.[45]

In quoting this passage, with its intertwining of racial, religious and sexual rhetoric, it is not my intention to vilify Albright the individual. Rather I suspect that his occasional flourishes of rhetorical excess shed light on attitudes that have often crept more subtly into much modern biblical and theological scholarship. In the wake of contemporary postcolonial critique, it is impossible to encounter rhetoric such as that found in the work of Albright without being struck by the extent to which its representation of the 'sensuous' Canaanites participates in a recurring sexualization of the 'Orient' that has been noted and analysed by others.[46] It is little wonder therefore that native American, Palestinian and Asian readers of the Bible, among others, have suggested that it is time to reconsider biblical religion, as well as modern communities of faith that understand themselves to be related in some way to biblical religion, from

44. William F. Albright, *From the Stone Age to Christianity: Monotheism and the Historical Process*, 2nd edn (Baltimore, MD: Johns Hopkins University Press, 1957), p. 23.

45. Ibid., pp. 280–1.

46. Edward Said, *Orientalism* (New York: Random House, 1978); Keith W. Whitelam, *The Invention of Ancient Israel: The Silencing of Palestinian History* (New York and London: Routledge, 1996), pp. 82–4.

the point of view of the Canaanites rather than simply adopting the Israelite subject position uncritically.[47]

To reconsider religious tradition from the position of the Canaanites is not, however, to assume any 'real', or at least any certain, identity. As I have already pointed out, the identity of the 'Canaanite' cannot today be given a great deal of firm, coherent content. The Canaanite, far from being a stable ethnic or religious entity, is something more like the 'constitutive outside'[48] of Israelite identity. And yet, ironically, as a 'constitutive outside', the Canaanite is to some extent a kind of necessary support for Israelite identity, helping to define the Israelite by means of differential relation and contrast. We know what the Israelite is by knowing what it is not; and in that respect Israelite identity is actually dependent for its existence as a coherent object upon the demarcation and exclusion of the Canaanite. Thus the Canaanite is actually not outside Israelite identity at all, but rather is always already inside Israelite identity as a kind of necessary support for the illusion that such an identity is coherent and secure. And precisely for these reasons it seems to me that those of us who are today defined largely in terms of deviance from normative heterosexuality have especially good reasons to identify with, rather than over against, the Canaanites. For as I shall now attempt to argue, the 'Canaanite' is positioned with respect to the 'Israelite' in something like the same way that the 'homosexual' is positioned with respect to the 'heterosexual'.

IV

Already in 1968 the British sociologist Mary McIntosh attempted to reflect critically upon the fact that homosexuality had come to be understood not simply as a collection of sexual behaviours but rather as a 'condition', a condition that one either has or does not have. While sexual contacts between persons of the same sex have occurred in many different societies across time and space, it appeared to McIntosh to have been only quite recently, and primarily in the modern West, that one could find widespread acceptance of the assumption that 'there are two kinds of people in the world: homosexuals and heterosexuals'.[49] In a move that has now become much more common, McIntosh suggested that this historical shift in conceptualization was due especially to the increasing authority of medicine and science in the modern West. Under the influence of medicine and science, studies

47. Kwok Pui-Lan, *Discovering the Bible in the Non-Biblical World* (Maryknoll, MD: Orbis, 1995); Naim Stifan Ateek, 'A Palestinian Perspective: The Bible and Liberation', in R.S. Sugirtharajah (ed.), *Voices from the Margin: Interpreting the Bible in the Third World* (Maryknoll, MD: Orbis, 1991); Francisco O. García-Treto, 'The Lesson of the Gibeonites: A Proposal for Dialogic Attention as a Strategy for Reading the Bible', in Ada María Isasi-Díaz and Fernando F. Segovia (eds), *Hispanic/Latino Theology: Challenge and Promise* (Minneapolis, MN: Fortress Press, 1996); Regina M. Schwartz, *The Curse of Cain: The Violent Legacy of Biblical Monotheism* (Chicago, IL, and London: University of Chicago Press, 1997).

48. Judith Butler, *Bodies that Matter: On the Discursive Limits of 'Sex'* (New York and London: Routledge, 1993), p. 8.

49. Mary McIntosh, (1968), 'The Homosexual Role', in Edward Stein (ed.), *Forms of Desire: Sexual Orientation and the Social Constructionist Controversy* (New York and London: Routledge, 1992), p. 25.

of homosexuality were increasingly being carried out along lines familiar from the study of illness. One first identified a population or cohort of individuals thought to be afflicted with the 'condition' and then used an analysis of these individuals to reach conclusions about the condition in question, including for example conclusions about its etiology, its proper diagnosis and prospects for its cure. It was the opinion of McIntosh that such studies were fundamentally flawed, for the conception of homosexuality as a 'condition' covered over serious ambiguities with respect to the phenomenon being considered. Arguing from within the tradition of the sociology of deviance, McIntosh therefore proposed that the study of homosexuality as a condition should be abandoned in favour of a study of the 'homosexual role'. Such an approach would serve among other things to reconceptualize homosexuality in terms of social processes rather than as an individual condition.

McIntosh's article is often forgotten or ignored today, but in the decades since it appeared a number of studies have made arguments that, while not identical, nevertheless have striking points of similarity. The best-known of these, and certainly the most influential within contemporary queer theory, is surely Foucault's *History of Sexuality, Volume I*. There Foucault highlights what he famously calls a 'veritable discursive explosion' around sexuality emanating from medical, psychiatric, legal and educational discourses. One effect of the power/knowledge mechanisms of the discourses of sexuality, Foucault argues, is that sexuality has come to be understood in the modern West as that area of life in relation to which the truth of one's self can most reliably be deciphered. In the process, homosexuality has been transformed 'from the practice of sodomy into a kind of interior androgyny, a hermaphrodism of the soul. The sodomite', Foucault goes on to say, in a much-quoted formulation, 'had been a temporary aberration; the homosexual was now a species'.[50]

Now this argument, grounded as it is in Foucault's discursive analysis of knowledge and power, is of course not identical to McIntosh's more explicitly sociological account. There is nonetheless clearly a parallel between McIntosh's interrogation of the processes by which homosexuality came to be understood as a 'condition', and Foucault's interrogation of the processes by which 'the homosexual' became a 'species'. Both arguments are mischaracterized, however, when they are conflated simplistically with debates about whether sexual desires for persons of a particular gender are innate or acquired, a matter of nature or a matter of nurture. In that respect it is important to recall that McIntosh, by abandoning the notion of a 'homosexual condition', hoped to get away from questions about etiology and causation[51] and to note that Foucault refused to give an answer when asked on one occasion whether he thought homosexuality should be understood in terms of 'innate predisposition' or 'social conditioning'.[52] To be sure, scientific research into questions about the origins of specific types of sexual desire has increased in recent years, and the political and ethical implications of this research continue to

50. Michel Foucault, *The History of Sexuality. Volume I. An Introduction*, trans. Robert Hurley (New York: Vintage Books, 1978), p. 43.
51. McIntosh, 'The Homosexual Role', pp. 26–7.
52. Foucault, *Ethics: Subjectivity and Truth*, p. 142.

be matters for debate.[53] For my purposes here, however, it is important to stress that the crucial insights of McIntosh and Foucault do not in the first instance concern the *causes* of particular sexual desires within the individual, but rather the *use* of particular sexual desires to construct conventional *identity categories*. The specific interpretive assumption, according to which human beings can be usefully and neatly categorized into types of human person on the basis of the gender of their preferred sexual partners, is now recognized to be a social, cultural and historical development rather than a universal, transhistorical fact.

The critical questions raised about the conceptualization of 'homosexuality' and 'the homosexual' by such writers as McIntosh and Foucault have therefore increasingly led contemporary queer theory to historicize and contextualize our notions about 'homosexual identity', and in particular to re-examine the ways in which 'homosexual identity' is differentiated from its supposed opposite, 'heterosexual identity'. Indeed, queer theorists now often argue that the binary opposition between 'homosexual' and 'heterosexual' functions not only to stigmatize individuals classified as 'homosexual' but also to cover over ambiguities in the notion of 'heterosexuality'.[54] 'Homosexuality' is in fact a kind of necessary support for 'heterosexuality', serving as its 'constituent outside' and helping to define it by means of differential relation and contrast. As with the 'Israelite', so also with the 'heterosexual', we know what it is by knowing what it is not; and in that respect 'heterosexuality' is actually dependent for its existence as a coherent object upon the demarcation and exclusion of 'homosexuality'. Thus 'the homosexual' is actually not outside heterosexual identity at all, but rather is always already inside heterosexual identity as a kind of necessary support for the illusion that such an identity is coherent and secure. The homosexual is therefore positioned with respect to the heterosexual in something resembling the way that the Canaanite was positioned with respect to the Israelite.

The loose structural parallel that I am proposing here between modern discourses of sexuality and biblical and scholarly representations of Israelite identity may surprise those who imagine that queer theory and questions about religion have little to do with one another. In that light it may be important to recall, however, that Foucault at one point also raises the possibility that some sort of relationship might exist between the development of modern systems of sexual identities and certain processes associated with religion. Where, after all, do we find roots for the notions (much emphasized by Foucault, though of course critically) that sex must be put into discourse and that sexuality can, in Foucault's words, 'tell us our truth'? As part of his attempt to answer this question, Foucault points to Catholic pastoral

53. For one recent discussion of the issues see Edward Stein, *The Mismeasure of Desire: The Science, Theory, and Ethics of Sexual Orientation* (New York and Oxford: Oxford University Press, 1999), p. 142. Much light is shed on the historical background of this type of research by Jennifer Terry, *An American Obsession: Science, Medicine, and Homosexuality in Modern Society* (Chicago, IL, and London: University of Chicago Press), p. 142.

54. David M. Halperin, *Saint Foucault: Towards a Gay Hagiography* (New York and Oxford: Oxford University Press, 1995); Annamarie Jagose, *Queer Theory: An Introduction* (New York: New York University Press, 1996); Jonathan Ned Katz, *The Invention of Heterosexuality* (New York: Dutton, 1995).

practices, which in his view underwent an important transformation beginning as early as the Counter-Reformation. Here we find, according to Foucault's interpretation, a growing imperative to disclose in confession or to one's spiritual director not simply practices and acts (which of course were always objects of confession) but also the minute workings of 'all the insinuations of the flesh: thoughts, desires, voluptuous imaginings, delectations, combined movements of the body and the soul; henceforth all of this had to enter, in detail, into the process of confession and guidance'.[55] As Foucault sees it, this development within religion opened a path, followed by the Marquis de Sade and eventuating in many of the human sciences, which involved 'an institutional incitement to speak about [sex], and to do so more and more ...'[56]

It is striking that this particular part of Foucault's argument, dealing with the contribution of Christian confessional practices to the development of modern discourses of sexuality and modern notions of sexual identity, has generated so little comment from those readers of Foucault most associated with queer theory, in spite of Foucault's phenomenal influence. And there can be little doubt, I think, that we see in this lack of attention one effect of both the limited interest in religious and theological questions on the part of most (though not all) queer theorists, and the limited interest in queer theory on the part of most (though not all) scholars of religion. It is perhaps true that Foucault's suggestion is made rather hastily and without the detailed analysis of Christian confessional practices that might be required to sustain it[57] But Jordan[58] has called attention to this oft-neglected element of Foucault's argument in order to argue among other things that *questions about sexual identity and questions about religious identity can and should be thought together*. It is this suggestion that I understand myself to be pursuing here by pointing out a sort of structural parallel between the terms 'Canaanite' and 'homosexual'.

Recognition of the parallel depends, of course, on acknowledgment that both the rigid binary distinction between 'Israelite' and 'Canaanite', and the rigid binary distinction between 'heterosexual' and 'homosexual', can be seen as, at least in part, effects of language, discourse, history and ideology. It may be objected by some of my readers that this emphasis on relational rather than substantive notions of identity (whether religious or sexual) is too negative to serve as a point of departure for a 'queering' of notions of religious identity. Indeed, just such complaints have sometimes been made against Foucault's approach to 'sexuality' by gay readers who fear that it undermines the basis on which a gay politics could be established.[59] And it is of course true that Foucault's work casts doubt on particular assumptions about the homosexual subject underlying certain discourses of sexual liberation. However David Halperin, in a discussion that has in my view

55. Foucault, *The History of Sexuality. Vol. I: An Introduction*, p. 19.
56. Ibid., p. 18.
57. Jeremy Carrette, *Foucault and Religion: Spiritual Corporality and Political Spirituality* (New York and London: Routledge, 2000), pp. 25–43.
58. Jordan, *The Silence of Sodom: Homosexuality in Modern Catholicism*.
59. Richard Mohr, *Gay Ideas: Outing and Other Controversies* (Boston, MA: Beacon Press, 1992), pp. 221–60.

much potential relevance for the 'queering' of theology, biblical interpretation and religious identification, has argued that Foucault's discursive, oppositional approach to 'sexuality' actually enables a more radical 'queer' sexual politics than Foucault's critics generally allow. Halperin points out that Foucault's controversial thesis is actually an attempt to call into question forms of power that claim to reveal the truth *about* homosexuality by making homosexuality always an *object* of knowledge. Such claims simultaneously allow *heterosexuality* to be constituted as a category of identity and assumed as an unproblematic norm. In the light of Foucault's work, Halperin refuses to give 'the homosexual' a substantive definition and argues instead for an understanding of homosexuality as a discursive position in a network of power/knowledge relations: 'The aim ... is to treat homosexuality as a position from which one can know, to treat it as a legitimate condition of knowledge. Homosexuality ... is not something to be got right but an eccentric positionality to be exploited and explored: a potentially privileged site for the criticism and analysis of cultural discourse'[60] For Halperin a queer politics does not acquire its shape from any assumed essence of homosexuality waiting to be liberated, but rather from the concrete processes of resisting and interrogating particular structures of power and knowledge strategically from the position of 'a new kind of sexual identity, one characterized by its lack of a clear definitional content'.[61] It is precisely the relational-oppositional, rather than the essential nature of this queer 'positionality' that Halperin finds most useful.

Now among the discourses that I believe need to be interrogated by queer readers of the Bible who are willing to adopt such a position are precisely those discourses on religious identity presupposed by arguments for 'inclusion' and 'welcome' within religious communities.[62] More specifically, it is in my view important to resist the implication that 'inclusion' within, or 'welcome' into, religious communities that identify with the Israelites and against the Canaanites could ever really be a sufficient goal for those of us who know too well the brutality of the policing of communal borders. Such resistance may entail, however, a new imagined relation to the biblical Canaanites. Advocates for lesbian and gay Christians and Jews have sometimes tried to argue that supposed biblical references to homosexuality in, e.g., Leviticus 18 and 20 are actually references to particular practices 'within the cult identified as Canaanite'.[63] I have already raised some initial critical questions elsewhere about the ideological assumptions at work in this kind of attempt to distance contemporary lesbians and gay men

---

60. Halperin, *Saint Foucault*, pp. 60–1. Halperin's language here is partly indebted to the fine discussion in Teresa de Lauretis, 'Eccentric Subjects: Feminist Theory and Historical Consciousness', *Feminist Studies* 16.1 (1990): 115–50.

61. Halperin, *St Foucault*, p. 61.

62. The term 'queer readers' is itself, of course, ambiguous and contested. For further discussion in relation to biblical interpretation see Ken Stone, 'Queer Commentary and Biblical Interpretation', in Stone (ed.), *Queer Commentary and the Hebrew Bible* (Sheffield and Cleveland, OH: Sheffield Academic Press/Pilgrim Press, 2001).

63. George R. Edwards, *Gay/Lesbian Liberation: A Biblical Perspective* (New York: The Pilgrim Press, 1984), p. 58.

from the biblical Canaanites.[64] Here I wish to go further and suggest that, rather than distancing ourselves from the Canaanites (or from whomever is being made today to stand in for the Canaanites) in order to be 'welcomed' into communities that identify with the Israelites, perhaps queer readers should actually be adopting the position of 'Canaanite' intentionally and strategically. This suggestion recognizes that the 'Canaanite' is, like the 'homosexual', not a self-evident object that can be given a firm substantive definition; it lacks, in Halperin's terms, 'a clear definitional content'. The 'Canaanite' as we encounter it today is, rather, constituted in opposition to its binary partner the 'Israelite' within a complex network of power/knowledge relations that itself needs to be interrogated. Such an interrogation might begin, I am suggesting here, by calling into question the sharp distinction so often made between the inside and the outside of the boundaries of religious identities.[65]

Thus we return full circle to the arguments for 'welcome' and 'inclusion' cited at the beginning of this essay. Rudy's discussion, referred to earlier, seems to suggest that we should exchange such binary oppositions as 'male/ female' and 'heterosexual/homosexual' for the binary opposition between 'Church' and 'world' (which is, after all, only a Christian version of the opposition between 'Israelite' and 'Canaanite'). I would prefer to ask whether such binary oppositions are not themselves an inadequate way of thinking about religious identities in our postmodern world. Given the troubling tendency of identity categories to establish themselves through stigmatization of the Other, and in particular through sexual stigmatization, perhaps the use of securely bounded identity categories as a way of thinking about our various affiliations, desires and commitments is itself problematic. Queer theory has already suggested as much with respect to sexual affiliations, desires and commitments; I would like to suggest as much with respect to religious affiliations, desires and commitments as well.

And so perhaps the biblical stories that queer readers need to focus upon are not, first of all, stories that construe religious identity in polarized terms or make absolute distinctions between insiders and outsiders. Perhaps we might cast our glance instead on such tales as that of Tamar, the daughter-in-law of Judah, whose story is told in Genesis 38. Tamar's ethnic and religious affiliations are, in the text of Genesis, quite ambiguous. She is arguably a Canaanite, like her mother-in-law, the wife of Judah (Genesis 38.2), and is frequently accepted as such in the commentaries; and yet her Canaanite origins

---

64. Ken, Stone, 'Lovers and Raisin Cakes: Food, Sex and Divine Insecurity in Hosea', in Stone (ed.), *Queer Commentary and the Hebrew Bible*.

65. Inasmuch as the term 'Canaanite' has been given not only religious but also (as we have seen) ethnic and racial connotations, a parallel argument might be made that critical reflection on the 'Canaanites' could and should lead to an interrogation of the widespread assumption that racial and ethnic identities are firmly bounded and substantive rather than relational and constructed. Cf. James L.F. Davis, *Who Is Black? One Nation's Definition* (University Park, PA: Pennsylvania State University Press, 1991); Michael Omi and Howard Winant, *Racial Formation in the United States: From the 1960s to the 1990s*, 2nd edn (New York and London: Routledge, 1994).

are never explicitly stated in the text. Her identity is further obscured when she disguises herself in order to achieve what she wants; and when she does so she is referred to by others first as a prostitute and then as a *qedeshah*, that is, the very cultic functionary from Canaanite religion which has caused so much confusion among scholars and motivated so much speculation about (to borrow again a phrase from Albright) 'sexual abuses in the service of religion'.[66] Tamar's story is frequently cited by those who wish to argue that there is a close connection between the roles of prostitute and *qedeshah*, which connection is usually explained by postulating the existence in Canaan of 'sacred prostitutes'. However Frymer-Kensky has suggested, in my view convincingly, that we can probably better explain the fact that Tamar is referred to first by one of these terms and then by the other when we recognize that women filling these two roles were perhaps the only women in ancient Israel who were 'at least in male eyes ... outside the family system and therefore approachable for sexual encounter or arrangement'.[67] Thus Tamar is represented as positioning herself at the margins of the gender, sexual and kinship systems of ancient Israel. The chain of events that leads her to do so, moreover, begins when two of her sexual partners die and her father-in-law comes to believe that sexual contact with Tamar will mean death for his youngest son. Thus, in the age of AIDS, gay men in particular might find it valuable to reflect upon the story of Tamar, in spite of (or perhaps, on the contrary, partly because of) the complexities of cross-gender identification that result from such a reading. For here we have a tale, after all, of someone who provokes in others – and, who knows, perhaps in herself as well – a fear that sexual intercourse might lead to death.

Tamar, of course, tricks her father-in-law into having sexual relations with her in order to receive the son that she believes she rightfully should bear. Her story is sometimes criticized for placing women yet again in the position of sexual seductress, and indeed we do have to acknowledge that it was produced (as were all the biblical texts) in a patriarchal society that heavily influenced its structuring. But rather than attributing to the story a single, stable meaning which places Tamar always in the position of victim, I prefer to emphasize the fact that, within a society organized to her disadvantage, Tamar is willing to use whatever tools are at her disposal to achieve her goals. She acts at first in secret, and only subsequently reveals more about her sexual contacts; and yet her decision to do so exposes the hypocrisy of those most eager to defend the system of sex, gender and kinship within which Tamar was expected to live. Her sexual actions, like those of many of us, stand outside the accepted conventions of her society, and at one point bring her quite close to being killed. As a woman, a Canaanite, and a participant in proscribed sexual activities, Tamar would seem to be the ultimate biblical outsider. Yet in the end her sexual relations with Judah produce a son who turns out to be the ancestor of David; her story is referred to positively (in Ruth 4.12) by

66. Albright, *Yahweh and the Gods of Canaan*, p. 132.
67. Frymer-Kensky, *In the Wake of the Goddesses*, p. 271.

the book of Ruth (itself a tale of a woman who crossed boundaries of ethnicity, religion and sexual propriety); and the reference to Tamar in the genealogy of Jesus in the New Testament Gospel of Matthew (Matthew 1.3) probably implies that her unconventional actions were understood ultimately to have made possible the birth of the Christian Messiah. Thus Tamar is neither inside Israel in any conventional sense, nor completely outside Israel in the position usually allotted to Canaanites. Existing upon, and ultimately destabilizing, the boundary between inside and outside, she both ensures the survival of the Davidic line and contributes to the birth of Christianity. In that respect she offers a biblical position from which, or in dialogue with which, a 'queering' of theology, biblical interpretation, and the conceptualization of religious 'identity' might usefully commence.

Demands to be allowed *inside* such institutions as the religious community, the ordained clergy, the socially sanctioned marriage contract, the heteronormative academy, and so forth, may be necessary as interim political goals for those of us who are currently excluded from, or marginalized within, them. But we should not ignore the extent to which such demands actually reinforce boundaries between 'inside' and 'outside', boundaries that undergird most identity categories but are themselves a primary support for stigmatization and oppression. Ultimately we may need to commit ourselves instead to the task of dissolving those very boundaries between 'inside' and 'outside'; or, like Tamar, using our marginality and proscribed sexual practices to turn those boundaries 'inside out'.[68]

---

68. Diana Fuss, 'Inside/Out', in Fuss (ed.), *Inside/Out: Lesbian Theories, Gay Theories* (New York and London: Routledge, 1991).